ID0205675

POSITIONING
SUBJECTS

Critical Studies in Education and Culture Series

Critical Multiculturalism: Uncommon Voices in a Common Struggle
Barry Kanpol and Peter McLaren, editors

Beyond Liberation and Excellence: Reconstructing the Public
Discourse on Education
David E. Purpel and Svi Shapiro

Schooling in a "Total Institution": Critical Perspectives on
Prison Education
Howard S. Davidson, editor

Simulation, Spectacle, and the Ironies of Education Reform
Guy Senese with Ralph Page

Repositioning Feminism and Education: Perspectives on Educating for Social Change
*Janice Jipson, Petra Munro, Susan Victor, Karen Froude Jones, and
Gretchen Freed-Rowland*

Culture, Politics, and Irish School Dropouts: Constructing Political Identities
G. Honor Fagan

Anti-Racism, Feminism, and Critical Approaches to Education
Roxana Ng, Pat Staton, and Joyce Scane

Beyond Comfort Zones in Multiculturalism: Confronting the Politics of Privilege
Sandra Jackson and José Solís, editors

Culture and Difference: Critical Perspectives on the Bicultural Experience in
the United States
Antonia Darder

Poststructuralism, Politics and Education
Michael Peters

Weaving a Tapestry of Resistance: The Places, Power, and Poetry of a
Sustainable Society
Sharon Sutton

Counselor Education for the Twenty-First Century
Susan J. Brotherton

POSITIONING SUBJECTS

Psychoanalysis and Critical Educational Studies

STEPHEN APPEL

Critical Studies in Education and Culture Series
Edited by Henry A. Giroux and Paulo Freire

BERGIN & GARVEY
Westport, Connecticut • London

Library of Congress Cataloging-in-Publication Data

Appel, Stephen.
   Positioning subjects : psychoanalysis and critical educational
studies / Stephen Appel.
     p. cm.—(Critical studies in education and culture series,
ISSN 1064–8615)
   Includes bibliographical references and index.
   ISBN 0–89789–442–1 (alk. paper)
   1. Educational psychology. 2. Critical pedagogy. 3. Educational
sociology. 4. Freud, Sigmund, 1856–1939. I. Title. II. Series.
LB1051.A619 1996
370.15—dc20   96–3624

British Library Cataloguing in Publication Data is available.

Copyright © 1996 by Stephen Appel

All rights reserved. No portion of this book may be
reproduced, by any process or technique, without the
express written consent of the publisher.

Library of Congress Catalog Card Number: 96–3624
ISBN: 0–89789–442–1
ISSN: 1064–8615

First published in 1996

Bergin & Garvey, 88 Post Road West, Westport, CT 06881
An imprint of Greenwood Publishing Group, Inc.

Printed in the United States of America

The paper used in this book complies with the
Permanent Paper Standard issued by the National
Information Standards Organization (Z39.48–1984).

10 9 8 7 6 5 4 3 2 1

Copyright Acknowledgments

The author and publisher gratefully acknowledge permission to reprint the following copyrighted
material:

Excerpts from Stephen Appel (1995), "Freud on Civilization," *Human Relations*, 48 (6) , 625–45.
Reprinted by permission of Plenum Publishing Corp.

Excerpts from Stephen Appel (1995), "The Unconscious Subject of Education," *Discourse: Studies
in Cultural Politics of Education*, 16 (2), 167–89. Reprinted by permission of Carfax Publishing
Company.

For Christine

The so-called contemplation from the standpoint of society means nothing more than the overlooking of the *differences* which express the *social relation*. . . . Society does not consist of individuals, but expresses the sum of interrelations, the relations within which these individuals stand.

—Karl Marx
Grundrisse

CONTENTS

SERIES FOREWORD

Within the last decade, the debate over the meaning and purpose of education has occupied the center of political and social life in the United States. Dominated largely by an aggressive and ongoing attempt by various sectors of the Right, including "fundamentalists," nationalists, and political conservatives, the debate over educational policy has been organized around a set of values and practices that take as their paradigmatic model the laws and ideology of the marketplace and the imperatives of a newly emerging cultural traditionalism. In the first instance, schooling is being defined through a corporate ideology which stresses the primacy of choice over community, competition over cooperation, and excellence over equity. At stake here is the imperative to organize public schooling around the related practices of competition, reprivatization, standardization, and individualism.

In the second instance, the New Right has waged a cultural war against schools as part of a wider attempt to contest the emergence of new public cultures and social movements that have begun to demand that schools take seriously the imperatives of living in a multiracial and multicultural democracy. The contours of this cultural offensive are evident in the call by the Right for standardized testing, the rejection of multiculturalism, and the development of curricula around what is euphemistically called a "common culture." In this perspective, the notion of a common culture serves as a referent to denounce any attempt by subordinate groups to challenge the narrow ideological and political parameters by which such a culture both defines and expresses itself. It is not too surprising that the theoretical and political distance between defining schools around a common culture and denouncing cultural difference as the enemy of democratic life is very short indeed.

This debate is important not simply because it makes visible the role that schools play as sites of political and cultural contestation, but because it is within this debate that the notion of the United States as an open and democratic society is being questioned and redefined. Moreover, this debate provides a challenge to progressive educators both in and outside of the United States to address a number of conditions central to a postmodern world. First, public schools cannot be seen as either objective or neutral. As institutions actively involved in constructing political subjects and presupposing a vision of the future, they must be dealt with in terms that are simultaneously historical, critical, and transformative. Second, the relationship between knowledge and power in schools places undue emphasis on disciplinary structures and on individual achievement as the primary unit of value. Critical educators need a language that emphasizes how social identities are constructed within unequal relations of power in the schools and how schooling can be organized through interdisciplinary approaches to learning and cultural differences that address the dialectical and multifaceted experiences of everyday life. Third, the existing cultural transformation of American society into a multiracial and multicultural society structured in multiple relations of domination demands that we address how schooling can become sites for cultural democracy rather than channeling colonies reproducing new forms of nativism and racism. Finally, critical educators need a new language that takes seriously the relationship between democracy and the establishment of those teaching and learning conditions that enable forms of self and social determination in students and teachers. This suggests not only new forms of self-definition for human agency, it also points to redistributing power within the school and between the school and the larger society.

Critical Studies in Education and Culture is intended as both a critique and as a positive response to these concerns and the debates from which they emerge. Each volume is intended to address the meaning of schooling as a form of cultural politics, and cultural work as a pedagogical practice that serves to deepen and extend the possibilities of democratic life. Broadly conceived, some central considerations present themselves as defining concerns of the series. Within the last decade, a number of new theoretical discourse and vocabularies have emerged which challenge the narrow disciplinary boundaries and theoretical parameters that construct the traditional relationship among knowledge, power, and schooling. The emerging discourses of feminism, postcolonialism, literary studies, cultural studies, and postmodernism have broadened our understanding of how schools work as sites of containment and possibility. No longer content to view schools as objective institutions engaged in the transmission of an unproblematic cultural heritage, the new discourses illuminate how schools function as cultural sites actively engaged in the production of not only knowledge but social identities. *Critical Studies in Education and Culture* will attempt to encourage this type of analysis by emphasizing how schools might be addressed as border institutions or sites of crossing that are actively involved in exploring, reworking, and translating the ways in which culture is produced, negotiated, and rewritten.

Emphasizing the centrality of politics, culture, and power, *Critical Studies in Education and Culture* will deal with the pedagogical issues that contribute in novel ways to our understanding of how critical knowledge, democratic values, and social practices can provide a basis for teachers, students, and other cultural workers to redefine their role as engaged and public intellectuals.

As part of a broader attempt to rewrite and refigure the relationship between education and culture, *Critical Studies in Education and Culture* is interested in work that is interdisciplinary, critical, and addresses the emergent discourses of gender, race, sexual preference, class, ethnicity, and technology. In this respect, the series is dedicated to opening up new discursive and public spaces for critical interventions into schools and other pedagogical sites. To accomplish this, each volume will attempt to rethink the relationship between language and experience, pedagogy and human agency, and ethics and social responsibility as part of a larger project for engaging and deepening the prospects of democratic schooling in a multiracial and multicultural society. Concerns central to this series include addressing the political economy and deconstruction of visual, aural, and printed texts, issues of difference and multiculturalism, relationships between language and power, pedagogy as a form of cultural politics, and historical memory and the construction of identity and subjectivity. *Critical Studies in Education and Culture* is dedicated to publishing studies that move beyond the boundaries of traditional and existing critical discourses. It is concerned with making public schooling a central expression of democratic culture. In doing so it emphasizes works that combine cultural politics, pedagogical criticism, and social analyses with self-reflective tactics that challenge and transform those configurations of power that characterize the existing system of education and other public cultures.

—Henry A. Giroux

ACKNOWLEDGMENTS

My wife has sustained me intellectually, materially, and emotionally throughout this difficult intellectual journey. She has paid as high a price as I have without getting any of the kudos. This book is dedicated to her with love.

My family, too, has supported me with pride on this curious expedition.

I have been fortunate enough to study with two important educational theorists, Johan Muller and Philip Wexler; they have been academic mentors of the most stimulating and rigorous kind. Any merit of the book belongs to them. Catherine Casey has been my closest colleague and friend through this long labor. She discussed many points with great insight and encouragement. I can only hope that I have managed to contribute something to her own work.

David Atwell, Megan Bowler, Pam Christie, Warren Critchlow, Roger Deacon, Jacqui Fisher, John Gultig, Ken Harley, Grahame Hayes, David Hursh, Said Karodia, Bruce Kimball, Bruce Lusky, William McGrath, Serge Moscovici, Doug Noble, Christine Parkinson, Michael Peters, Yael Shalem, Tom Smith, Otto Thaler, Lynn Vacanti, Volker Wedekind, and Heather Worth all read or discussed bits of my work in the best spirit of academic collegiality.

Parts of the book-in-progress were presented to the Education Forum (University of Natal, Pietermaritzburg), the Science and Vision Conference (Human Sciences Research Council), the Department of Education at the University of Auckland, and the Auckland Family Counselling and Psychotherapy Centre (AFCP). The participants are thanked for their thoughtful comments and questions, as are my students for their lively responses to my infliction on them of psychoanalytic theory. My colleagues and clients at AFCP generously provide an environment for me to see and feel the impact of psychoanalytic ideas and therapy on people's lives.

The financial assistance of the Centre for Science Development is hereby acknowledged. Opinions expressed in this publication and conclusions arrived at are those of the author and are not necessarily to be attributed to the Centre for Science Development, or to any of the following who also generously provided funding: the Ernest Oppenheimer Foundation, the Scandling Scholarship Fund, the University of Rochester, and the University of Auckland's Staff Research Fund.

INTRODUCTION

In the preface to *Totem and Taboo*, Freud's first attempt at "applying the point of view and the findings of psycho-analysis to some unsolved problems of social psychology," he was aware of the problems of trying to please both social scientists (as they would be called today) and psychoanalysts. Such attempts

> cannot offer to either side what each lacks—to the former an adequate initiation into the new psychological technique or to the latter a sufficient grasp of the material that awaits treatment. They must therefore rest content with attracting the attention of the two parties and with encouraging a belief that occasional co-operation between them could not fail to be of benefit to research. (1912-13: xiii)

This remains true, not only of Freud's own brilliant initiatives, but of those of Roheim, Reich, Marcuse and the many others who have attempted unions of psychoanalysis and sociology. It is true too, of course, of this modest attempt to introduce Freudian psychology to critical educational studies.

This book is simultaneously a part of, an engagement with, and a contribution to the discipline of critical sociology of education, (CSOE) which has been part of a larger tradition—broadly speaking, that of Western Marxism. (It does not take much imagination to read between the lines of practically all CSOE to find Marxist traces, even if only in the Leninism of the authors.) This tradition covers a bewildering array of political movements and strategies as well as theoretical interpretations. At bottom, though, Western Marxism has it that capitalism is characterized and driven by class conflict. Opposed to economic reductionism, Western Marxism gives great emphasis to the political and cultural sphere: the "superstructure". Here, probably, all agreement ends. Nevertheless this is enough to have driven much political and, more to the point for the purposes of this book, theoretical work.

If Marxism has been a major intellectual strand this century, so has psychoanalysis. Indeed, several intellectuals of the last hundred years, from Fromm to Habermas, from Sartre to Kristeva, have understood that the central intellectual and political questions of our time should be addressed in some sort of dialogue with Marxism and with psychoanalysis. Some, seeing deep similarities between these great minds, have tried to unite the works of Marx and Freud. Marx demonstrated that beneath the apparent "fair wage" of capitalism is the hidden extraction of surplus value. He argued that every aspect of capitalist culture tends to take on the commodity form. Freud, for his part, showed that behind the "I" that appears to be rational and free is the id, a dark recess of desire. He extrapolated this insight outwards and argued that large social structures behave in many ways like the individual child. The similarities, then, are immediately striking. Both Marx and Freud addressed the "macro-" and the "micro-"; both demonstrated that the individual is not a free agent at the center of the social and mental universe; and both developed dialectical or dynamic models. While no satisfactory synthesis exists, there is a strong, if small, tradition within Western Marxism of considering both the economic base and the unconscious, alienation and repression.

> If one idea can be termed primary in Marx, it is that consciousness mediates the relations between human and nature through the active transformation known as the labor process. . . . Thus Marx is fully aware of the dialectic between humanity and nature, and he places subjectivity, i.e., consciousness, at its center. However, for Marx consciousness is purely active; it has no passive relation to nature, as is contained in the notion of desire. This is a serious deficiency—just as the Freudian downplaying of the active relation to nature is a serious deficiency. For both sides are needed in a full view of human nature. (Kovel 1988b: 390)

The first few years of life, Louis Althusser has argued, are not to be explained by Biology, although they are supported by biology. History, Sociology, and Anthropology, dealing as they do with society or culture, cannot offer anything to our understanding here. Psychology—which sees the infant as an instance of human nature—is also lost, as is Philosophy when it is disabused of "God, reason, consciousness, history and culture" (Althusser 1964: 206). In the abyss between Nature and Culture the human subject is born; "humanization" is the specific domain of interest of psychoanalysis.

Chapter 1 shows, while there is much learn from CSOE about the business of schooling, too little attention has been paid to the operations of schools with regard to the intricacies of human motivation and "socialization," to rework an old-fashioned term.

"Until now, radical education theory has refused to have any dealings with the question of 'psychology of education'" (Wexler 1985a: 233). Here Wexler is not advocating the incorporation into CSOE of mainstream academic psychology, but he is pointing instead to the need for a psychodynamic "social psychology of classes"; we need to investigate the "differential relations" between institutional and self-formative processes (1992: 128-29). To provide a foundation for this, Chapter 2 is an account of Freud's sociological writings.

When asking this order of question, one is concerned not so much with this or that form of domination or resistance, but rather with how the overt and covert social lessons of schooling are learnt; how precisely does the social become personal? It is not enough to assert that schools socialize; how does this happen?

One never addresses questions "cold." There are personal factors that make particular questions live. One's own history guides one in the search for answers. This is not bad academically—it is inevitable. In my own intellectual background the figure of Louis Althusser looms large. The reason for this is at once close at hand and out of reach. At the most obvious level, I was influenced by a teacher, Johan Muller, who demonstrated the importance of Althusser. To work out why this made an impact is a task beyond my interests here. Althusser, I came to see, was one of the few who has written about education who asks, *How* is it that people learn the know-how and the values that society requires of them? The family/school nexus, he says, forms the individual at a deep psychological level. And the medium through which this happens is ideology.

Althusser's work has been badly treated in CSOE, rejected as the worst type of economistic Marxism. However, as I show in Chapter 3, his work is a serious attempt to grapple with the processes whereby the animal infant becomes a human child: what he calls humanization. Although he is remembered particularly for his contributions to Marxist philosophy, it is Althusser's integration of psychoanalysis that gives his theory of ideology its rich soil.

This book is a critical and synthetic instance of theory building. It is an attempt to reintroduce Althusser's notion of ideology into educational studies. This involves developing Althusser's skeletal model psychoanalytically, and suggesting how this new view may prove to be useful.

The basic idea on which the book builds is Althusser's famous statement, "Ideology interpellates individuals as subjects." Believing that in this elementary formulation lies the possibility of a sophisticated theoretical alternative to both naïve notions of agency and to theories of economic determination endemic in CSOE, I occupy myself in this book principally with developing and expanding a psychoanalytic theory of ideology, while maintaining the form of Althusser's definition. While his usage of and contribution to Marxism is famous, it is to psychoanalysis that one must turn in order to capture what it is that he suggests in the above axiom. Its three key words are therefore each developed by the addition of psychoanalytic flesh.

Chapter 4 deals with Althusser's theory of ideology. Because the word "ideology" has come to have so many meanings in everyday language and in social theory, a construct of "ideology-in-general" is proposed. By this is meant not particular ideolog*ies*, but the universal cultural condition of ideology: lived experience.

According to this view, human beings are "positioned" by ideological discourses, such discourses being systems of social practice constituted by beliefs, values, norms, myths, customs, common sense, philosophy, and all the activities that enact and reconstitute them. Ideological discourses can be as vast as the discourse of male supremacy, and as small as the as the particular ways of a family (clearly, these are not independent of each other).

In order to articulate this theoretically, I turn to Gramsci and to Freud. Antonio Gramsci formulated a notion of ideology that, despite the fact that he wrote in the 1930s, remains one of the richest models yet proposed. He argued that ideology operates at various over-lapping levels. At the highest and most elaborated level is "philosophy". Below that are levels of "common sense" and "popular religion," and below these "folklore." The lower the level of ideology the less formal and deliberate it is, and the more obvious and simply accepted. No person or class exists at any one of these levels, rather these are levels that are always present in mixtures of different strengths for everyone. And these levels do not exist in sync with each other; any one person can quite possibly exist within a quite inconsistent ideological system.

A crucial aspect of this understanding of ideology is that, while none of it can be said to be independent of the socio-political in a broad sense, each individual within a particular society will have a particular, and changing, ideological personality based on experience and make-up.

Sigmund Freud's psychic model is not, it seems to me, very far away from the picture Gramsci has produced. Without collapsing the one into the other, it may be that by superimposing Freud onto Gramsci we will get a fuller understanding of how incompatible thoughts and ambivalent feelings come to coexist within the same person. And, moreover, we will see that (and why) these do not bear equal weight or exist in peaceful harmony.

For Freud, the mind of the philosophers—a rational, self-aware, intentional mind—is but the visible tip of the psychic iceberg. This "I," or ego, in fact develops out of the unconscious, which in turn is the product of channeled biological drives and repressed thought. While the unconscious id is pleasure seeking and avoids pain, the ego—the person's window to the world—has the task of dealing with reality, and these two operations are often in conflict. So the id may motivate one to want to eat, drink, steal, have sex, assault, or sleep in order to satisfy the pleasure principle; but the ego, learning that pain may follow the immediate gratification of these aims, holds back. Over time the ego develops the superego, a part of itself that is repressed into the unconscious. The superego is an internalization of familial and wider social strictures of what is good and bad. Freud's model is a dynamic one. So it happens that the id craves something, say the death of a sibling, a thought that is intolerable to the superego. It may therefore be that the superego does not allow the unwanted thought into consciousness and represses it. The ego is thus unaware of the existence of the thought and yet feels an uneasy and unaccountable guilt. What is more, the repressed thought may, evading the censor of the superego, emerge into consciousness in distorted form as symptom and dream.

With the benefit of Freud's conflictual analysis, Gramsci's theory of ideology gets a dialectical structure that it previously only alluded to. In a sense this book is simply here continuing a task that Althusser himself started, viz., developing Gramsci's notion of ideology by using Freud's depth psychology.

Chapter 5 focuses on "interpellation," which Althusser called the process whereby a person, imagining that he or she is a free and volitional individual, is unconsciously placed in various subject positions. While this idea is rich in implications, Althusser has left this crucial socializing mechanism very vague. The book turns to Melanie Klein's concept of "projective identification" in order to elaborate what happens in the process of interpellation. For Klein, projective identification consists of the phantasy expulsion from the self of bad or good feelings into objects (people). These objects are thereby changed and are then reinternalized in modified form. (British and French writers tend to adopt the spelling "phantasy" to distinguish unconscious phantasy from conscious fantasy; their American counterparts prefer the spelling "fantasy" to refer to both processes. As I rely heavily on Klein and Lacan, I use the former spelling.) This is one of the principal ways in which the person creates his or her internal world. Subsequent to Klein, writers like Betty Joseph, Wilfred Bion, and especially Thomas Ogden have argued that projective identification is a crucial part of the transference and countertransference experienced in psychoanalytic treatment. During this relationship the patient can, through various means, actually alter the emotional state of the analyst, and vice versa. This means that projective identification not only involves the changing of internal phantasy objects, but also of real, external objects. If it is considered that transference relationships exist in all human relationships, usually at lower magnitude than in the psychoanalytic room, it then becomes clear that the theoretically well-developed mechanism of projective identification is precisely what Althusser was getting at with his brief inauguration of the concept of interpellation.

Ernesto Laclau, for one, has extended Althusser's notion of subjectivity beyond that of only class interpellations. He speaks of multi-faceted subjectivities, meaning that each person is an amalgamation of shifting, conflictual, and concurrent subjectivities.

Chapter 6 considers subjectivity. For Althusser, as for Marx and Freud, human beings are not independent, volitional beings, free to see themselves and their environment as it is and rationally to impose their will upon the world. Marx has shown, for example, that beneath the appearances of society are invisible forces that have a determining effect upon what people can and cannot do. And Freud established the fact that the human mind is far more than rational consciousness and that people are driven and constrained by unseen, unconscious forces.

Human beings, then, are "split"; we experience ourselves as free, whole, and rational beings, but this consciousness is only a small part of the mind. Structuralist and poststructuralist theories have as a basic tenet that the human subject is "decentered," and Althusser, via Marx and Freud, has attempted to formalize this point. He does this by borrowing heavily from Jacques Lacan's theory of subject formation.

For Lacan, the infant at birth is not yet human. A mass of need, the infant does not yet distinguish between itself and its environment. The infant's unconscious becomes structured by the ways in which need is fulfilled or frustrated, and it begins to perceive the mother as a separate being. At the mirror stage, says Lacan, the infant for the first time experiences itself, not as a disjointed apparatus of ebbing and flowing emotion, but as a whole, coherent person. But this is necessarily "imaginary"; the child does not see itself as it *is*, but rather sees an *image* of itself. This mirror image is the prototype of the subject. We feel ourselves to be complete and free beings, but this is only a representation of what we are and how we relate to the world.

When Althusser asserts that individuals are interpellated as subjects, he means that it is through the process of subject formation that human beings come to conceive of themselves as individuals—independent, free agents.

At the risk of laboring the point, the theory developed is that of Althusser, "Ideology interpellates individuals as subjects." Although the book deals with ideology, interpellation, and subjectivity in separate chapters, there is increasing reference in each particular chapter to the other concepts. Althusser's structural logic is maintained; it is through ideological processes that human subjects come to live as (or, as *if* they are) individuals. But this is not a closed system or a static process. The key question for cultural studies is "the *failure* of ideology" (Donald 1991: 7); this book's embellishment of Althusser's theory addresses precisely that task. Althusser's axiom will be elaborated as follows: Ideology-in-general is the social field where the split, lacking, alienated, desiring subject is positioned as a coherent, volitional "individual" by the externalizing and internalizing unconscious interpsychic mechanism projective identification.

Along the way, the place of this conception in other important social theoretical work will be indicated. Representation is at the heart of Lacan's notion of the "Symbolic" and also of Althusser's work. Without any difficulty, Althusser's notion of subjectivity can be seen as compatible with, indeed formative of, poststructuralist ideas of the de-centered, fluctuating subject. Poststructural theory is concerned with the micro circuits of power, and a version of how these operate on an interpersonal level is provided by the way transference has been developed here. The humanistic concept of human agency is seriously undermined by the work of the book; any concept of free individuals is, to use Freud's word, an "illusion": a wish fulfillment. In short, Althusser's ideology-in-general, when filled out, shows itself to be concerned with the same issues as poststructuralist theory. Where Althusser's theory differs from poststructuralism is that the latter denies the existence of fixed structures. (A case can be made, though, that whenever poststructuralists explain any phenomenon, they in fact do so by proposing new axes, slices, oppositions, and models, i.e., structures.)

Without pretending that this represents anything like a full and final explanation, this book offers—via Marx, Freud, Lacan, Althusser, and others—a theory of socialization; socialization that is both inescapable and that always "does not work" (Walkerdine 1990: xiv). And I assert that this new-fledged theory may have several uses in the study of education.

The question arises as to why psychoanalysis has made no impact thus far on CSOE. This problem deserves closer attention, but there seem to me to be at least two ways to begin answering it. First, Freud repeatedly predicted that psychoanalysis is too degrading to people's narcissism to ever become widely accepted. It was more likely, he said, that relatively harmless elements would become popular; we see this with the incorporation in everyday language of words like "Oedipal," "repressed," and "anal" to describe people in trivial and isolated ways.

Second, the broadly left intellectual groupings that have formulated CSOE have for various reasons rejected psychoanalysis. To generalize, psychoanalysis has very seldom been part of Left analysis in Britain. Aside from writers like Juliet Mitchell, British Left intellectuals have found particularly inventive other ways of adapting Marxism to the problems at hand. Psychoanalysis in Britain has by and large remained the domain of therapy. In the United States, on the other hand, the situation is more puzzling. The influence of the Frankfurt School has, after all, been a major one on the American Left. Why, then, is the name of Freud not found in the writings of American CSOE theorists? For some reason it seems that, while a thinker like Herbert Marcuse was influenced as much by Freud as by Marx (as is Jürgen Habermas who followed), the third generation of the Frankfurt School in the United States has split into those like Christopher Lasch who look to Freud and are suspicious of the Left, and those like Bertell Ollman who lean principally toward Marx. To continue this over crude description, as CSOE is a broadly Left discipline, it is more likely that the latter group of thinkers would be influential in the United States: psychoanalysis, especially in its American variations, regarded as pessimistic and conservative. Of course there are exceptions to this; around the world there are educational thinkers who can be seen to be sensitive to what can be called the flavor of Freud's work: Basil Bernstein, James Donald, Maxine Greene, Stuart Hall, Johan Muller, Valerie Walkerdine, and Philip Wexler. The bulk of the new generation of CSOE scholars, though, if the journals are anything to go by, are continuing the non-Freudian trends of their predecessors, or jumping straight into post-structuralist theory without recognizing the relation of this work to the grand theories of either Marx or Freud.

CSOE, this book argues, cannot deal with questions of *how* reproduction happens, or *how*, given the socialized nature of human beings, people and institutions are able to change. Psychoanalysis, it is suggested here, is a profitable way of thinking about these problems. Socialization and social consent happen at two levels. First, people enter language and, thus, human culture generally. This humanization involves the infant's unavoidable channeling of instinctual drive, a process that structures the unconscious; no normal person can escape this introduction into culture-in-general. Second, each person internalizes the values of his or her particular milieu in that unconscious part of the ego, the superego.

Now, it may seem that such a view can deal with the question of reproduction and its mechanisms, but not with oppositional behavior. But a careful and sympathetic reading of Freud reveals that no-one is the perfectly tamed product of family or society. Culture, or "civilization," is characterized by a conflictual relationship between selfish desire and self-sacrificing society; these forces inhabit each person in a psychic field of contradiction, overlap, repression, guilt, symptom formation, and, above all, ambivalence. So, just as in the physical world, human beings viewed from a macro- or species perspective have, says psychoanalysis, universal, law like, predictable *ways* of becoming human. But at the unpredictable level of individual thought and behavior, the most that the social theorist can do is to describe trends and tendencies. As opposed to the theories that form the backbone of CSOE, psychoanalysis emphasizes not either/or, but both/and answers.

Chapter 7 discusses recent social theory that, arising in significant ways out of the work of Althusser, can be used to study society in a psychoanalytic way. For example, building on the Laclau and Mouffe notion of the social as being structured around antagonisms, the Lacanian Slavoj Žižek places desire at the center of these splits.

Psychoanalysis, if taken on board, has enormous and far-reaching implications for many a field of human study. One only has to look at its varied influences on literary and film studies, anthropology, broad social analysis, biography, and, of course, psychological development and therapy to get a feel for what Freud's legacy has meant and can mean. This book does not attempt to argue for anything like the full range of psychoanalytic concepts and applications. In an attempt to address a weakness in the parent discipline of CSOE, it highlights, hopefully in a faithful and responsible way, a handful of concepts that can be used in further educational research. Here I refer not to, say, the unconscious or drives, or to ideology-in-general. Rather than being sensitizing concepts, these are the underlying metaphors of the whole enterprise.

While one cannot investigate something psychoanalytically without acknowledging the determining influence of unconscious forces, the unconscious itself is not a refined enough concept to be useful on its own in research; it is the perspective, not the tool.

A concept that this book does promote as being vital is that of the subject. If one takes psychoanalysis seriously, one cannot any longer speak of human agents who, either altruistically or malevolently, decide how to live. Human beings are, to use the language of Lacan and Althusser, positioned in ideological discourses; although they can choose whether to lift a hand or to drop it, they are not free to choose their sexual preferences, the values they hold dear, or what they feel about their fellows. However, this is not to say that people are unflinching, static end-products of their social experience. Emotional ambivalence, it seems to me, is a human characteristic that can contribute much to critical analyses of education. Educational researchers will offer valuable findings when we conceive of human beings as being in constant relationships of struggle with themselves and their worlds. Immediate satisfaction versus delayed gratification, fear of pain versus the pleasure of doing good deeds, selfish wants versus social needs: these are the unresolved and unresolvable stuff of human life. When speculating on the effects of particular pedagogic policies or measures, or on the motivations of students and teachers, it is crucial to consider that every person has mixed and changing feelings about everything significant in his or her life, and, moreover, that no two individuals have the same experiences.

The clinical practice of psychoanalysis heightens and highlights transference phenomena, and these are also phenomena to be sensitive to when studying educational relationships. More specifically, the concept of projective identification gives the researcher an elaborated model of personal interaction that can help to describe what is happening in particular educational situations, showing that all such relationships are relationships of shifting power, and demonstrating how real psychic changes occur.

Freud often referred to himself as a conquistador. If I may develop this analogy a little, Freud courageously and carefully charted a dark and uninhabited continent that had been fleetingly visited by only a few poets and visionaries; the existence of which was largely unsuspected by humankind at large. After him, several travelers have visited this strange place mapping these lands in closer detail, some of the most daring—Ferenczi, Klein, Winnicott—wandering off Freud's tracks and inspecting new regions. Some parts of the territory have become well known and safe for comfortable travel, these parts avoiding the most inhospitable and inaccessible areas surveyed by Freud. Many intellectual groups have explorers who venture into this dark continent in search of treasures and mystery. Some even treat a trip into this wilderness as an initiation. However, there are whole fields of exploration that ignore the land of the unconscious, sometimes because a journey previously made is no longer in vogue, or in the belief that the area has been conquered and tamed. Sometimes the avoidance is the result of a cold terror of the monsters and the danger that rumor has reported lie there. My fellow searchers in education are examples of those who, for one reason or another, steer clear of these shores. I have taken it upon myself to act as a tour guide, introducing those who may be frustrated by the ruts of well-traveled roads or whose curiosity may be excited. Perhaps this proffered day trip into the rich and singular country first delineated by Freud will attract a wanderer or two from the mainland.

POSITIONING
SUBJECTS

1

CRITICAL EDUCATIONAL STUDIES

> At the centre of modern social thought there is a well-known theoretical puzzle. The social world is constructed by ongoing social activities, and if not continuously reproduced by our ongoing practices, it would immediately cease to exist. How come, then, that we nevertheless experience this universe of ongoing practices as some external opaque reality, even as such an unbending force?
> —Bernhard Peters
> "Why Is It so Hard to Change the World?"

Education is unendingly ambiguous: uniting and dividing, building up and breaking down, encouraging both critical and conformist thought, overtly political and relatively autonomous, scene of community and of isolation, of joyfulness and of misery. What, one wonders, are schools for? How do they do what they do? And what are schools capable of doing?

The discipline of critical sociology of education (CSOE) has managed to cast some light on these questions. It has shown that educational knowledge is not a neutral body of facts (Young 1971), that it is structured in particular ways (Bernstein 1990), and that much of it is invisible "cultural capital" (Bourdieu and Passeron 1977). It shows, further, that there are connections between what happens in schools and what happens in the world of work (Bowles and Gintis 1976; Livingstone 1995), and that mass schooling has been characterized by the production and reproduction of racism (Demaine 1989; McCarthy 1988) and sexism (Arnot and Weiner 1987). CSOE argues that schooling is a system that, far from being the great social equalizer (Wexler 1976), socializes the next generation of citizens. And it describes examples of school students manufacturing their own meanings within the limits of these institutions (Walker 1988; Willis 1977).

The impetus for CSOE comes to a large extent from the social activist consciousness of those who make up the field. However, there has been a theoretical short-circuiting that is the product of that which gives CSOE its very strength—progressivism: the belief in, and drive for, social change and betterment. The realization that schooling has not lived up to hopes for equality has led critical educationists to look below the surface of the school and at the "hidden curriculum" (Apple 1971). There have been scores of studies claiming to have uncovered the ways in which educational practices "attempt to assure acceptance and conformity to [dominant] beliefs, attitudes and interests" (Barton, Meighan and Walker 1980: 2). Such studies consider, to mention just a few areas, the hidden politics of textbooks (Du Preez 1983) and readers (Burbules 1986), of literacy (Lee 1989), sex education (Fine 1988), tracking (Ball 1986), and compulsory education (Williamson 1981). There have also been any number of studies asserting the ability of students to cut through the official veneer of the school (Critchlow 1992; Everhart 1983; Molteno 1987). In recent years there have been attempts to incorporate postmodern notions into CSOE (Aronowitz and Giroux 1991; Ball 1994). Even though, as R. Moore (1991) points out, postmodernist views of education have not been able to maintain either CSOE's progressive impulse or the possibility of theory, such efforts have in fact tended to force postmodern notions into the existing "critical pedagogy" (McLaren 1988). By and large, critical educationists have resisted the radical nature of postmodern and poststructuralist ideas, thereby domesticating them. Together these trends—ideology-critique, critical ethnography, and politics of difference—constitute a valuable antidote to the commonsensical acceptance of the curriculum as worthwhile knowledge. But deeply inscribed in CSOE is a notion of ideology as false consciousness and thus of the potentialities of raising consciousness; the progressive imperative leads a majority of writers to suggest that the very laying open of what has been hidden will "conscientize" students. There is a belief that scratching below surface appearances reveals the truth about education and that this revelation liberates. However, neither a deeper intellectual understanding of schooling nor the rebellious classroom has produced the politicized student body sought after by progressive educators. (In countries like South Africa and South Korea where students have become political forces, the contientizing role of teachers and educational academics has been negligible.)

This chapter indicates a failing in CSOE, namely an inability to theorize identity formation in schooling; it sides with a growing strand within CSOE that looks toward the unconscious. Finally, it suggests that psychoanalytic theory may change the tradition in educational theory of viewing society and the self as a dualism.

CSOE AND EDUCATIONAL CHANGE

Stasis and change, reproduction and action—these have been the primary concerns of CSOE from the start. However, they have seldom been theorized; rather, they have been assumed and described. In his article entitled "Why is it so hard to change the world?" Bernhard Peters persists: "Now why *is* it so hard? At some point in your life you may have asked the question yourself. You noticed that our world keeps changing all the time, sometimes rapidly—but often not in ways that we had intended or even foreseen" (1994: 275). The answers, he argues, lie in historical contingency, the vagaries of human nature or motivation, and problems of representation and cognition; even in the most transparent and voluntary arrangement imaginable, these factors would necessarily continue to render the social opaque and inertial (290).

Sometimes change is cheerfully imputed on shaky evidence in CSOE; sometimes its absence is admitted with surprise and disappointment. Maarit Lindroos is "discouraged" to find that, despite legal efforts at gender equality, "girls" and "boys" are still being produced in Finnish classrooms. To her credit, the author realizes that the question is profound: "one cannot *take* the issue of equality from somewhere; one has to *experience* it very deeply through the body" (1995: 154). Chris Shilling has also noted the "curiously disembodied" (1992a) views of sociology of education; he uses the work of Bourdieu to argue that habitus is "physical capital" that "educates the body" (1991).

And when change does happen in the classroom, there is little confirmation that the writer knows *why* and *how* this change has occurred. J. Alleyne Johnson (1995) describes two innercity US classes where violence and death were formally acknowledged and discussed; in one class the teacher's efforts were angrily rejected, in the other the students seem to have dealt with the trauma in a new and personally useful way. The author cannot explain the difference except call the second "critical pedagogy" and to say that the first teacher did not ask for the students' permission. It seems clear to me that the psychodynamics are rather more complex than this; a useful place to begin to look might be Shoshana Felman and Dori Laub's (1992) notion of the deep psychological value of testimony—bearing witness to trauma.

CSOE, as several have noted, remains by and large divided into macro- and micro-levels, where macro- includes analyses of social systems and national policies, and micro- involves studies of schools and classrooms. This split focus manifests itself in a pair of quite different arguments—the "structure-agency" partition. To my mind this is a misnomer; the cleft is better labeled "system-agency" because on the whole, educational studies have not been centrally informed by the French tradition of structuralism (a view that most usefully transcends the need for this dualism, as my own work attempts to show). Ironically, both the "system" and "agency" approaches carry the same humanistic notion of human beings. The pawns and ciphers of system-level analysis are potentially the active, rational, self-conscious individuals described by agency-level studies.

The barrenness of CSOE's cul-de-sac has been demonstrated to me by the vain gropings of generations of education students. In an attempt to meld personal history, politics of education, and education theory, my colleagues and I require undergraduate students to write educational biographies. Although they find the experience challenging and worthwhile, it is clear that their efforts are hampered by the limitations of CSOE metatheory. In the typical essay the student hops awkwardly, now standing unsteadily in system-level theory, now precariously poised in the realm of agency. Once the world has been split in this way, these students, like many of the writers they read, literally cannot speak of themselves as subjects.

Peters puts it thus: "The social world *is us* . . . and we, on the other hand, our selves, our identities, are nothing without this social world that we both 'interiorize' and help to produce" (1994: 276). Or to put in the terms of French philosophy, "the speaking subject is never innocent" (Kristeva 1993).

There is much of interest in CSOE with regard to the question of *what* schools do. Critical education studies also have interesting things to say about *why* schools do what they do. But on the question of *how* schools do what CSOE asserts they do, the discipline offers very little. Schools reproduce the status quo, yes. But CSOE cannot explain how this happens, only state that it does. Among activist intellectuals this situation is particularly chronic. This chapter is an argument that much of what ails CSOE, both in academic theory and in classroom enactments, revolves around the "delusory Enlightenment concept of culture and the self" (Donald 1992a: 137). In our attempt to show just how dastardly capitalist schooling has been and how heroic the struggle of the students, leftist intellectuals in education have, almost without exception, ignored the intricacies and incongruities of motivation and socialization.

Institutions prevail, in the last analysis, "by and through the formation (fabrication) of the human raw material into a social individual, in which they and the 'mechanisms' of their perpetuation are embedded" (Castoriadis 1987: 40).

AFTER "STRUCTURE-AGENCY"?

There have been attempts to merge "structure" and "agency" via, for example, the work of Gramsci (Giroux 1983b) or Giddens (Shilling 1992b), and now postmodernism and poststructuralism are regarded as most promising in this regard. Notions of power, meaning, desire, discourse, difference, and textuality are gaining currency in education studies. Of course, employment of such terms does not necessarily equate with acceptance of the traditions from which they arise. Barry Kanpol, for one, wants to fashion "a postmodern theory of 'similarity within differences'" (1992a). Without displaying any qualms about theoretical incommensurability, this is to be, he says, "a postmodernism *which includes* the modernist tenets of possibility, community, dialogue, and hope" (220, emphasis added): "a celebration of difference, a fundamental coming together in union and solidarity" (Kanpol 1992b: 134). Cleo Cherryholmes, to cite another who adheres to modernism while denouncing it, sees poststructuralism as a "critical pragmatism" which puts one "in a stronger position to deal with, anticipate, and sometimes, perhaps *predict* the fate of the latest proposal to guide curriculum" (1988: 149, emphasis added). In the work of Bronwyn Davies (1992), discourse analysis becomes the now familiar educational pairing of ideology-critique plus humanist agency. Burbules' article on *Tootle* is but one of a multitude of studies in the CSOE literature which *is* textualist; it "analyses" the children's reader in order to reveal its "ideological content and implicit normative commitments" (1986: 239). Another instance is that of J. Nespor and L. Barber who confusingly argue for rhetorical analyses that, on the one hand, move us "toward weak, irreductionist explanations that make problematic our explanatory practices," and that on the other hand inform us that the "*only* function" of a particular boundary distinction is to "obscure the *nature* of our practice." Unsurprisingly, their paper ends with a claim for the "increased scope of our opportunities for political mobilization and action" (1991: 431-32). (Evans, Davies and Penny [1994] astutely point to the absence of the subject and the state in the Foucauldian textualist approach to policy research; they argue for a return to the work of Bernstein.) The incorporation of poststructuralist notions of discourse into a putative activism is an insistent thematic in the recent literature. Carmen Luke (1994) avers that women should and can "take charge of the rules and of those discourses that define centre and margin, insider and outsider, ruler and ruled." And, using the critical theory of Habermas, Robert Young (1990) still wants to partake of postmodernism, and he therefore claims to reject grand narratives while inconsistently insisting that "what is at stake is a struggle for authentic agency" (1992: 139). Lyn Yates pours cold water on postmodernism, feminism, and cultural politics as employed in CSOE; once we eradicate the vestiges of master narratives, she says, we are left with "general posturing on the one hand and insightful but limited local projects on the other" (1992: 132). Given the field's progressivist drive, I believe that it has been nearly impossible for educationists to adopt the sang-froid and ironic distance of postmodernism.

A poststructuralist feminist strand of research moves beyond simply counterposing the socialization of boys and girls and acknowledges various subject positionings in multiple locations (Bromley 1989; Jones 1993; Lather 1991). But the presence of the agent is strongly to be felt here. Davies and Chas Banks, for example, state that people "actively take up *as their own* the discourses through which they are shaped" (1992: 3), and that these are not only rational selection processes. Davies does not shy away from conspiracies in her preemptive strike:

> Of course the major source of resistance to liberating children in [a feminist poststructuralist] way will come from those who wish to control them and who recognise that people are in fact less controllable if they are not tied to liberal humanist rules of consistency and predictability. (1992: 65)

So, although the door has been opened to theorizing about *how* self-positioning might happen, that threshold has yet to be crossed. Shirley Grundy, in her portrayal of a lesson characterized by "traditional Australian values such as fairness and equality" (1994: 17), assumes that this leads to the construction of the identity of "Australian." She does so without any evidence that this is the case or any explanation of how this might happen; rather, she has detected something being said, therefore that thing must have been produced. So far, little more has been offered in educational studies than an acknowledgement of the possibility of "a range of subject positions around which subjectivities tend to cluster and/or resist each other" (Giroux and McLaren 1992: 15).

While some in CSOE willingly incorporate and adapt the words of postmodernism and poststructuralism, there are those who resist it. Such rejection is defended on two grounds. First, postmodernism is said to offer nothing new: "I can find very little of any use in postmodernism and even *that* has been said before in a different form" (Skeggs 1991: 255). Second, postmodernism is critiqued because it is seen to hinder radical educational alternatives (Beyer and Liston 1992). It is this determination to be seen as positively active that leads Nicolas Burbules and Suzanne Rice to reject more powerful explanatory theory (what they call "antimodernism") for more exhortatory conjecture ("postmodernism *per se*") purely on the grounds that the latter seems to offer "more fruitful educational implications" (1991: 399). When it *is* accepted, postmodernism (this term is habitually taken as synonymous with poststructuralism) in many educationists' hands becomes a kind of hesitant certainty, but certainty nonetheless. Rather than theorize a connection between progressivism and poststructuralism, CSOE writers have tended to deny the serious conflicts and incommensurabilities between these and have simply advocated a modernist "enlightened subject" *and* postmodern "diversity, contingency, and cultural pluralism" (Aronowitz 1991: 82). (For critiques see Ball 1992; Schrag 1992.) It is becoming something of a doctrine in postmodernist sociology of education that mere awareness of discursive practices enables one to be a postmodern modernist; to have "a validation of both difference and conflict, but also an attempt to build coalitions around common goals rather than a denial of differences" (Weiler 1991: 470). Again, the touchstone of ideology-critique.

Although this is not the place to defend the point, this chapter proceeds on the assumption that, despite efforts to add on recent developments in social theory, two pillars of critical sociology of education remain (even though these props have been severely critiqued by social theory outside education): the individual and society, with education seen as mediating between the self and the social. Paul Auerbach has put it most clearly: "Education, properly concept-ualised, is an end in itself—part of the path to self-realization and democracy" (1992: 33), democracy here being a synonym for social community. Similarly, McLaren sounds "an invitation posed by critical pedagogy which is to bend reality to the requirements of a just world" (1991: 33). Radical teachers who subscribe to this captivating view are, Walkerdine has argued, "the guardians of an impossible dream, reason's dream of democratic harmony" (1986: 60). I would differ from Shilling who says that blame for the "demise" of sociology of education should be attributed in part to those theorists who "celebrate difference rather than engage *seriously* with problems of community (e.g. see the recent work of Giroux and McLaren)" (1993: 112). A serious engagement with Derrida, Lacan, or Foucault does not lead to a celebration, but to an acknowl-edgement of difference; it does, however, also lead to radical problematizing of the metaphysical concepts of self and community. For the moment, let me suggest that the self ("inside") and the social ("outside") are two sides of the coin of subjectivity; the development of the human subject is that involuntary journey from nature to culture—"the growth of an 'it' into a he or a she" (Mitchell 1988: 80). And this is precisely the domain of psychoanalytic theory.

VIA THE UNCONSCIOUS

So, as an alternative set of theories to functionalist educational research, CSOE has greatly increased the scope of what we can say about education and schooling. And yet, the traditional question of "socialization" has been inadequately treated in this broad set of analyses. Starting out with the best of emancipatory motives, much of what we read flounders around the questions of how people become social beings and why predictable social change is so difficult to effect. If one can speak of an academic discipline as experiencing emotions, critical sociology of education can be described as feeling ambivalent in this regard. To cite a few examples of this unease, Patti Lather agonizes over the question: "How do our very efforts to liberate perpetuate the relations of dominance?" (1991: 16). The same qualms are reflected by Julie Mathews (1994), and in the cry of the students of Elizabeth Ellsworth: "Why doesn't this feel empowering?" (1989). As Roger Dale puts it, "the pessimism and the optimism were symbiotic. The pessimism arose from a failure to fulfil a set of possibilities that could only be seen as possibilities when they were generated by an optimism of the will that ignored the essential basis of its own optimism"

(1992: 205).

It is my contention that critical educational analysts have been disappointed and frustrated in part because of an undeveloped understanding of the complexities involved in becoming educated/socialized/"civilized." We have failed to engage with the actual processes of educational socialization because we have been ignorant of the fact that these processes are largely *unconscious.* We have not pursued with any rigor Basil Bernstein's codes—the "structuring of pedagogic discourse" (1990)—through which power inequalities determine ideological subjects. We have not asked enough how it is that homo sapiens become persons, i.e., about what Althusser called "humanization" (not the same as socialization, in the sense of von Wiese's "sociation" as patterns of behavior, neither is it to be confused with humanism.) There has been very little detailed consideration of the "war" declared on all children, "who, projected, deformed and rejected, are required, each by himself in solitude and against death, to take the long forced march which makes mammiferous larvae into human children, *masculine* or *feminine subjects*" (Althusser 1971b: 206). In short, CSOE lacks a theory of the psychic economy of subjectivity: a theory that can account for the ambivalences and resistances, the "emotion and pedagogic violence" (Worsham 1992/1993), and the erotics in education settings (Gallop 1992).

Some others have, it is true, pointed to this weakness in educational studies. John Furlong, noting the importance of attempting to make sense of the lives of disaffected students, argues that studies with such students require more complex notions of social structure and of individual psychology than have been used up to now. We need to understand, he says, how it is that "educational structures—the power of education—is used not just to *impose* certain sorts of behaviour, but to *construct* young people in certain sorts of ways" (1991: 298). Philip Wexler has called for a "social psychology" of education that will understand mass culture and its relation to production and to the individual unconscious (1985a: 227): an analysis of "becoming somebody" (1992). Henry Giroux, one of the most "redemptive" (Dale 1992) of educational writers, has also long acknowledged that what is needed is a "depth psychology that can unravel the mechanisms of domination and the possible seeds of liberation [which] reach into the very structure of the human psyche" (Giroux 1983a: 39). Grappling with the problem of teaching feminism to men, Jane Kenway points out to her colleagues that this work "touches deep psychic sensitivities"; she suspects that "good will and/or rationality and/or professionalism have very little to do with the change process" (1995: 78). Felman (1986) has written a paper that directly uses psychoanalysis to try to understand teaching, as have David Bensusan and Yael Shalem (1993). Concentrating on the emotion of shame, Lindsay Fitzclarence (1992) has begun to develop a theory of conflict in order to understand the place of emotions in school violence. Also, in Australia Roslyn Arnold (1994) has sketched the outline of a "psychodynamic pedagogy" centered on empathy. Bell hooks has touched on the taboo subject of "eros, eroticism, and the pedagogical process" (1994). Somewhat notoriously, so has Jane Gallop (1995), arguing that teaching and learning are erotic. (See also Gurko 1982; Kulevski 1984; Talbot 1994; Unger 1986.) (Michelle Fine's work [1988] on the "missing discourse of desire" is far more specific than being a theory of desire. It postulates that there is an "anti-sex rhetoric" around sex education in the United States, and that this contributes to teenage pregnancy, disease, violence, and harassment. Barbara Dafoe Whitehead finds comprehensive sex education to be have a "technocratic understanding of teenage sexuality; it envisions a regime of teenage sexual self-rule" [1994: 64].)

Continuing along this path, this book argues that unconscious desire is a dimension missing from most notions of subject positioning in educational theory. It is my contention that until sociologists of education grasp the difficult conceptual nettle of the unconscious, it is unlikely that we will transcend the present reliance upon one of the humanistic assumptions of the existence of free, volitional individuals, or the functionalism of macro-sociological explanations. While much writing in education appears to accept this point, it invariably reverts to a bravura language of action and choice. So Luke (1994), for example, encourages readers to "de-essentialize experience, identity and location," at the same time calling for a "united front" of women engaged in "a full-scale, concerted, and politically cohesive assault." For Paul Kringas and Ian Steward, dialogue leads to critical consciousness, that leads to political praxis: "enlightenment, rather than mystification, is the goal" (1992: 34). This is of a piece with the Freirean (1970) notion of "conscientization" which drives the advocacy of teachers as "transformative intellectuals" (Aronowitz and Giroux 1985). Armed with "the means to challenge . . . painful circumstance," such teachers are said to be able to get out of the "cycle of cultural maintenance" (Britzman 1986: 454), and thereby they "make the political personal" for their students (Dippo et al. 1991: 81). Ellsworth has tellingly pointed to the "repressive myths of critical pedagogy" (1989).

It should be no surprise that critical sociology of education wrestles, whether it is aware of the fact or not, with the defining characteristic of modern- ity—rationality; nor should it be unexpected that CSOE is hamstrung in this battle by a deep-rooted prejudice against psychological causes, explanations denounced as "individualism" or "psychologism." What *is* odd, though, is the extent of the reluctance of educational theorists, relative to the clusters of theorists in feminist, literary, film, and cultural studies, to deal seriously with the unconscious. Recently, though, three authors have published books that attempt to drag educational theory toward an acknowledgment of unconscious forces: Wexler (1992), Valerie Walkerdine (1990), and James Donald (1992b). It is the task of these books to introduce into the study of education some of the questions raised by psychoanalysis—not in the adaptive forms of mainstream psychoanalysis, but in ways richly informed by recent social theory. Interestingly, all three books insist on considering education as extending far beyond the school, to the family, popular culture, and the media. As of yet, although cited now and then, these authors have not made the kind of impression on CSOE that their work deserves.

Wexler finds the identities of high school students to be inauthentic self-conscious images. Each broad social class produces an organized set of self-images: "it is not simply a question of deficits or deprivations and advantages, but of different lifeworlds and of the dynamic organizational economies that generate and sustain diverse understandings and aspirations" (Wexler 1992: 8). Students take these on board defensively, he says, to compensate for what is lacking in schools: interaction, society, and self. For example, rather than seeing aggression among African American youth as the result of the loss of communal values and traditions (e.g., Ward 1995), Wexler sees it as a defensive measure against an assault on the self in inner-city schools. The prison-like atmosphere of these schools means that something is missing in the teacher-student relationship. Pedro Noguera, too, has found a common idea among the students, namely that "adults don't know who their students are" (1995: 204).

Walkerdine argues that it is through conscious and unconscious phantasy that we confront the world and take on social identities; these are not, she insists, easily shrugged off. "We are not simply positioned, like a butterfly being pinned to a display board. We struggle from one position to another and, indeed, to break free—but to what?" (1990: xii). Her bravely told story of her childhood phantasy of being a "fairy" illustrates identity formation that occurs "at the unstable point where the 'unspeakable' stories of subjectivity meet the narratives of history, of a culture" (Hall 1987: 44). Pam Nilan comes to a similar point when she discovers that male and female students in a secondary drama exercise of collective script creation produce different, but stereotypical, representations of men. In order to explain this, Nilan suggests that the answer may lie in part in the students' "personal and collective fantasy lives" (1995: 175).

Donald speculates about how it might be that we construct such self-images or phantasies. He postulates an "impossible" intermediate psychic space that mediates pedagogical and disciplinary measures and produces the structured agent, the imagining subject: "Norms *and prohibitions* instituted within social and cultural technologies are folded into the unconscious so that they 'surface' not just as 'personal desires' but in a complex and unpredictable dynamic of desire, guilt, anxiety and displacement" (Donald 1992b: 94). Bernstein has asked: "How does the outside become the inside, and how does the inside reveal itself and shape the outside" (1990: 94). If the words "inside" and "outside" are placed in quotes, this is Donald's question too. Earlier I spoke of subjectivity as a coin with two sides: self and society. As arresting as that image might be, it has the flaw of presenting subjectivity as a seamless whole. In contrast, "psychoanalysis focuses on the caesura between the *structure* of social determination and the psychic effect of *feeling*" (Donald 1991: 5)—a split in the self between perception and understanding. What does it mean to be an "agent" within psychoanalysis? "Freud's subject is both active agent, frustrated by forces beyond his or her control, and knower, gauging its world by what is represented to it through the inner eye" (Forrester 1987: 15). To put Donald's point in more mainstream language: "psychic experiences filter the social and pedagogical ones" (Arnold 1994: 32).

TOWARD A PSYCHODYNAMIC ECONOMY OF IDEOLOGY

Freud called psychoanalysis, government, and education "impossible professions" (1937: 248). Cornelius Castoriadis offers one way to understand this comment with regard to education. An impossibility of pedagogy, he says, "lies in the attempt to produce autonomous human beings within a heteronomous society, and beyond that, in the paradoxical situation of educating human beings to autonomy while—or in spite of—teaching them to absorb and internalise existing institutions" (Castoriadis 1994: 7). Impossibility, though, should not necessarily lead to despair; human beings have alwyays operated "in the teeth of paranoia and institutionalized power" (Wilson 1986: 53). For CSOE it means, rather, that we need to grapple with the "paradox" of human subjects having to "serve, simultaneously, as both the cause and the effect of social structures and, ultimately, of history itself" (Grossberg 1993: 117).

Our lives are part and parcel of natural events and socio-political oppression and exploitation; ideology refers to the ways we live our social relations. These relations do not exist in the ether, but are the productions of a psychodynamic economy of interpersonal externalizations and internalizations, processes Althusser (1970) has indicated schematically with his notion of "interpellation." It is probably true that his famous ISA paper is the closest that CSOE has got to Continental social theory and to psychoanalysis; his work made a brief impact on educational studies, but has left almost no lasting impression.

Ideology-in-general is the ubiquitous atmosphere of cultural life, of social relations. This (as opposed to either the notion of ideology as false consciousness or of ideolo*gies* as systems of belief, both of which inevitably lead to dualistic ideology-critique) is the theoretical route of the book. The field of study, then, is the human sciences in an age when the myths of individualism and of community have supposedly been irreparably damaged. The problem is the construction of *homo sociologicus*, and the sociological study of education. The method is the analysis of intra- and inter-psychic processes, indicating a return of depth psychology. The subtext is a dispute with liberal humanistic notions of the self.

Although the point cannot be developed here, it should be noted that the effect of the avoidance and repression in educational studies of the notion of unconscious desire (and also perhaps the motivation for this neglect) is the same as that of all the many neo-Freudian moves in social analysis: denial of the "cloven hoof of sex" (Riesman 1950: 187). Why is it that in sociology of education, which is after all a "sub-discipline" of the sociology of culture (Muller 1989a: 79), the unconscious subject is all but absent? It may be that social reformism is so much part and parcel of the practice of education that those who are drawn to education have little tolerance for Freud's remorseless message. As Lacan says, "we place no trust in altruistic feeling, we who lay bare the aggressivity that underlies the activity of the philanthropist, the idealist, the pedagogue, and even the reformer" (1949: 7). Compare this view with that of critical pedagogy: "By applying Freire's pedagogy to learning, students and teachers have the opportunity and the means to do more than learn language: they can win the freedom to think and act as critically conscious beings. This is the humanizing purpose of education" (Gramm 1988: 448). C. Breen intends for students to "have the confidence and vision to 'choose their own adventure'" (1991/1992: 42); subjects can, according to this view, be freed to decide upon their own positioning (Davies and Banks 1992). In response to this type of statement, C.A. Bowers has referred to critical pedagogy's "messianic self-assuredness" (1991: 244). But enough, the point has been made. If it can contribute anything, psychoanalysis offers at least a certain modesty—giving up the narcissism of the ego through the recognition of the Other within.

Let us leave for another time the fascinating question of why the Freudian unconscious has made even less impression on the sociology of education than on the rest of sociology where several of the dominant figures—from Marcuse to Parsons to Giddens—have been students of Freud. John Wilson speculates on how being an educator "regenerates one's own paranoid feelings" so that for the radical pedagogue the unconscious *idea* of a highly punitive adult becomes "more ferocious and threatening when the adult resigns his authority and tries to behave more like a child himself" (1986: 48). For now it may be sufficient to read the mixed feelings, unease, and tension—which surface more and more in the "obsolete, even quaint" (Wexler 1985b: 391) mainstream of critical sociology of education—as justification for introducing some psychoanalysis into our discipline. This is not a matter of applying psychoanalysis to education, but rather of considering how educational analysis changes once one accepts the place of the unconscious: "What does it mean to be a reader *after* Freud?" (Felman 1987: 24)

Sprinkled through CSOE literature are instances of terms like "desire" (Davies 1990; Walcott 1994), usually unburdened, intentionally or in ignorance, by any reference to psychoanalysis or Freud. But, "what would one be trying to forget about reason, for what reasons, if, today, one was trying to forget the unconscious?" (Derrida 1990: 7). It is to remedy this forgetfulness that Chapter

2 consists of a reasonably full account of the sociological work of Sigmund Freud.

2

FREUD ON SOCIETY AND THE SELF

His conclusions were, it is true, founded on the psychology of the individual, but it was Freud more than anyone else who taught us that every aspect of that individual is really a social one.

—Ernest Jones
The Life and Work of Sigmund Freud

In a recent article, the social psychologist Serge Moscovici (1993a) describes the discovery of the unconscious as "the most significant discovery in the history of psychology and its greatest contribution to world culture." He points to the rich correspondence between the "constructive" unconscious of psychoanalysis and the "functional" unconscious of cognitive psychology, and sketches an outline for a reconciliation in social psychology of the two streams. Both of these, he argues are crucial to a proper "collective psychology" of culture and social movements. One of the many obstacles to the actualization of Moscovici's scenario is what he calls "an embarassing silence in the books and articles published by social psychologists—those I have read, of course—concerning the ideas put forward by our classic writers, including Le Bon, MacDougall, and Freud" (1993a: 53). That is not to say that excellent prehistories have not been written; Jaap van Ginneken (1992) has written the most recent such study, showing the relations between the nineteenth-century "theorists of the crowd" and twentieth-century social psychology, and establishing Gabriel Tarde as a key linking figure. Rather, Moscovici is pointing here to the general absence of this history from the work of actual social psychologists. Behind this neglect, he suggests, lies a profound uneasiness with any association with the "immense presence of Freud" (Moscovici 1993a: 53), who, when considered at all in this regard, is treated either as an historical figure in psychology or as just another crowd theorist.

It is not the case that the Freudian unconscious has been surpassed by social psychology, but rather that it has been repressed. Chapter 1 has shown that this is also the case in critical educational studies. Moscovici calls explicitly for the remembering of the penetrating early theorization into collective behavior, and it is to partially fill that intellectual gap that this chapter is written. It provides backing for two central assertions of this book: that psychoanalysis is a *social* theory, and that psychoanalysis has potential value for educational theorists. This review systematically outlines Freud's own writing on religion, history, groups, and the origins of social life. While far from a comprehensive account of the work of this disregarded corpus, the chapter does attempt to synthesize Freud's writing on "civilization," as well as to explicate his engagement with the work of other turn-of-the-century theorists of collective behavior, particularly Gustave le Bon.

Despite the fact that Freud wrote many works on socio-cultural matters, and despite the proliferation since him of applied psychoanalytic studies, there is an assumption that Freud himself was principally a psychological clinician, the wider implications of whose theory need to be extracted by social theorists. One seldom reads today of the sociological content of Freud's own writings. In an attempt to remedy this situation, what follows provides a brief chronological overview of his discussions of society. It is hoped that this reading of the sociological Freud will accomplish two functions besides telling a story that is seldom heard today. First, it will provide ample evidence for the relevance of psychoanalysis for the study of social phenomena. Second, and more specifically, this exposition will highlight some of the concepts that when developed into a model of the self/society relation, might well be useful contributions to the theoretical problems currently facing social research.

Since it is Freud's one book that focuses precisely on the problem of understanding the behavior of people in groups, the greatest attention will be paid to *Group Psychology and the Analysis of the Ego* (1921). This chapter, then, is divided into three parts: a section on Freud's writings before the publication of the group psychology book, a second on the book itself, and a third on Freud's work after that date.

PRE-1921

Sigmund Freud, the founder of psychoanalysis, described his intellectual career as following "a long *détour* through the natural sciences, medicine and psychotherapy" only to return to "the cultural problems which had fascinated me long before" (1935: 72). He returned "with increasing regularity" to the study of culture, which for him included not only theories on art but also questions about the origins of civilization, social life, and the relation of the individual to society. Freud's long life was devoted to understanding the human condition: "human civilization, by which I mean all those aspects in which human life has raised itself above its animal status and differs from the life of beasts—and I scorn to distinguish between culture and civilization" (1927: 5-6).

His very first published case history argued that as much attention should be paid to the patient's "purely human and social circumstances" as to the clinical facts (1905a: 18). In fact his cultural or sociological work was really no more than a wider application of the psychological theories he developed based on clinical casework; there was never a separation for Freud between matters psychological and matters social. This is, of course, further borne out by the centrality of the primary social group—the family—in psychoanalysis.

Repression of Instinctual Drive

While it is true that Freud's cultural theories grew in complexity and frequency throughout his life, a basic theme was stated in a letter written to Wilhelm Fliess on May 31, 1897: "Civilization consists in . . . progressive renunciation. Contrariwise, the 'superman'" (in Masson 1985: 252). Cultural development, Freud insisted, depends upon the increasing repression of the individual's instincts. In his early psychological work, however, Freud postulated both external and internal sources of repression. On November 14 of that same year, Freud wrote to Fliess of his suspicion of an organic feature of repression originating, for example, in the human adoption of an upright stance and the replacement of smell by sight as the most important sense (78-80). This problematic continued in *Three Essays on the Theory of Sexuality* wherein Freud allowed both for an "inverse relation holding between civilization and the free development of sexuality" and for an "organically determined" repression (1905b: 242, 117-18). The evaluation of the external sources of repression as dominant had to wait for Freud's concept of the superego emerging from early object relations (1923). ("Object relations" here simply means the earliest relations to love objects.)

An instinctual drive, unlike other physiological stimuli, is a stimulus operating on the mind from within the organism. Undiminished by muscular flight, an instinctual drive is a need that can be gratified. Noting that all mental functions are regulated by the pleasure/unpleasure principle, Freud postulated that feelings of pleasure or unpleasure "reflect the manner in which the process of mastering stimuli takes place," the former representing a decrease and the latter an increase of stimulus. An instinctual wish, then, is the psychic representation of the instinctual drive originating in the organism; it exists "on the frontier between the mental and the somatic" (1915a: 118-22).

An instinctual drive, Freud showed, may reverse into its opposite, turn around upon the subject's own self, be repressed, forced out of consciousness into the unconscious, or be sublimated, be ready for use by a drive "that is higher, and perhaps no longer sexual." These vicissitudes are ways of dealing with "the unserviceable aim of various impulses" (1910a: 54). His next formulation of the instinctual drives postulated the existence of two drives, the sexual and the aggressive (1920). Although more is known about the former, both instincts are always mixed, though in different strengths. And in each manifestation of the instincts a different amount of psychic energy is invested—cathexis—in the mental representation of a person or a thing.

The sexual instinct, libido, then, is capable of displacement without diminishing in strength, a process he called "sublimation." Or sexual thoughts can be outlawed and repressed into the unconscious, revealing their continued existence in slips, dreams, jokes, free association, or in neurotic symptoms.

Mental slips or parapraxes, Freud showed, can be traced to strong unconscious motives. All people, he found, forget proper names, foreign words, and impressions and intentions. They commit slips of the tongue and other errors for reasons unknown to themselves. Parapraxes are not chance accidents. For example, when an uncle, after a long-awaited visit, bade farewell to his relatives with the words: "I hope from now on I shall see you still *more seldom* than in the past," he had unknowingly taken offense at the long gap between visits (1901: 7).

Dreams are another example of how the healthy person can be shown to have a motivating unconscious. Dreams, like pathological thought, operate according to "primary process thinking." Primary process is the "language of the unconscious," the laws of which govern the translation of manifest to latent dream content. Typically, day residues, thoughts aroused during the course of the day, connect during the night with unconscious memories of early life that have been repressed. Via mechanisms of condensation, displacement, and "concern for representability" (1900: 339), the dream-work activities, day residues, and repressed thoughts are distorted according to these unconscious laws. And, above all, dreams are wish fulfillments. For example, an aunt who dreamt of her nephew lying in his coffin unconsciously longed to see this loved relative whom she had last seen beside the coffin of another nephew. As she did not experience grief in relation to the dream, in this case the dream was not a wish for the death of the nephew (1900: 152-54, 248). Phantasies or day dreams are like dreams in that they are also distorted wish fulfillments that are expressed as a result of relaxed censorship (1907b).

The psychological function of jokes is the satisfaction of lustful or hostile instincts inhibited by the obstacle of social distaste at the undisguised expression of such desires. While "a dream is a completely asocial mental product," a joke "is the most social of all the mental functions that aim at a yield in pleasure" (1905c: 179).

The derivatives of unconscious drives can be made to enter consciousness, but this requires exertion. The individual who tries to dredge up the contents of his or her unconscious encounters a feeling of repulsion; in the same way, during analysis patients resist gaining insight. We can therefore distinguish between preconscious ideas that can easily be made conscious, and unconscious ideas that are forcefully prevented from direct expression. Each psychical act, Freud said, begins as an unconscious one. Whether or not it can become conscious depends on whether it meets with resistance (1912: 264).

Hysterical patients, Freud discovered early on, are often driven by hidden motives and feelings of ambivalence. Anna O, for example, developed paralysis of her right arm. Although she did not know the cause of this symptom, it was discovered after laborious analysis that in a semiawake state she had phantasized that a snake was approaching her ailing father and she had felt unable to lift her arm to protect him as her arm had fallen asleep. From then on her arm had become rigid whenever the sight of an object reminded her of a snake (Breuer and Freud 1895: 21-47).

Civilization and Repression

Civilization, or social life, depends upon the repression of raw, unmodified instinctual drives that, if strenuously pursued, are asocial. Society demands that each individual give up "some part of the sense of omnipotence or of the aggressive or vindictive inclinations in his personality" (1908: 186). Excessive repression of sexual drive, however, results, as Freud's clinical work clearly shows, in neurotic illness. Freud therefore questioned whether the civilized sexual morality of his day, which permitted only reproduction as a legitimate sexual aim, was worth the price of increased neurotic illness.

Religion and Magic

Freud's views on religion were intimately tied to his ideas of the development of cultures and the development of the individual mind. The mythological view of the world evident in most modern languages is the projection of inner psychological processes into the world. This notion he illustrated by comparing religious ceremonial acts to the rituals of the obsessional neurotic (1907a). Just as the obsessional neurotic attempts to ward off sexual temptation by invoking various personal rituals (an individual religiosity), so religion analogously combats aggressive and antisocial desires (a generalized obsessional neurosis).

Freud mentioned a second feature of the development of civilization. Human consciousness widens as societies become more complex and, rather than this fact counteracting simultaneous repression, the widening of interests and capacities is won at the expense of the instincts. In his psychological biography of Leonardo da Vinci, Freud made the parallels between religion and psychopathological struggles even more plain (1910b). Stemming from the

Oedipus complex, God is the representation of an exalted father image.

Totem and Taboo was Freud's first comprehensive attempt to deal with basic questions of culture and religions (1912-1913); it is an effort to synthesize the findings of psychoanalysis and those of anthropology. Freud used the examples of childhood and neurotic mental processes as well as those recorded by anthropologists to demonstrate commonalities and links.

Anthropologists studying "primitive" cultures around the world confirmed one common social fact: the fear and harsh punishment of incest. Freud argued that groups impose strict rules for those crimes that the people are strongly tempted to commit. The incest taboo therefore stems from a deep desire to commit incest. Such desires become repressed and denied. When considering totemic worship, Freud reiterated a theme broached earlier, namely equating such practices with the Oedipus complex. Both the incest taboo and the protected totem, the latter of which represents the father, stem from incestuous desires for the mother and the consequent hostility toward the father. Freud told "a just-so story," which he suggested recurred in essentially the same way over thousands of years. Darwin had postulated the existence at the beginning of humankind of a primal horde ruled over by an old man who posessed all the women. Driven by their desire for the women and their growing hatred for the "father" of the horde, the younger men set about murdering the older man and eating his flesh. After a brief period of free expression of instinctual drive, this crime was followed by remorse, repressions, and inhibitions, and lived on as guilty conscience.

The underlying motives of the complex rules of primitive societies are revealed during totemic feasts during which taboo sexual relations are permitted and the totem animal is ceremoniously slaughtered and devoured by the entire clan. Similarly, for Freud, children have sexual desires toward one parent and aggressive feelings toward the other in the Oedipus complex. A crucial conclusion reached here is that all human relationships are essentially ambivalent.

When considering animism and magic, Freud found—just as with obsessional neurotics and with the unconscious generally—that thoughts are regarded as omnipotent. Superstitions are based upon the belief that wishes can influence reality: wish fulfillments. With children one also finds drives of murder, cannibalism, and incest. Now, if we combine with these desires the omnipotence of thoughts, it is not hard to see that whether or not one actually commits a phantasized forbidden act has no relevance as far as feelings of guilt are concerned: the wish is the same as the deed in the world of the unconscious.

Religions, then, are the products of the guilt that groups suffer for their terrible desires. They are, in this sense, ancient memories. But they are historically based in that "God the Father once walked upon earth in bodily form and exercised his sovereignty as chieftain of the primal horde until his sons united to slay him" (1919: 262).

Referring fleetingly to a concept that was to take on greater significance in his later work, Freud wrote in his essay on narcissism that the ego ideal has an individual side, which "binds" narcissistic libido and much homosexual libido, and a social side, which is the "common ideal of a family, a class or a nation" (1914b: 101).

Politics and Groups

Reflecting pessimistically on the problem of war and death, Freud showed the two ways in which innate selfish instincts are transformed into altruism, viz. internal and external (1915b). The internal way is the influence of erot- icism—the need for love—on self-directed libido. The combination of eroticism and egoism produces social attitudes. People accept the love of others in return for the renunciation of their own desires for immediate instinctual satisfaction. The external way consists of the environment, both the immediate cultural environment and the traces of ancestral cultural history. But external compulsion, which can by rewards and punishment produce changed behaviour, does not necessarily involve "ennoblement of instinct" (1915b: 283). Freud continued to worry that because modern society assumes that all people's social behaviour is the result of real psychological altruism, it tightens moral standards beyond a level attainable by most of its members. Lives lived in accordance with standards based upon instincts that have not in fact been transformed are mentally troubled lives. Also, however, since mental development involves not the replacement of individualistic stages by higher social stages but the coexistence of stages, regression to the more primitive mental mode is always possible. "Thus the transformation of instinct, on which our susceptibility to culture is based, may also be permanently or temporarily undone by the impacts of life" (286).

Freud, although not a sympathizer with Marxism, acknowledged that work and the economy were crucial factors in human life. As society needs its members to work to survive, it controls the numbers of those members and it redirects their sexual energies toward work. "The motive of human society is in the last resort an economic one" (1916-1917: 312). So, infants are taught very early on to excrete on demand, "to exchange pleasure for social respectibility" (315). The "ego-censor" has its origins in "the influence of parents, educators and social environment—from an identification with some of these model figures" (429).

Throughout Freud's life there was in Europe an intense interest in the new disciplines of sociology, anthropology, and psychology, as well as heightened political interest in urbanization, industrialization, democracy, socialism, and fascism; in short, a widespread interest in understanding and influencing people in groups (see Barrows 1981; Nye 1975). Because the works of the French writer Gustave Le Bon were so influential both in Europe generally, and in Freud's study of group psychology, it is worth a short detour through his life and work.

Le Bon

Gustave Le Bon (1841-1931), well known in his day as a popularizer of science, is best remembered for *La psychologie des foules* (known in English as *The Crowd*), until recently the best-selling scientific book in history. Published in 1895, this psychological study of the crowd has been described as possibly "the most influential book ever written in social psychology" (Allport 1968: 35). A political conservative, Le Bon was a strenuous opponent of the democratic socialism of the Third Republic, and was one who set out with some success to influence political and military elites; indeed, his work was known to both Hitler and Mussolini. The latter was an ardent reader of Le Bon's works, and received the "conditional" support of the author for the Italian dictatorship (Nye 1975: 177-79). Le Bon was, however, only the most popular of a host of crowd theorists, and Susanna Barrows has traced the emergent discipline's history and intellectual roots, as have Erica Apfelbaum and Gregory McGuire, Patrick Bratlinger, Dieter Groh, Serge Moscovici, and most recently van Ginneken. Robert Nye (1973) has also shown that later totalitarian theories of the masses emerged at least partly from these turn-of-the-century intellectual detestations of the crowd.

In *La psychologie des foules*, Le Bon argued that the individual in a crowd behaves like the hypnotic, and that the irrationality of crowds can thus be attributed to the suggestibility of their members, who act in increasingly primitive and instinctual ways (Le Bon 1895). This analysis Le Bon extended to all groups, both law-abiding and criminal: to juries, parliaments, social classes, electorates, and academies, as well as to violent strikes and workers' riots. Realistically, however, he realized that crowd behavior was inevitable and that politically motivated crowds were of growing importance. The only hope for Western civilization was the governance of such crowds by leaders who understood how to manipulate the imagination of crowds. Leaders needed prestige and virtuous reputations in addition to knowledge of the rules of crowd psychology, which Le Bon said are essentially emotional rather than logical. Le Bon thereby ingeniously turned growing bourgeois dismay at Western decadence into crowd psychology, a tool for controlling the masses. Crowds, arrogant in the face of weakness, are servile before authority, and the statesman who learns to move crowds by "images, words, and formulas" could use illusion to master them, he wrote (1895: 90-96). His Machiavellian text told the new prince precisely how to sway crowds. The art of persuasion, he said some years later, has "five chapters: affirmation; repetition; prestige; suggestion; contagion" (1913:

273). This aphorism of Le Bon summarizes his theory about the member of a crowd: "A man who is part of a crowd ceases to be himself. His conscious personality vanishes into the unconscious soul of the crowd. He loses all critical spirit, all ability to reason and returns to primitiveness" (276).

GROUP PSYCHOLOGY AND THE ANALYSIS OF THE EGO

This work by Freud is, as the title suggests, both a theory of group formation based on individual psychology and a contribution to Freud's model of the mind, which was fully developed as the structural model in *The Ego and the Id* (1923). *Group Psychology* begins with Freud's insistence that, except with respect to narcissistic processes, individual psychology cannot be separated from the relations between the individual and others: "From the very first individual psychology, in this extended but entirely justified sense of the words, is at the same time social psychology as well" (1921: 69).

Freud argued against the existence of a social instinct, a popular idea of the day—Le Bon, William McDougall, and Wilfred Trotter—showing the folly of attributing to sheer numbers the ability to ignite an instinct otherwise dormant. Rather, he suggested that social behavior is reducible to a more basic group; its origins are in the family. Just as family life inevitably involves the controlling of desires and a loss of privacy and individual identity, so the social group demands sacrifices from its members while offering them certain advantages.

What, Freud asked, is a group? How is it able to influence the behavior of the individual? How do people behave in groups? Although it contributed nothing new, he said, Freud was attracted to Le Bon's analysis of the behavior of crowds because of the place in Le Bon's theory for unconscious processes and because of the elaboration of the impulsiveness, credulity, intolerance, obedience, illogicality, and susceptibility of crowds to the power of words. The morals of people in crowds, Freud agreed, differ from the morals of their individual members: in crowds people are capable both of cruel and destructive behavior, and of high and unselfish acts. He asked, if crowds are united, what unites them?

While Le Bon asserted that in a crowd individual differences disappear and are replaced by an "average character" and some new characteristics, Freud pointed out that the unexpected behavior of people in crowds was better explained as the throwing off of repressions (which Le Bon's notion of the unconscious did not include). Le Bon argued not simply that the crowd behaves *like* a hypnotic subject, but that it actually *is* a hypnotic. But where, then, is the hypnotist? Freud saw that Le Bon had misunderstood the importance of the leader, and that *La psychologie des foules* lacked an explanation for group cohesion. Le Bon's leader of the instinctually submissive herd had only to have a strong faith himself as well as "prestige." But prestige exists only in its ability to evoke suggestion, so this description was not sufficient to explain the function of the leader or the nature of prestige; nor were shared interests, the sense of belonging, or fear of separation sufficient explanations for the existence of groups. Instead of focusing primarily on people's suggestibility, Freud emphasized that this characteristic was itself a derivative and could only be explained by considering the libidinal bonds between members of the group, and between members and the leader.

Libido, the energy of the instinctual drives called "love," encompasses sexual union as well as the aim-inhibited forms of love: self-love, love for parents or children, friendship, love for humanity in general, love of things and of abstract ideas. Libidinal ties, or, more neutrally, emotional ties, are, as in hypnosis and in the family, aim-inhibited bonds thar counter individual narcissistic self-love. It must be remembered that psychoanalysis has shown that every intimate relationship is ambivalent, the "sediment of aversion and hostility" (1921: 101) routinely made invisible by repression.

Freud was principally concerned here with those groups that have a leader but that have not acquired the characteristics of the individual person. While Le Bon had accurately described short-lived crowds, the more lasting associations and institutions of society deserved a more friendly description: "Groups of the first kind stand in the same sort of relation to those of the second as a high but choppy sea to a ground swell" (1921: 83). Following W. McDougall's distinction between temporary crowds and the more stable groups of society (McDougall 1920), Freud pointed out that the former type of group regressed in behavior and thought to an earlier stage, thereby lowering the individual's intellect, distinctiveness, and sense of identity.

While Freud said that the average intelligence of unorganized crowds is low, the group mind, he agreed, is capable of creative genius. He gave language, folk song, and folklore as examples of such genius. The more organized a group, the greater the control of unconscious drives, the lower the vulnerability to suggestion and regression, and the greater the coherence of the sense of individual identity. In other words, the highly organized group is not unlike the individual prior to his or her renunciation of instinctual aims in group formation. Like a pristine individual (who, aside from the cases of infants and narcissism, only exists theoretically) the group develops continuity, self-consciousness, traditions and customs, particular functions and positions, and separation from rivals. But this does not contradict the two basic facts regarding groups, the general intensification of emotion and the inhibition of intellect:

> We are reminded of how many of these phenomena of dependence are part of the *normal constitution of human society*, of how little originality and personal courage are to be found in it, of how much *every individual* is ruled by those attitudes of the group mind which exhibit themselves in such forms as racial

characteristics, class prejudices, public opinion, etc. (1921: 117; italics added)

Acknowledging the complexity of groups in society, Freud used two examples of highly organized, lasting, and artificial groups. The Catholic Church and the army demonstrate the attachments between members and the leader and between members themselves. The leaders, the symbolic fathers of these groups, are believed by the members to love each member equally. All groups are loving communities internally while cruel and intolerant toward outsiders. Acting as social cement, the illusion that they are loved equally by the leader unites members into a community: "brothers in Christ," or comrades in arms. Conversely, a group, say an army, disintegrates not only because of increased danger but because of a loss of the libidinal forces of attraction in the group. The perceived loss of the leader himself, or misgivings about the leader's love, results in the disintegration of the group into selfish individuals.

It should be noted that for Freud the "leader" can be a living or non living figure, an ideal, or even an interest or shared wish. He insisted, too, that the ideal expressed or presented by the leader has to correspond closely with the ideals of the followers. Also, identifications with each other and those with the leader can be accompanied by object ties.

Libido and Identification in Individuals

While in the former the boy wants to have the object, in the latter he wants to be like the object. Identification is an ambivalent relationship. In the Oedipus complex the boy wants to possess his mother and to be like his father. He therefore wants to take the place of his father in the eyes of his mother, and as a result wishes for the removal and death of the father at the same time as he feels a tenderness towards him. The libidinal ties of groups are different from sexual object-cathexis. Far from simple object-cathexes, the libidinal ties of groups are desexualized identifications. Identification, the earliest example of an emotional tie, is a remnant of the oral stage and involves symbolically eating (introjecting) and thus destroying the loved object.

Sensual love expires when its aim of direct sexual satisfaction is reached. Affectionate love, on the other hand, involves a libidinal object-tie that is aim-inhibited, primarily the product of the repression of the infant's sexual desires for a parent. Every affectionate feeling is the successor to a "sensual" tie with the object or with the object's prototype. Desexualized drives form more lasting bonds because, unlike sexual cathexes, they cannot achieve total satisfaction. In romantic love—the state of "being in love"—earthly love (sexual) and heavenly love (spiritual affection) are combined.

Being in love is typified by idealization, the overvaluation of the loved object. Here, Freud says, the object is treated like the individual's own ego:

LIBRARY
OF
MOUNT ST. MARY'S
COLLEGE
EMMITSBURG, MARYLAND

being in love involves "narcissistic libido overflow" (1921: 112) onto the object. The similarity between the idealizing aspect of being in love and the sublimated devotion to an abstract idea are clear. Devotion of this type, where the object can do no wrong, involves the cessation of the critical agency, at that time called the ego ideal: "The object has been put in the place of the ego ideal" (113). Being in love is similar to hypnosis where the figure of the hypnotist replaces the ego ideal. Freud pulled these threads together by arguing that aim-inhibited libido and devotion to an idealized object are common features of romantic love, hypnosis, and group formation.

Identification is the original form of link between a person and an object and therefore a libidinal tie may become an identification. In contrast to Le Bon's argument, for Freud identification with another does not occur through sympathy, but through a wish shared as "a point of coincidence between the two egos" (1921: 107). Identification is closely linked to empathy, a felt under-standing of another's mental life.

Identification in Groups

Identifications in groups arise from a perceived, shared, common quality, specifically the common tie with the leader. Freud made a distinction, as we have seen between the ego identifying with an object and the ego ideal being replaced by an object. For example, the soldier takes his superior officer as his ideal, but identifies with his comrades and not with the leader. In the Catholic Church, on the other hand, the Christian identifies with other Christians, takes Christ as his or her ideal, *and* identifies with Christ (1921: 134). There is, though, a causal link between identification and alteration of the ego ideal. "*A primary group of this kind is a number of individuals who have put one and the same object in the place of their ego ideal and have consequently identified themselves with another in their group*" (116).

Freud found the concept of a herd instinct of humanity (as in W. Trotter's *Instincts of the Herd in Peace and War*) unacceptable in its postulation of this "instinct" as irreducible and in its total disregard of the leader: "the herd . . . without the herdsman" (1921: 119). Nonetheless, the book did lead Freud to a consideration of the bonds between members of groups. The manifestations of group formation among nursery children, for example, Freud showed to be the results, not of an innate herd instinct, but of a slow realization by each child that envy of the other children is not possible without self-injury. Consequently, the child identifies with the other children. In other words, the apparently natural sociability of children is a development from an earlier individualistic phase. *Gemeingeist, esprit de corps*, or "group spirit" is derived, therefore, from envy. Social justice is the result of the willingness of the members of the group to share their love object on the condition that no one receives favoritism. A group of individuals identifying with equals and with a superior leader is more properly called a horde than a herd, Freud said.

Returning to the hypothesis of *Totem and Taboo*, Freud postulated original human beings as individuals living in a horde ruled by a chief. This leader, loving no one but himself and restricting none of his drives, is like Nietzsche's "superman," except that for Freud he existed at the beginning of civilization and not in the future. Freud again argued his point that the primal father, possessing the females and oppressing the members of the horde, was killed by the younger men who subsequently became "brothers." The memory of this murderous and cannibalistic event (or, as we have seen, the desire for the event) survives as "indestructible traces upon the history of human descent" (1921: 122) and plays a part in totemism (the basis of religion), morality, and all group formation. The contrivance, or illusion, of groups according to which the leader loves all members of the group equally is an "idealistic remodeling" (124-25) of the situation of the primal horde where all the sons were equally persecuted by the father and feared him equally: "Just as primitive man survives potentially in every individual, so the primal horde may arise once more out of every random collection; in so far as men are habitually under the sway of group formation, we recognize it in the survival of the primal horde" (112-23). Hypnosis depends on the reawakening of the individual's relation to the father and, further back still, a memory of the relation of the member of the primal horde to the leader. Similarly, "the leader of the group is still the dreaded primal father" (127).

Using the example of melancholia, characterized by self-reproaches linked to the loss of an object, Freud added a new development to his earlier topographical model of unconscious, preconscious, and conscious regions of the mind. Emerging out of the ego, Freud realized, is a structure that becomes largely unconscious and that, containing the introjected object, criticizes the conscious part. The unconscious critic he here called the ego ideal. As yet undifferentiated by Freud into the super-ego and the ego ideal, the ego ideal concept at this date also served as the model of perfection that we strive to attain. "A feeling of triumph" follows the coincidence of the ego and the ego ideal, and a sense of guilt and inferiority is "the expression of tension between the ego and the ego ideal" (1921: 131). Freud gave as an example of these effects manic depression in which the ego ideal, after ruling with particular severity, temporarily "resolves into" the ego (132). Analogously, the primal father (or the group leader) is the group ideal "which governs the ego in the place of the ego ideal" (127).

To condense this complex and innovative volume into one sentence, one can say that individuals behave as group members as a result of the ambivalent identificatory libidinal bonds with the leader and with other members that produce a group ego ideal.

POST-1921

The process whereby selfish instincts become affectionate, as Freud discussed in *Group Psychology*, is a generalized expression of a process that occurs in more particular instances. For example, Freud argued that male homosexuality can be the consequence of a boy's intense jealousy of his older brothers. In order to conquer his destructive death wishes for the brothers, the boy identifies with them and so the objects of his hatred become his love objects (1922).

Religion

The Future of an Illusion (1927) further developed Freud's earlier ideas about religion. For Freud, religion is an "illusion," but he made it clear that an illusion is not necessarily an error; an illusion is a belief primarily motivated by wish. Although he demonstrated the roots of all religions, these origins are grossly distorted within each religion by hopes derived from wishes and needs. While Freud had, up to this point, placed stress on the wishes related to children trying to come to terms with their parents, he now also emphasized the needs arising from human helplessness in general. In the face of the dangers of the outer world, inner mortal weakness, and troublesome social relations, "man's helplessness remains and along with it his longing for his father, and the gods" (1927: 17-18).

At this point Freud enunciated his thinking on the relation of religion and society. Human civilization has two aspects: (a) acquired knowledge, the ability to control nature and to extract wealth to meet human needs, and (b) mores and regulations that adjust social relations especially with respect to the distribution of wealth. These two aspects are related in three ways. First, the form of social relations is closely linked to the extent of instinctual satisfaction wealth will allow; second, an individual can serve as wealth for another as a worker or as a sexual object; and third, every individual is "an enemy of civilization" at the same time as "civilization is supposed to be an object of universal interest" (1927: 6).

The internalization of external coercion into what Freud by now called the super-ego, and the latter's consequent strengthening, is "a most precious cultural asset" whereby the opponents of the culture become its vehicles (1927: 11). The earliest cultural strictures are attributed to God, and "through some kind of diffusion or infection" divinity is spread to every other cultural rule (41). But this is far from a fait accompli. While most people have internalized the taboos against incest, cannibalism, and murder, they are still avaricious and lustful, they lie, commit fraud, and so on. The obvious (and, for Freud, understandable) objections of the suppressed and deprived classes to many cultural norms overshadow the fact of "the more latent hostility" of the wealthier classes. He predicted justifiable revolt by the rebellious lower classes and a curtailed existence for any civilization that leaves unsatisfied so many of its members (12).

Despite the fact that religious ideas are wish fulfillments that contain historical recollections and can spare people from the development of personal neuroses, Freud insisted that religion is a universal neurosis we can well do without. He argued instead for rational and scientific thinking that would reconcile people to "the burden of civilization" by their realization that laws are in their interests: that laws can be improved upon, but not abolished (1927: 41-43).

Civilization

Civilization and Its Discontents (1930) was an attempt by Freud to uncover the nature of the relationship between people and the universe. While people are driven by the search for happiness, because of bodily suffering, external dangers, and poor relations with other people, "one feels inclined to say that the intention that man should be 'happy' is not contained in the plan of 'Creation'" (1930: 36). Civilization originated, as Freud had said before, when a number of people limiting their gratifications found that they were stronger than a single powerful man satisfying all his desires. The assurance that no law will be broken for any individual is, for all cultures, justice. Social life, then, is essentially a contradictory compromise between the claims of the individual and the claims of the group. The institutions that protect the people at the same time produce their discontents.

But not only is Eros repressed in civilization: so are the aggressive instincts. Menaced by the aggression of its members, society must prevent it at all costs, although aggression directed against enemies—"narcissism of minor differences"—strengthens the bonds of the group (1930: 114). Pathologically, however, aggression is internalized into the super-ego, which exerts the harsh aggression on the ego that the ego actually wants to inflict on others. The tension produces guilt and feelings of inferiority. The "cultural super-ego" is the production of many such internalizations of aggresive feelings back into the self (141-43).

Freud's objections to religion's "prohibition against thought" were again raised in the *New Introductory Lectures* (1933: 171). He considered institutionalized Marxism to be a religious-type illusion that stifles thought. While he dismissed Marxism's view of history and its predictions for the future, he saw the strength of "its sagacious indication of the decisive influence which the economic circumstances of men have upon their intellectual, ethical and artistic attitudes" (178). He said the task of a scientific sociology—"applied psychology"—is to show in detail how inherited human dispositions (both the ancient history of civilizations and cultural transformations) affected one another while taking into account social rank, profession, and earning power (179).

The *New Introductory Lectures* again makes direct connections between culture and the super-ego: Freud stressed the importance of considering the super-ego for the understanding of social behavior. Parents and other authorities, for example, forget their own childhoods and educate their children (and thereby the super-egos of these children) according to their own super-egos. Thus the super-ego is filtered down the generations with these "time-resisting judgements of value" (1933: 67). Returning to his partial agreement with some Marxist notions, Freud said of the "materialist" doctrine that ideologies are the products of contemporary economic conditions: "That is true, but very probably not the whole truth." Living as we do, as least partially in the past, the ancient traditions of people live on in "the ideologies of the super-ego, and yield only slowly to the influences of the present and to new changes." The past, via the operation of the super-ego, "plays a powerful part in human life independently of economic conditions" (67).

In his final book, *Moses and Monotheism* (1939), Freud attempted to uncover the origins of the Jewish and Christian faiths, and he also considered the general significance of religion. The book's first two sections propose that Moses was an Egyptian nobleman who advocated a monotheistic religion that he borrowed from pharoah Amenhotep IV (circa 1375 B.C.); Moses then led the oppressed Jewish people from Egypt only to be murdered by his followers. The Jewish people then reverted for several generations to worshipping Yahweh, a cruel volcano god. After several centuries a new prophet (with whom the story of Moses has been condensed in biblical myth) adopted the name of Moses and imposed his predecessor's religion upon his people. In both the Jewish and Christian religions Freud uncovered the murder of the original leader (Moses and Jesus) and, after a period, the emergence of a new leader (the new Moses and Paul), who advanced the creed in the name of the dead progenitor. In the Christian communion, when symbols for the body and the blood of the crucified Christ are consumed, Freud found the traces of the totemic feast: the symbolic destruction and introjection of the original leader.

In the third and final section of the book Freud reasserted the familiar theme of the neurotic nature of all religion and added the notion of a latency period—between the primal crime and the return of the repressed guilt—to account for profound "oceanic" religious feelings. The "archaic heritage" that Freud mentioned more and more often exists, he said, in the id. At birth, people have not yet developed an ego, but via "phylogenetic" inheritance they come into the world with preexisting tendencies, for example, the predisposition for suggestion (1921: 128) and also symbols (1939: 102, editor's note).

CONCLUSION

George Orwell once said that one of the most pressing questions is not only why the dog bites the hand that feeds it, but why it licks the hand that beats it. The irrationality of human social behavior is as intriguing and vital today. While Moscovici criticised only social psychology for having forgotten Freud, he could quite justifiably have included vast tracts of philosophy and sociology, as well as whole disciplines like education and academic psychology, all of which seem determined to fight with one hand tied behind their backs. Indeed, Moscovici has gone a lot further when he argues that sociologists can describe and prescribe, but are not able to *explain* without reverting to what they have expressly forbidden themselves, viz. psychology; the great sociologists, he says, were "great psychologists who scorned psychology" (1993b: 21). Implications for social research generally can be drawn out of Moscovici's article. Most importantly, analyzing the achitechtronics of human subjectivity cannot credibly ignore the social expression of both "compelling reflexes and irresistible compulsory ideas" (1993a: 91). And this should not proceed without an appreciative taking into account of what has already been discovered.

This chapter has provided an inkling of the enormous scope of Freud's sociological writing. The range of this work, and the half-century across which it was produced, transcends many particular interests, emphases, interpretations, and explanations of his contribution, and renders it nigh on impossible to summarize. However, it is possible to extract certain themes that emerge with some regularity: the ego is not master in its own house; individual psychology—inextricably linked to upbringing, cultural environment, and ancient historical traces—is always also social psychology; the importance of the Oedipus complex in history and prehistory; the demand of civilization for instinctual repression; the central role of the leader in social life; group formation and religion as the result of repressed wishes and distorted memories of real events; the ambivalence of all libidinal ties; and the super-ego and ego ideal as the sites of cultural ideals.

It must be said, however, that if psychoanalysis is to be more than either a means to "scientific" social psychological ends, or a merely source of social classifications, the spirit of Freud's writings should not be missed. It is a fascinating proposal that social psychology (broadly defined) could be both humanized and more rigourous through the *anti*humanism and refinements of psychoanalysis. But that is the subject for another occasion. This review chapter hopefully leaves little doubt as to the crucial place of the unconscious in the behavior of social collectivities, and thus the potential usefulness of psychoanalysis to their study. In this regard both Freud's psychological and sociological writings warrant rereading.

Having (1) identified a gap in CSOE with regards to unconscious processes, and (2) demonstrated the extent of Freud's own sociology, Chapters 3, 4, 5, and 6 will undertake the principal task of the book: the development of a psychic economy of subjectivity.

NOTE

This chapter has been reprinted from the 1995 article "Freud on Civilization," *Human Relations*, 48 (6), pp. 625-45.

3

ALTHUSSER:
THE TROJAN HORSE

The only way *beyond* Althusserianism is through it, not round it.
—Tony Bennett
"The Not-So-Good, the Bad and the Ugly"

The work of Louis Althusser has been almost completely repressed in critical educational studies. When his name is mentioned, it is dismissed in a most perfunctory fashion. It may be strange in the age of "the crisis in historical materialism" (Aronowitz 1981) not to mention the collapse of communism in Eastern Europe, to attempt to blow air into the lungs of the this "dead dog" (Alain Lipietz, quoted in Elliott 1987: 1). However, Althusser's work may be uniquely suited to addressing the problems of critical educational studies, namely its total lack of sophisticated psychological concepts with which to understand motivation and socialization. Stephen Crook has called Althusser the Trojan Horse of recent social analysis: "He smuggled a series of anti-humanist, anti-idealist, anti-historicist themes into radical social theory" (Crook 1991: 146). I too use Althusser to convey a way of thinking into the fortress of educational theory, and as a way to organize my introduction of psychoanalysis.

Rather than itself being an encomium to Althusser, though, this chapter is anti-anti-Althusserian (Elliott 1987: 10) as well as post-Althusserian (Donald 1991). Seeing Althusser as a highly provocative and unjustly rejected thinker, I will attempt to use his later theory of ideology as a foundation upon which to build a more sophisticated, psychoanalytic theory of the identity-formation processes of socialization, especially those that arise in education.

The chapter is arranged in four sections. First, it places Althusser's work in context both politically (inside and outside the French Communist Party, or PCF) and intellectually (in Marxist and European thought generally). Second, it considers his *For Marx* and *Reading Capital* (written with Etienne Balibar), both first published in French in 1965, and *Lenin and Philosophy and Other Essays*, which appeared in 1971. In the process it outlines Althusser's major theoretical innovations and notes the development of his thought. All this is framed in the political events that so influenced his intellectual labor. Third, some common criticisms, particularly those of Paul Ricoeur (1986), as well as Althusser's own *Essays in Self-Criticism* (1976), are considered. While some of these criticisms are shown to be based on misunderstanding of his project, others are trenchant. Some basic themes are rejected, but Althusser's radical theoretical intervention is confirmed. Fourth, the theory of ideology is briefly introduced in light of what has been retained and what discarded from his corpus. The relevance of ideology-in-general to critical educational studies is proposed.

CONTEXT AND EARLY WORK

Althusser joined the PCF in 1948 when it was still strongly identified with the heroic Resistance to Nazism. Under the rigid control of Moscow, though, the PCF did not allow thinkers in its midst to develop theories in opposition to the party line. One either toed that line, trusting implicitly in its revolutionary role, or dissented and resigned, or was purged. (See Derrida 1993 for a non communist description of those difficult days.) Althusser meanwhile became a professor of philosophy at the École Normale Supérieure. Then at the Twentieth Party Congress of the Communist Party of the Soviet Union, Krushchev delivered his critique of Stalinism. This started an intellectual thaw, which opened the way for critical theoretical work within communist parties. Althusser's work was a response to this opportunity.

In the light of the summary ways in which Althusser has been dismissed as a "Stalinist," "economistic," "reproductionist," "reductionist," and so on (Barrett 1993; Clarke 1980; Giroux 1983b; Thompson 1978), it is crucial to understand how he viewed his own project. His major texts *For Marx* and *Reading Capital*, while operating in the realm of philosophy, had a dual political object, he said: opposition to both Stalinist economism ("dogmatism"), and to Krushchev's humanistic Marxism ("the rightist critique of dogmatism" [1976: 168-69]). The long overdue critique of Stalinism was to be made from the left, not from the right.

Althusser's opposition to the French Communist Party's allegiance to Moscow was initially only pursued obliquely in theoretical papers, but his favorable references to Mao in an essay on contradiction and overdetermination (1965a), and his incorporation of major ideas from non-Marxist European thought, were viewed askance by the PCF leadership, and he was censured throughout his career (Benton 1984). He was not expelled from the party nor, however, did he ever leave it—a matter of grave concern to his critics outside the PCF. His justification for remaining in the party was that the Communist Party was "not a biographical accident to me" (1978, quoted in Elliott 1987: 313), it was the only path to the revolutionary working class—without it his work would be over.

After representing the high point in the reemergence of Marxist theory in the 1960s and early 1970s, the name of Althusser has been either generally repressed and forgotten or continues to be cited only in the act of rejecting his work. Some of the embarrassment surrounding his name is undoubtedly attributable to "the tragedy of the Althussers" (Karol 1980; Althusser 1992): Althusser was admitted to St. Anne's Psychiatric Hospital in November 1980, having confessed to killing his wife Hélène. While the exact circumstances of this event are not clear, it is known that he had suffered from severe depressions for thirty years. On October 22, 1990, Althusser died at the St. Louis Hospital (Balibar 1991). His autobiography *The Future Lasts a Long Time* (published in English in 1993) is his attempt to understand why he perpetrated this ghastly act of madness.

But, of course, there were political events and intellectual trends, too, that drove Althusser's work from the high place it once enjoyed. In France, Marxism largely fell out of intellectual and political favor following the discrediting of East European communism with the invasion of Czechoslovakia, the demise of Maoism in China, and the defeat of the worker's movement in Southern Europe: this to the extent that "Paris today is the capital of European intellectual reaction," according to Perry Anderson (1983: 32). On the intellectual stage, the structuralism upon which Althusser's Marxism is based has been supplanted by non-Marxist poststructuralism and by Anglo-American analytical Marxism.

In Britain Althusser's work has also become marginalized after enjoying a high status, when it was discussed regularly in *New Left Review* and was called "scientific" by Barry Hindess and Paul Hirst (1975, 1977; Hirst 1985). This glorification is no longer the case. The most famous critique of Althusser in English is E.P. Thompson's essay, "The poverty of theory: Or, an orrery of errors" (1978). Thompson rejected the view that Althusser's later self-criticisms represented real movement. He baldly stated: "Althusserianism *is* Stalinism reduced to the paradigm of theory" (Thompson 1978: 374). This is a gross misreading; contrary to Thompson's accusation, Althusser's project was in large part an attempt to escape from the strictures and terror of Stalinism.

Althusser was eager by the late 1970s to extricate himself from political criticism after his poor record vis-à-vis the 1968 Paris uprising and the 1969 invasion of Czechoslovakia. At last he was openly critical not only of the PCF's theory but of its politics, which had lead to the electoral defeat of the Left in France in 1978. For many this was a case of too little, too late. Irrespective of his political record, however, we should study his theoretical work.

REREADING MARX

Althusser was opposed to economism, the teleological doctrine that socialist revolution is inevitable because of the conflict between the forces of production (land, technology, raw materials, labor power) and the relations of production (the relations between owners and nonowners of the means of production). This economism, first espoused late in his life by Engels, had become official Communist dogma after Stalin's *Dialectical and Historical Materialism* was published in 1938.

Nor does the principal contradiction between Capital and Labor inevitably lead to revolution, Althusser said. This contradiction only becomes "active" as "a ruptural principle" in "fusion" with historical circumstances and currents (1965a: 99). Taking political specificity seriously, Althusser rejected any economism that posits the political arena as simply a reflection of the economic base. The economic contraction does not determine other regions of social practice in any simple or direct way, but is, as history has shown, "inseparable" from its social conditions; it is radically *affected by them* (101). Echoing Mao (1953) and Freud (1900), Althusser said that every contradiction is an overdetermined contradiction; "complexly-structurally-unevenly-determined" (107). Overdetermination refers to the multiple and complex nature of the influence that levels of social practice bring to bear on one another. This overdetermined contradiction, as distinct from the simple Hegelian dialectic, was for Althusser "*the Marxist dialectic* itself" (1965g: 217).

The Social Formation

Althusser and Balibar did not claim that the social formation is a synonym for the mode of production (e.g., feudalism, capitalism, communism). Indeed, periods of transition are marked by "*the coexistence of two* (or more) *modes of production* in a single "simultaneity," with one being dominant (Althusser with Balibar 1965: 307).

Althusser argued that Marx and Engels had not only changed the terms of Hegel's state (passive)/civil (active) conception of society, they had also changed the relations between these terms. The social formation is rather characterized by "determination in the last instance by the (economic) mode of production" and "the relative autonomy of the superstructures and their specific effectivity" (1965g). So, Althusser developed the metaphor of Marx and Engels in *The German Ideology* whereby the social formation is likened to a building with the economic "base" represented by the foundations, and politics, law, values, norms, culture, education, art, theory, etc., represented by the visible edifice, or "superstructure." Althusser developed a theory of "social practice" that is constituted, as has been said, by distinct economic, political, ideological, and theoretical practices. The economic is the realm of production, the political is where social relations are transformed into new social relations, the ideological transforms "men's consciousness," and the theoretical is scientific thought (1965g: 229). Each of these domains is structurally the same but unique in content, each having different objects, means of production, and products, and each is articulated with, but relatively autonomous from the other practices in this "complex unity of practices in a determinate society" (1965f: 167). This complex structure is so arranged that the economic is determinant but not dominant.

Each of Althusser's levels operates according to "differential historical time," so that each type of social practice—economic, political, artistic, scientific, etc.—operates according to different time scales and tempo. "These differential histories are said to be *dislocated* with respect to one another in order to stress their irreducibility, the real difference between their respective rhythms, continuities and discontinuities" (Geras 1972: 112). Althusser refined Marx's notion of the labor process as developed in *Capital*. For Althusser "social practice" is made up of four main practices, with each practice having three moments: raw material, means of production, and product. A "practice" is any process of "transformation" through human labor (1965f: 166-67); "practice in the narrow sense" is the determinant element, "the moment of the labor of *transformation* itself" (167).

Engels had said that the economic is determinate "in the last instance" (Marx and Engels 1975: 393). In Althusser's hands, this does not constitute economism, however: "The economic dialectic is never active *in the pure state*. . . . From the first moment to the last, thel lonely hour of the last moment never comes" (1965c: 113). This does not mean that society is a plural collection of equal instances, but that the "*complex whole has the unity of a structure articulated in dominance*" (1965f: 202). Each social formation is a "*variation of the—'invariant'—structure in dominance, of the totality*" (209).

For Althusser, both Stalinism and its corrective, Hegelianism, were incorrect. Both of these views were teleological: consequentialist notions of events being driven by their functions and purposes in the future. Hegelian, or humanistic, Marxism sees history as a process with a subject (Man) and an end (communism). Stalinist economic evolutionism similarly sees the coming of communism as inevitable, as the necessary development of the productive forces. To sum up, the transitive causality of Stalinist Marxism posited a mechanistic relationship as seen in its economism. The expressive causality of humanist Marxism suggested that causation lies in an omnipresent essence, for example "agency." Althusser's theory proposed a quite new model: a structural causality that describes the effect of the whole on the parts without either essentializing that whole or reducing it to one of its parts (1965f: 186).

He opposed Krushchev's "de-Stalinization" (which, ironically, now allowed

Althusser's own intraParty theoretical speculations), seeing it as a right-wing move. In this he adopted a position similar to the Chinese Communist Party's criticism of Krushchev and all the western communist parties. Althusser wanted a critique of the Stalinist "dogmatist night," (1965b: 31), not from the right, but by a return to revolutionary Marxism—a "return to Marx." He wanted to be the "Luther of French Marxism" (Daniel Lindenberg, quoted in Elliott 1987: 32n).

Theoretical Antihumanism

Althusser's critique of Krushchev's "socialist humanism" continued in an essay on Marxism and humanism (1965g). Noting an alliance between socialist humanism and bourgeois humanism, he warned that "humanity's millenarian dreams" may become realized and "the reign of Man will at last begin" (1965a: 222).

Althusser's arguments for "theoretical antihumanism" coincided with the rise to prominence of structuralism in European intellectual circles and the rejection of humanism. In an essay on Freud and Lacan, Althusser made this theoretical antihumanism very clear. He referred to the radical decentering of cosmology, history, and the human subject in the work of Copernicus, Marx, and Freud (1964: 218-19). Speaking of Marx's decentering of Man, Althusser said that it is "impossible to *know* anything about men except on the absolute precondition that the philosophical (theoretical) myth of man is reduced to ashes" (1965g: 229-30).

Humanism and historicism were under attack in French intellectual culture in general. The sudden rise of structuralism over phenomenology made the theoretical mores of humanist Marxism that Althusser criticized very quickly dated. This fortuitous conjuncture caused Althusser to be catapulted for a time to the status of one of Europe's most important intellectuals. His antihumanism was to remain a major element of his work. It is clear from the start, though, that antihumanism opposes the *theoretical* notion of free, volitional human beings, and not real people and their struggles; it is not anti*human*, as some seem to think.

The Two Marxes

A related and continual emphasis of Althusser's work was his opposition to the attempt to conflate the young Hegelian Marx and the mature Marx. For Althusser, Marx and Engels made a clear "epistemological break" with the publication of *The German Ideology* (1846). Historical materialism, "the science of History" (Althusser 1976: 151) separated the ideological (i.e., humanist) Marx and the scientific Marx. "Science" as the scientific status of Marxism, then, was a basic concern of Althusser's writing.

Using a term that he was to change the meaning of himself, Althusser early on saw only the specter of "ideology" (socialist humanism and economistic Marxism) that was to be opposed by "science" ("true" Marxism). This early phase of his career, up to 1967, has been called High Althusserianism, a stage marked by the struggle to establish the scientific credentials of his work. As early as 1967, however (with the publication of "To my English readers" in the English edition of *For Marx*,) the second stage of Althusser's career began, the time of "auto-critique"; it is this Althusser that this book puts to work.

Marxism As a "Science"

Besides rejecting Stalinism and the young Marx for the mature Marx, Lenin and Mao, Althusser asserted against most of western Marxism that Marxism is a science like the natural sciences. The scientific status of Marxism, he said, is based on the fact that it discovers objective knowledge. The method of Marxism, however, is antiempiricist. Gregory Elliott characterizes Althusserian Marxism in the following judicious mouthful: "his epistemological anti-empiricism and his social-scientific anti-historicism, anti-humanism and anti-economism" (1987: 53). Dialectical materialism is a science for Althusser, because Marxism is the only philosophy which is "*capable of accounting for itself*, by taking itself as it own object" (1965b: 39).

The earlier Althusser wished to complete an incomplete project in Marxism, to produce a scientific theory that would be recognized as such by the natural sciences. From Spinoza, Althusser borrowed the distinction between the "true idea" and its "ideate" (for example, the difference between the idea of a circle and the circle itself). "Opinion, or imagination" is formed by random sense experience ("idea"), while "reason" and "intuition" ("ideate") produced true knowledge. He used this schema to make his early distinction between science and ideology. Science is distinguished from Althusser's early understanding of ideology or prescientific thought by "the indispensable theoretical minimum" (1965d: 14) for a science, which are the criteria that the theory be a coherent system or "problematic," and that the content of the theory represents an "epistemological break" between lived experience and scientific knowledge.

Althusser, in advocating Marxist science, rejected both empiricist science, which is simply an apprehension of the real, and dogmatic (Stalinist) science, which sees itself as complete. Rather, Althusser's science, like that of Copernicus, Marx, and Freud, calls everyday experience into question and breaks with it. Scientific knowledge recognizes the unbridgeable gap between the object and the concept, while at the same time such knowledge comes from that object. Building on Spinoza's notion that knowledge production is a process of production of "intellectual instruments," Althusser argued that there is no actual "practice in general," only "distinct practices," one of which is "theoretical

practice" (1965d: 58). Theoretical practice realizes that it is a representational
construction of reality, while "ideological thinking" believes that it is a true
representation of reality.

Theoretical knowledge is "relatively autonomous" from the social. This
means that while theoretical practice is a "historically constituted system"
"defined by the system of real conditions" (1965c: 41), knowledge production
itself happens within the problematics of theories.

Highly questionable as Althusser's science/ideology distinction is, it does
have several suggestive and potentially useful features for understanding the
nature of the theoretical labor of intellectuals. For example, while "science is a
process of *transformation*, ideology . . . is a process of *repetition*" (Alain
Badiou, quoted in Elliott 1987: 100).

The epistemological break, then, is characteristic of "scientific-thinking,"
reflexive "theoretical practice," a counter-intuitive process distinct from
ideological or common-sense knowledge.

Structuralism

Although he later claimed that he and his followers had never been
structuralists but rather Spinozist rationalists, this point can be regarded as a
philosophical quibble. (Alison Assiter [1984] argues intriguingly that Althusser
is both a structuralist and a Marxist, but never both at the same time.) There is
little doubt that Althusser's work—in the exciting French intellectual milieu of
structuralism—was in large part an attempt to theorize the structure of the social
order. The structuralism of Althusser, widely denigrated today as crude
reproductionism and reductionist, is actually a "complex unity" (1965f: 199)—a
unity of practices that are distinct yet articulated, and that are not simply
reducible to one practice or manifestation of the essence, whether Stalinism's
Economy, Hegel's Absolute Spirit, or the young Marx's Man.

Having established to their own satisfaction that dialectical materialism is a
science, Althusser and Balibar set out to show in *Reading Capital* (1965) that
Marx's own career was divided into "ideological" (1840-1844) and "scientific"
(1845-1883) phases. Indeed, only after his epistemological break from Hegel did
Marx became a Marxist, they argued.

Human agents do not create society, they are its "bearers." Relations of
production are the ways the means of production (land, technology, raw
materials, capital) are distributed, as are the social relations (into classes). The
true constitutive subjects of the social formation—the social relationships
themselves—are "the definition and distribution" of the "places and functions";
"concrete individuals," or "real men," are the "supports [*Träger*]" of these
functions (1965e: 180). Class struggle, not as the activity of agents, but as the
"non-correspondence" in the relations of production and between levels of the

social formation, remained for Althusser "*the motor of history*" (1965f: 215).

CRITICISMS

While many have criticized his work, often quite unjustly, the writer who most clearly summarizes the problems with Althusser, while taking his contributions seriously, is Paul Ricoeur (1986: 103-180). Ricoeur poses five interrelated problems, which should each be addressed.

1. The Problem of Science. "First is the question of the scientific claim of Marxism: in what sense is it a science?" (Ricoeur 1986: 151).

Althusser's attempt to move away from Stalinist notions of Marxism as a finished science, while avoiding positivist correspondence thinking, took him back toward the former. In his insistence that Marxism, as a science, cannot be evaluated from without, he echoed communist orthodoxy of dialectical materialism as "the science of the more general laws governing the development of nature, society and thought" (Boguslawsky et al., quoted in Elliott 1987: 104). The "relative autonomy" of science, Althusser's great contribution, becomes, in his ultimate adherence to Marxism, the Truth about the social, absolutely independent from history. Dialectical materialism construed as revealed truth unfortunately minimizes the developmental aspects of "theoretical practice" that he himself had identified.

Yet, this is not sufficient justification for brushing off Althusser as "Stalinism at last, theorised as ideology" (Thompson 1978: 374). In wanting to get rid of the scientific aspirations of Althusser's work one does not have to agree with John O'Neill: "The problematic of Marxist theory is *not* the role of humanism in Marxist science. On the contrary it is the role of Marxist science in humanism" (1982: 15). Nor is it necessary to side with Steven Smith here: "It may well be true that the doctrine of 'theoretical anti-humanism' is the highest expression of the soul of bureaucratic rule, or what Hannah Arendt once called 'a kind of no-man rule,' 'the rule of nobody'" (1984: 218). This amounts to a common criticism. But where does the writer stand when uttering such views? The zeal to reinsert agency and experience leads precisely back to the Hegelian Marxism which Althusser was correct to dissect in the first place. Humanism cannot explain history except by appealing to human agents, motivated it cannot say by what. Althusser was theoretically justified in trying to develop an explanatory theory. It seems, however, that his work suffers a great deal by the drive toward science, and that it loses nothing by dropping such pretensions.

If, however, one regards his development of dialectical materialism as but *a* rigorous philosophy, as it undoubtedly is, it is a theory whose relative openness should be recognized and commended. "There is no longer any simple unity, only a structured, complex unity. There is no longer an original simple unity (in any form whatsoever), but instead, *the ever-pre-givenness of a structured complex unity*" (Althusser 1965f: 198-99). Althusser's work tries to be at once anti-idealist ("pre-givenness"), antiempiricist ("structured unity"), and antihistoricist ("complex unity").

Althusser never dropped the word science from his vocabulary. It is clear, however, that the term came to mean something quite different for him from both the positivist notion of science and the Stalinist notion of Marxism as a finished science. "A science (Lenin repeats it again and again when he talks about historical materialism) never comes to an end" (1974: 112). Althusser makes a crucial distinction here in a footnote where he argues not for science "in the singular" but rather the "*minimum of generality*" necessary for scientific explanation (112n). Scientific thinking, "theoretical practice" generally, is to be regarded as "science." Althusser's insistence on using the word science is based upon tactical and theoretical assumptions: "fighting for the *word*" (1974: 116). So for Althusser the revolutionary movement could not exist without a revolutionary theory.

High Althusserianism viewed Marxism as the science of the social. Thus, as a science, Marxism was a system of thought of and about itself: not a reflection of real objects, but the construction of theoretical objects about the real. On the one hand, this distinction removes Marxism from the naïvety of positivism. On the other hand, however, it severs theory completely from reality, thus refusing to compel theory to correspond in any way to the empirical world. The result of this is the unwitting closure of Althusser's "science," as well as the neglect of the necessity to change—on what grounds is the scientist to question his or her science (except in terms of internal theoretical logic) if science does not have to try to explain the real object?

Althusser, then, may then be "accused of confusing truth with internal consistency" (Smith 1984: 215). Steven Smith shows precisely where the strengths and weaknesses of Althusser lie on this question:

> The purely formal criterion of logical consistency runs the risk of falling into a kind of epistemological agnosticism. We are left at best with a criterion for making a plausible explanation, but if we are looking for something more than mere plausibility, Althusser is unable to help us. (215)

Ted Benton is in agreement with this point. For him, Althusser "has difficulty in avoiding relativism (there are *differences* between the problematics of the earlier and later Marx—that is all), but relativism is of no use if the requirement is for a seal of scientific *authority*." What Althusser's whole exercise is about is not the establishment of a new science (in any usual understanding of that term) but "providing an authority for a *particular reading* of Marx in opposition to others" (Benton 1984: 29).

Although later Althusser softened his notion of science even further, and although it is important for the Left to struggle to win over important words (Hall 1981), it is my contention that the word "science" has been more trouble than it has been worth. Despite his sophisticated attempts to distance science as "theoretical practice" from positivism and from diamat, the mere mention of science tends to produce a reflex action in those who hear it: science as "reification." Althusser's theories, as suggested in the response to Ricoeur's fifth problem below, are powerful enough not to need the rhetorical status of science.

2. The Problem of the "Break." "Is a complete break understandable without some kind of intellectual miracle, a sense of someone emerging from the dark?" (Ricoeur 1986: 152).

Norman Geras makes the same point: "If he begins by affirming the universality of knowledge *in its content*, he ends by denying the historicity of its *conditions and processes of production*; their autonomy has become, quite simply, absolute" (1972: 123).

It is a point well taken. It is difficult to sustain the distinctive break that Althusser insists upon, particularly if Marx's own development is shown to have been gradual. In fact, Althusser's auto-critique does acknowledge that the "break" is misleading. He insists that Marx did make such a break with his Hegelian past, but then Althusser wanted to refine this. Marx's break, he now said, was not with "ideology in general," but with "*bourgeois* ideology" (1974: 120). Subsequently, in response to such accusations of idealism, Althusser has elaborated upon his notion of the break. Every science, he said, emerges from a process of labor and also from its own philosophical history. This is a complex matter where the "child *was born without* a (single-identifiable) *father*" and where "every recognized science not only emerged from its own prehistory, but continues endlessly to do so" (112-14). It should be pointed out that Althusser's pinpointing of the moment of Marx's break does not mean that this break was as clean as Ricoeur (and Althusser himself, sometimes) suggests. Althusser noted the following gradations in Marx's development:

a.   1840-1844, the "Early Work," comprised of:
          1840-1842 "the liberal-rationalist moment"
          1842-1844 "the communalist-rationalist moment"
b.   1845, the "Works of the Break" (*Theses on Feuerbach, The German Ideology*)
c.   1845-1857, the "Transitional Works" (*The Poverty of Philosophy* to the *Grundrisse*)
d.   1857-1883, the "Mature Works" (especially *Capital*)
       (Althusser 1965b: 34-35)

Indeed, a clean epistemological break would imply a strangely undialectical and ahistorical view. Althusser admits to an early error: "I reduced the break between Marxism and bourgeois ideology to the epistemological break, and the antagonism between Marxism and science and ideology" (1974: 123).

3. The Problem of "Base-Superstructure." Viz., Althusser's "conceptual framework of infrastructure and superstructure [which] is a metaphor of a base with stories, an edifice with a base" (Ricoeur 1986: 153).

The base-superstructure model may, it is true, have been dogmatically implemented in those political policies which have insisted that, say, art should reflect the economic base. Althusser does not use the model in this way, however. For him base-superstructure is indeed a metaphor—just as the foundation of a building sets limits on what *can* be built upon it while not prescribing what *is* built, so *in the end* the economic determines the superstructure (in the sense of setting limits). This is the flexible use of the word "determines" also preferred by Mao (1953) and Williams (1980). We are still left, however, with the uneasy question: Yes, but has the metaphor become irrevocably tainted by dogmatism? This author would claim that as long as Althusser's particular understanding of "determination" and "overdetermination" is explained, base-superstructure is a metaphor that can still usefully be employed. However, much of the general aversion to the metaphor can be attributed to a widespread distaste for what is perceived in Althusser's structuralism. It may therefore be necessary in this case to enlarge upon this structuralism, pointing out its difference from functionalism.

Althusser's paper on ideology (1970) is divided in three parts: a theory of Ideological State Apparatus (ISAs) and the Repressive State Apparatus (RSA); a theory of ideology; and a postscript emphasizing the importance of class struggle. This has been regarded as evidence that "Althusser's study is marked by an unresolved tension between functionalism—an automaticity of social *reproduction* via State apparatuses—and voluntarism—a contingency of social *transformation* via the *deus ex machina* of class struggle" (Elliott 1987: 225). That so astute a reader of Althusser as Elliott can so readily utter the cry of "agency not structure" is evidence of how poorly structuralism has been grasped in the English-speaking world. A few references to pertinent structuralist concepts may help to go beyond this automatic criticism.

Saussure (1915) developed the linguistic model of *langue* and *parole*, language and speech. The rules and vocabulary of language "determine" what *can* be said in conversation without determining what *is* said. Not only that, structural linguistics theorized that systems of selection and differentiation, of foregrounding and backgrounding, are the ways in which meaning is constructed out of the meaningless world around us. It is possible, then, to understand that for Althusser "ideology-in-general" is a theoretical account of the processes whereby human subjectivity is constituted and not a condemnation of real people to absolutely defined (damned) lives. This in no way precludes the possibility of rational action (practice guided by rigorous thought), nor does it predict precisely what will be done, thought, or said. Ideology-in-general, to be more fully discussed in the next chapter, is the mode by which class relations (necessarily antagonistic relations) are transmitted to subjects. "Class relations" is used here in Basil Bernstein's sense of "inequalities in the distribution of power" which "have their source in the social division of labour" (1990: 13).

Consider, too, Freud's (1923) notion of the id, out of which the ego grows. The unconscious determines what comes into consciousness in the sense that it is the psychic vehicle through which powerful urges demand satisfaction. The ego represses unbearable thoughts into the unconscious. But what is repressed returns to the unwilling ego in various forms, thereby demonstrating that the ego is not master of the psyche. While there are unlimited different ways of thinking and behaving, and while the influence of the id can be modified through strenuous analytic work, only in a limited and structured sense can human action be said to be free rather than determined.

Benton very insightfully suggests three "methodological principles" that need to be accepted from structuralism:

a. Structural determinants are not external to the subject. "Unconscious determination of conscious life provides theoretical space for a conception of human actors as more than 'bearers' of external structures, without resorting to the essentially theological notion of action as an "uncaused action" (Benton 1984: 213). (The latter is a reference to the impossibility of theories of human agency to *explain* history.)
b. Structural conditions are not constraints, but "facilitating conditions, or conditions of possibility of action" (Benton 1984: 214). Without linguistic structures, for example, intelligible language is impossible.
c. Structures are not *immutable*. "The susceptibility of relationships to deliberate dissolution or transformation by agents is . . . immensely variable." (Benton 1984, 214)

If the above detour can at least be intellectually accepted, it is odd that Althusser's work has been so severely condemned for placing historical human action within an historical and transhistorical structure. Critics who dismiss Freud because he argued that we are not free, indeed that our lives are dominated by id, are suspected of resisting knowledge of their own cognitive limitations and their pervasive sexual and aggressive desires. This author will do no more than suggest that those who decry the limitations on humans that Althusser has seen may also be victims of denial and wishful thinking.

4. The Problem of "Particular Ideologies." "We may start here from the previous question and ask what makes these particular ideologies specific" (Ricoeur 1986: 156).

Althusser argues that particular ideologies, like all social practices, are "relatively autonomous" from one another and from the economic base. There is a problem here over exactly how autonomous such practices are and exactly to what extent they are determined by the base in the last instance. But rather than reject this welcome sophistication of older, ossified ideas, the exact nature of specificities should be, and can only be, examined in concrete studies of actual, particular circumstances.

5. The Problem of "Ideology-in-General." "The fifth and final problem to arise from our reading is that of ideology in general. This raises the most radical question: what is distorted if not praxis as something symbolically mediated?" (Ricoeur 1986: 157).

The last problem that Ricoeur focuses on is the distinction between science and ideology—the "cardinal principle" of Althusser's epistemology (Elliott 1987: 110).

For Althusser, science in principle has an "openness" to problems and a capacity for self-correction and development, while the equivalent feature of ideology is closure and repetition (1965d: 51-69). "A science which repeats itself without discovering anything is a dead science, is no longer a science, but a frozen dogma. A science only lives from its development, i.e. from its discoveries" (quoted in Elliott 1987: 108).

Just as base-superstructure may be fixed in critics' minds as crude economism, so too, we have seen, is the notion of science. Althusser was adamant that Marxism is, or could be, a science, but in the process he so altered the notion of what science is that the natural sciences he aspired to emulate no longer themselves fit his own description of science. On the other hand, for earlier High Althusserianism, experience produces only false consciousness, and only science produces knowledge. The difficulties of Althusser's Marxism stem from this "bifurcation between experience, on the one hand, and claims of science, on the other" (Smith 1984: 215). This author is in complete agreement with Smith here. Although Marxist writers like Aronowitz (1988) and Lucio Colletti (1972) would disagree, it is preferable to drop all pretensions of Marxism as a science. It has been argued above that the explanatory power of Althusser's ideology-in-general concept is not diminished by this. Instead of ideology and science, it is more helpful (and less politically dogmatic) to speak of levels or forms of ideology as does Gramsci (1971). It must be acknowledged, of course, as a valid criticism that the narrow-mindedness of Althusser's rejection of all other western Marxist writing, while being understandable given his project of returning the party to revolutionary Marxism, shows his scientific aspirations to be theoretically arid.

Many writers (Clarke et al. 1980; O'Neill 1982; Thompson 1978) have dismissed Althusser's theories because he rejected human agency. This is strange, as that rejection was precisely Althusser's project. It is like criticizing Nietzsche for not having a place for God in his theory, or Kuhn for not describing the history of science as a steady accumulation of new facts. Nevertheless, even sympathetic readers want to know, "Where within the cohesive, self-reproducing social whole is the principle of its subversion and transformation to be found?" (Elliott 1987: 180). In "Elements of Self-criticism," Althusser himself says that by seeing "ideology as the universal element of human existence" he has "disregarded the antagonistic class tendencies which run through them, divide them, regroup them and bring them into opposition" (1974: 141). Althusser produced self-criticisms, many of which were overly severe. It could be argued that here he has undermined precisely what is powerful in his original formulations.

It is useful to turn again—in regard to the criticism over the supposed lack of a principle of antagonism in Althusser's work—to a writer influenced by both Freud and Althusser: Bernstein. He renders Althusser's theory of ideology as one of "codes." "*Power relations position subjects through the principles of the classifications they establish*" (Bernstein 1990: 24). "Classifications" are the relations between "categories," and these categories are separated by degrees of "insulation." Insulations in turn are the

> intervals, breaks, delocations, which establish categories of similarity and difference: the equal and the unequal; punctuations written by power relations that establish as the order of things distinct subjects through distinct voices. Indeed, insulation is the means whereby the cultural is transformed into the natural, the contingent into the necessary, the past into the present, the present into the future. (Bernstein 1990: 25)

But classification itself is arbitrary—it suppresses "the contradictions and dilemmas that inhere in the very principle of the classification" (24). So, between the categories of dominant and dominated classifications resides a necessary "potential oppositional 'yet to be voiced' which may be suppressed or rendered unthinkable" by insulation (30). The structuralist answer to the question posed above, Where within the structure is the principle of its transformation? is: It resides within the arbitrary and antagonistic construction of the structure itself.

What precisely this means for political practice should be beside the point here. Althusser's work, in my opinion, provides powerful ways of theorizing cultural reproduction. The problem lies in the direct translation of this *explanatory theory* into a *particular political project*. It is absurd for Althusser's critics to criticize and reject his work on the grounds of its perceived political implications (and then to complain if the implications dredged up appear to be pessimistic). First, Althusser was precisely opposed to this ontological interpretation of Marxism as a science that predicts exactly how history will proceed. Second, to criticize a social theory for being pessimistic is to demonstrate "illusory" thinking—thinking that is not necessarily true or false, but governed by a wish (Freud 1927). In this case it is the desperate wish to be reassured of the immanent end of capitalism.

The theories of the great Marxist thinkers illuminate in various ways the hidden structures of capitalist society. Their critiques are prophetic in that they show, for example, that the structure of capitalism is *historical* and therefore *capable* of being changed. However, when such speculations, no matter how brilliant, have been directly translated into political doctrine, left-wing totalitarianism has been the result. If this argument is true, Althusser's theories should not be used to drive political practice (even if he sometimes said that they should). Nor should he be castigated for downplaying the revolutionary role of the working class simply because the reader may wish to be told something more affirmative. Rather, Althusser should be read as a social analyst and judged strictly on the explanatory value of his work. Without pretending in any way that intellectual labor is, or should try to be, neutral or apolitical, I insist that theoretical work be judged by different standards to political policies (Appel 1993). Only where, for example, Althusser makes direct reference to particular current events, making overt strategic interventions, should he be evaluated by the standards of political efficacy.

Althusser devoted his life to the reconstruction in theory of revolutionary Marxism.

IDEOLOGY

The science/ideology distinction made by the early Althusser has been discussed and rejected as a false dichotomy. At most what needs to be maintained is a range or continuum of theoretical practices whereby a particular theoretical practice can be judged as more or less "mystified"—under the illusion that it is true, or aware of itself as an interpretive practice. Neither of the words "science" nor "ideology" is best employed in this regard.

The later Althusser developed a theory of ideology far superior to the earlier simple categorization. As developed in the "Ideology and Ideological State Apparatuses" paper (1970), ideology is developed as a concept with which to address the problems of why people consent to oppress and to be oppressed. It is obvious why people can be easily coerced through force and Marxism has explained how, for example, the capitalist mode of production exploits workers. But what is truly mystifying is that large area of socio-political life wherein people appear to cooperate in their own oppression. Traditionally, Marxism has resorted to the pseudo-explanation of false consciousness. Althusser, to his great credit, has located the answer within human subjectivity itself, arguing that this has to be fully theorized if Marxism is to understand social reaction, inertia, and change.

The ideology paper will be fully discussed in the next chapter, but suffice it to say here that Althusser has developed what can be called a theory of ideology-in-general that provides some basic tools needed to understand how it is that people *become*, not misled dupes, but subjects interiorizing sets of meanings and practice that determine their very consciousness. Indeed, it is a theory of socialization—how it is that the biological homo sapiens becomes a person. This book is devoted to explicating and elaborating what is only implied in Althusser's famous dictum, "ideology interpellates individuals as subjects."

There was a time when Althusser's paper on ideology was occasionally critically addressed in critical educational studies, but with very few exceptions these readings were fairly complete misunderstandings, not only of his project but even of the content of his famous essay. Michael Erben and Denis Gleeson have produced a typical version of this inability to read what actually appears on the page.

> It is within the activity of men experiencing such contradictions that they may act to transform realities. . . . Althusser is merely telling us "what we know," rather than considering how "what we know" may be made problematic in order to enhance those conditions through which change may be possible. . . . Therefore, we argue that in order to demystify ideological oppression in education there is a need initially to question what counts as a "problem," in terms of such oppression, by those who work and study in education. It is one thing to describe education as reproduction, but it is another to explain this phenomenon as transcendable. It is this problem, neglected in Althusser's thesis, with which this paper has been concerned. (1977: 89)

Erben and Gleeson reproduce (without any suggestion that they are aware that this is precisely what Althusser is getting at) the humanist Marxist faith in experience. Althusser is obviously not telling these authors "what we know," as they plainly do not know what it is that he is saying. All of Althusser's theorizing on ideology is reduced in their account to "ideological oppression," oppression, moreover, that needs to be "demystified" with the help of "those who work and study in education." Here, the humanists appear as omniscient party intellectuals who, able to perceive "the problem," will "demystify" "man." Reproduction is "transcendable," they assert, thus contradicting Marx's insistence that *no* social formation can "last the year" without reproducing itself. Erben and Gleeson end by confirming the depths of their misunderstanding: the problem of transcendence of reproduction has been "neglected" by Althusser. The authors have completely missed the point that it is the nature of social reproduction that Althusser's essay addresses.

Staggeringly few writers in critical educational studies have recognized the power of Althusser's contribution, perhaps because of the foreignness of his project and his writing style. But a more probable reason lies in the overweening political mission of the bulk of critical educational studies practitioners to be relevant and to make a difference—this too often at the price of rigorous intellectualization. It may not be too rhetorical a device to make an analogy between the theoretical state of critical educational studies and the theoretical opponents whom Althusser challenged. It has been shown that critical educational studies has two major strands, one fairly crudely reproductionist and the other of rather naïve resistance. We have also seen that Althusser's work was devoted to combatting rigid economism and voluntaristic humanism. While the specific trajectories of these pairs of tendencies are different, they are very similar in underlying assumptions. Critical educational studies' system model (what CSOE calls "structure") and economism generally are both teleological, seeing forms as more or less precise predictors of necessary developments. And the critical educational studies' resistance emphasis and humanism generally are both voluntaristic, believing in history as the product of volitional agents. If this analogy works, then it is conceivable that Althusser's theoretical proposals with regard to his opponents within Marxism may also help to extricate critical educational studies from its own cul-de-sac. Most notably, the concept of ideology-in-general with all its attendant ramifications is one that needs to pursued.

The discipline of critical educational studies as a whole has not been able to recognize the term ideology in its ubiquitous sense, concentrating as it has on interpreting ideology as a form of domination. Philip Wexler is one critical educational theorist who has identified a sense of ideology beyond that of straight oppression through false thinking. He talks of a positive moment "in the individual actualization and collective mobilization of social action" (1982b: 55). Wexler turns to Gramsci and Rudé to propose that "*ideology is analyzed in relation to the formation of struggle and collective historical action*" (Wexler 1982b: 64). Johan Muller and Mary Crewe (1983) claim that Althusser is correct that we cannot escape ideology-in-general, but they note an optimistic suggestion that it *is* possible to escape bourgeois ideology, which has placed the individual at the center of the universe. A new, more social interpellation is compatible with the socialist project.

Bernstein is another who has understood Althusser's contribution. Critical educational studies generally uses ideology in the "descriptive" and "pejorative" senses of Dieter Guess' (1981) typology. Ideology, according to these views refers to a system of ideas: ideologies-in-particular, and/or ideology as false consciousness. Bernstein has a different understanding: "Ideology is not so much a content as a *mode of relation for the realizing of contents*" (1981: 327).

> Codes are culturally determined positioning devices. More specifically, class-regulated codes position subjects with respect to dominant and dominated forms of communication and to the relationships between them. Ideology is constituted through and in such positioning. From this perspective, ideology inheres in and regulates *modes of relation*. (Bernstein 1990: 13-14)

Ironically, given the nature of the criticisms leveled against him, it is thus a "deepened appreciation of the 'realm of necessity,' which both defines and determines the 'realm of freedom' within practical life, that may constitute the highest teaching of Althusserian Marxism" (Smith 1984: 210-11). Research by critical educational studies theorists has generally done itself a disservice by neglecting to seriously and creatively incorporate Althusser's work.

Althusser has argued that the Law of Culture, in other words, the structure of all culture, is "*formally* identical with the order of language" (1964: 211) as explicated in the work of Lacan. It is the task of historical materialism to investigate the variable aspects of kinship structure and determinate ideological formations (211n.). The notion of subjectivity is useful for understanding our reality as a construction of both universal unconscious and culturally specific signifying practices. As we have seen, critical educational studies has done some work on the last of these, some on the second, and none on the first, that which is primary. In other words, critical educational studies has yet to begin addressing the question of the relation between language's structure, concrete kinship structures, and the "concrete ideological formations in which the specific functions implied by the kinship structures (paternity, maternity, childhood) are lived" (217).

We have come on a long excursion from the starting point of critical educational studies. Some of what is psychoanalytic social theory has been presented, as has the work of Louis Althusser; indeed, Althusser himself incorporated the work of Freud and Lacan. The detour of this chapter has been necessary because critical educational studies has by and large neglected these theoretical territories, which therefore needed to be fairly thoroughly outlined and developed in new ways. It is now time to return to the original task, the remedying of critical educational studies' theoretical lacuna by the introduction of psychoanalytical concepts of externalization and internalization, and a theory of ideology-in-general. Psychoanalysis, I will attempt to show, "may perhaps lead us some day to a better understanding of this *structure of misrecognition*, which is of particular concern for all investigations into ideology" (Althusser 1964: 219).

This chapter ends with a quotation that asserts the importance of proceeding in this way, and that criticizes its repression by the ideology-critics and humanists who typify the theorists of critical educational studies.

> Althusser has opened up the theoretical space for thinking the frighteningly real terms of our psycho-social oppression, *as well* as for thinking ways of combatting it. It is quite certain for Althusser and for us that any theorising that takes the category of unitary individual and his appurtenances—"autonomy," "freedom," "will"—as theoretically central, runs the grave risk of mystifying a very concrete oppression and of trivializing the way in which it could be opposed. (Muller and Crewe 1983: 6)

4

IDEOLOGY-IN-GENERAL

Freud has discovered for us that the real subject, the individual in his unique essence, has not the form of an ego . . . that the human subject is de-centred, constituted by a structure which has no "centre" either, except in the imaginary misrecognition of the "ego," i.e. in the ideological formations in which it recognizes itself.

—Louis Althusser
"Freud and Lacan"

I have asserted that critical sociology of education does not have an explicit theory of human socialization, and it has been further claimed that psychoanalysis can throw considerable light on the processes whereby the baby becomes a human being. Our socialization into human culture, is, as the terms suggests, a social process, but this does not imply that it is one whose nature we can change; the biological infant encounters society in active ways, but along paths, nonetheless, that are predetermined. Dennis Wrong makes precisely this point when he shows that "socialization" has two possible meanings that when confused, produce an "oversocialized" view. Socialization refers to, on the one hand, the transmission of particular culture, and, on the other, to becoming human.

All men are socialized in the latter sense, but that does not mean that they have become completely moulded by the particular norms and values of their culture. All cultures, as Freud contended, do violence to man's socialized bodily drives but this in no sense means that men could possibly exist without culture or independently of culture. (Wrong 1961: 193)

This book has the tasks of elaborating a theory of how human socialization happens and of showing how such a view can bolster studies in education. The first of these tasks is undertaken in the three chapters that follow, where Althusser's theory of ideology is developed through incorporation of certain psychoanalytic processes.

This chapter will begin by describing Freud's model of the mind and by considering the theory of ideology developed by Antonio Gramsci, the source of several of Althusser's own ideas. Gramsci's notion is articulated with Freud's psychic model. It is suggested that the levels of consciousness portrayed in these two perspectives have much in common, and that Freud's model may provide Gramsci's notion of ideology with the dynamism alluded to, but undeveloped, in *Selections from the Prison Notebooks* (1971). Next, the chapter introduces Althusser's notion of ideology-in-general, spelling it out in some detail along with some of the criticisms of it.

FREUD'S DISSECTION OF THE PSYCHICAL PERSONALITY

Absolutely fundamental to the entire science of psychoanalysis is an objection to the belief that "conscious" is a synonym for "mental." Even if included under conscious are those thoughts that, while not in awareness at one moment might become present the next, Freud believed that there exists a deeper "unconscious." "Preconscious" ideas are those that can easily be made conscious, while unconscious desires and thoughts are those which are forcefully prevented from direct expression. As discussed earlier, Freud postulated this on the basis of various signs or symptoms displayed by both himself (1925) and his patients. Posthypnotic suggestion, parapraxes, dreams, daydreams, and jokes were all sources of evidence of unconscious mental determinism.

Let us pause here to consider Freud's initial "topographical" psychic model. Psychic acts originate in the system unconscious (Ucs.). Tested by an internal censor, these acts are either repressed, thereby remaining unconscious, or, if passed by the censor, enter the system preconscious (Pcs.), where they are "capable of becoming conscious," entering the system conscious (Cs.) without strenuous resistance. Psychoanalysis, a depth psychology, thus first operated according to a mental model that was both dynamic and topographical (Freud 1915c: 172-73). But it is still not clear exactly what repression is or why secret wishes, obliquely revealed in parapraxes, dreams, and symptoms, are kept at a distance from consciousness. Or, more precisely, the nature of the unconscious and its drives thus far remain a mystery. There are two theoretical links between biology and psychoanalysis. One link is the focus on the psychic functions related to sense perception—the topographical schema considered above. The other link concerns the instinctual forces or drives.

What constitutes the unconscious? We have seen that its primary contents are repressed thoughts and representations of the drives seeking discharge, wishful impulses. These impulses do not contradict each other, but coexist, thereby revealing the absence of logic in the unconscious; the logically impossible happens freely in dreams. Instead, negation, doubt, and degrees of certainty are imposed upon the unconscious through censorship by the super-ego, as we shall see. "In the Ucs. there are only contents, cathected with greater or lesser strength" (Freud 1915c: 186). These contents are mobile and capable of displacement or condensation of their cathexes. The unconscious is also timeless; in other words its contents are not influenced by the passage of time. Again, in a dream events or people—in reality separated by several years or great distances—may occur simultaneously. Subject to the pleasure principle, the unconscious is unconcerned with external reality.

The contents of the unconscious are not free to flow into consciousness. Indeed those desires seeking fulfilment may meet resistances that repress them. As the satisfaction of all instinctual impulses would be pleasurable, we need to ask why wishes are often repressed. Repression, Freud saw, occurs when the potential pleasure of a wish fulfillment is outweighed by the unpleasure it would cause. Thus, for example, our moral sense may find the expression of a desire too distasteful to permit it access to consciousness. It demands the constant pressure of resistance to repress a desire, and even so it may emerge in a disguised form as affect, anxiety, or other symptoms (Freud 1915d).

The unconscious is only indirectly accessible to us via the interpretation of its products (dreams, slips, neuroses). Describing it as "a chaos, a cauldron full of seething excitations," Freud summarized the unconscious as being "filled with energy reaching it from the instincts, but it has no organization, produces no collective will, but only a striving to bring about the satisfaction of the instinctual needs subject to the observance of the pleasure principle" (Freud 1933: 73).

Once the existence and characteristics of the unconscious had been firmly established, Freud diverted his attention "from the repressed to the repressing forces, and we faced the ego." It may seem that the psychology of the ego is confronted by a paradox: the ego is both the subject and object of study. The solution to this theoretical riddle lies in the fact that the ego can be split; "the ego can take itself as an object, can treat itself like other objects, can observe itself, criticize itself, and do Heaven knows what with itself" (Freud 1933: 58).

Convinced that there exists a distinct observing agency of the ego, Freud considered the delusions of paranoids. Complaining that even their most intimate actions are observable to unknown persons, paranoiacs have externalized the universal observing ego. Such close observation, Freud suggested, is not far from judging and punishment. A special agency of the ego, he said, has the functions of self-observation and of conscience. He named this agency the "super-ego." The example of melancholia (depression) shows us the severity of the punishing super-ego (Freud 1917b: 246-47); representing, as it does, moral standards, the super-ego comes into conflict with the ego, whence come feelings of guilt.

Unlike the drives, though, the super-ego is not present from birth. Infants possess no inner restraints to their striving for pleasure; the authority of parents—external restraints—influence the child with love and lack of love. Gradually, external restraints are internalized and the super-ego replaces parental agency by itself observing, directing and punishing the ego, and also censoring dreams. Importantly for education, Freud says that while later identification with teachers and other influential people affect character formation, these change only the ego and not the super-ego "which has been determined by the earliest parental images" (Freud 1933: 64). Here we find, along with self-observation and conscience, the third function of the super-ego; the ego ideal is an image of the magnificent figures the parents once were to the child. The ego ideal is a standard of perfection that the ego tries to emulate, and according to which it judges itself.

This author suggests that the three functions of the super-ego work together in this way. The super-ego observes the ego, comparing it with its ego-ideal. The inadequacies of the ego thereby detected produce the guilt of conscience, while meeting the standards of the ego ideal result in feelings of joy and satisfaction. The child's super-ego is modeled not on the parents themselves but on their super-egos; the super-ego is, therefore, in this respect, distinct from the child's real parents—"it becomes the vehicle of tradition and of all the time-resisting judgements of value which have propagated themselves in this manner from generation to generation" (Freud 1933:67). Freud criticized "materialistic views" for underestimating the importance of the past in individual lives. Acknowledging the relation of "ideologies" to economic conditions, he reiterated that "mankind never lives entirely in the present" (67). The fundamental and unconscious place of tradition remains a trenchant critique of ideology-as-false-consciousness dogma, as tradition is seen here to be far deeper and more formative than simply a set of ideas and actions.

So far we have considered the super-ego as a special agency of the ego dealing with the external world. The super-ego, however, also operates in and on the unconscious. While the repressed thought or impulse strives to break into consciousness, the resistance of the ego keeps it in the unconscious. Repression, the product of our moral character and the reality principle, is enforced by the super-ego or by the ego under the instruction of the super-ego. But psychoanalytic practice has revealed that resistances are not conscious. Thus we are forced to acknowledge the fact that regions of both the ego and super-ego are unconscious.

A complication has arisen. While in the topographical psychic model it made sense to speak of a conflict between the ego and the system Ucs., it has now become apparent that regions of the ego itself are unconscious. Freud therefore labeled the innate unconscious region out of which the ego develops as the "id"

(1923: 23). And in 1923 he proposed his final psychic model usually referred to as the "structural model"—whereby the mental apparatus is constituted by the id, super-ego and ego. Let us be clear here. None of the Ucs., Pcs., or Cs. are equivalent to id, super-ego or ego. In order to illustrate the relationship between the topographical and structural models, Freud provided the following analogy. Imagine a country made up geographically of hill country, plains, and chains of lakes, and populated by Germans, Magyars, and Slovaks. It is likely that for various reasons the people would not live exclusively in specific regions. In the hill country, mainly suitable for the German cattle farmers, for example, there is also agricultural land that supports the Magyar cereal and wine farmers. So, while our first assumptions are largely correct—fish, and therefore Slovaks, are not found in the mountains, say—things are not quite as neat as we expected.

The ego, originally part of the id, becomes organized as the mediator between the outside and the inside of the mind. The ego is, via the system Pcpt.-Cs. (perceptual-conscious), the sense organ of the psyche: observing the world, accurately remembering it, and testing that reality. Between the drives of the id and conscious action, thought occurs. Thus the ego, with greater chance of satisfying the id by first considering reality, overcomes the pleasure principle (Freud 1911b). "To adopt a popular mode of speaking, we might say that the ego stands for the untamed passions" (Freud 1933: 76). But the ego, derived as it is from the id, is weak and it borrows energy from the id. One of the ways it does this is by identification with libidinal objects; the ego thereby itself becomes a love-object of the id. Often, however, the horse (id) forces the rider (ego) to travel its way, Freud said.

Indeed the ego serves three "tyrannical masters," the external world, the super-ego and the id (Freud 1933: 77). Failure to satisfy these masters results in realistic anxiety, moral anxiety, and neurotic anxiety respectively. He represented the self in a famous diagram (78), about which he commented that in at least one respect his "unassuming sketch" is incorrect; the unconscious should occupy an "incomparably greater (space) than that of the ego or preconscious" (79). "We shall now look upon an individual," Freud wrote in *The Ego and the Id*, "as a psychical id, upon whose surface rests the ego, developed from its nucleus the Pcpt. system" (1923: 24).

GRAMSCI ON IDEOLOGY

The object of this section is not to provide a full elaboration of my contention that Gramsci's notion of ideology is compatible with Freud's psychic model. Rather, that idea will be pointed to, illustrated, and left for another time. It will be enough merely to demonstrate that the theory of ideology expounded in this book (it originates with Gramsci) operates most importantly at the level of the unconscious, and that this necessarily leads us to Freud's work. "Everyone is a philosopher, though in his own way and unconsciously," Gramsci said, "since even in the slightest manifestation of any intellectual activity whatever, in 'language,' there is contained a specific conception of the world" (1971: 323).

Chantal Mouffe is the Gramscian theorist who has best pulled out the strands of Antonio Gramsci's theory of ideology from his writings. Gramsci, she asserts, "must surely be the first to have undertaken a complete and radical critique of economism, and it is here that his main contribution to the marxist theory of ideology lies" (1981a: 220). His contribution includes a rejection of two economistic notions of ideology: the superstructure as epiphenomenon, and ideologies as class ideologies. Althusser, we have seen, had the same goals.

In formulating a non reductionist conception of ideology, Gramsci insisted upon two principles: overdetermination of contradictions, and determination in the last instance. So

> if the ideological elements referred to do not *express* social classes, but if nevertheless classes do, in the last instance, determine ideology, then we must thereby conclude that this determinism can only be the result of the establishing of an articulating principle of these ideological elements, one which must result in actually *conferring upon them* a class character. (Mouffe 1979: 171-72)

For Mouffe, the Gramscian notion of hegemony involves the operation of this antireductionist theory of ideology. In *Selections from the Prison Notebooks* Gramsci fully developed the notion of hegemony as a cross-class alliance, or bloc, that provides a society with an amalgam of political, intellectual, and moral leadership. A class rules in two ways, he said, "it is dominant and ruling" (1971: 57):

> the integrative state = dictatorship + hegemony (Mouffe 1979: 182)

Hegemony, then, refers to leadership and not to domination (Sassoon 1980). Althusser owes his theory of the state directly to Gramsci.

For Gramsci there are three principal levels of forces in society: social forces, linked to the nature of production; political forces, or the levels of consciousness and organization; and military forces. The most developed moment of political consciousness is hegemony, when it is realized that one's interests transcend that of one's class and must become the interests of other subordinate groups (Simon 1982). Ideological struggle then emerges on a "universal" level. The class alliance of hegemony involves the "complete fusion" of economic, political, intellectual, and moral objectives "*through the intermediary of ideology*" (Mouffe 1979: 181). So, although a hegemony is a shifting alliance of a range of consensual social groupings, it is articulated by a hegemonic class. This is not to be seen as a cynical conspiracy, but involves genuine concern for other groups and also making sacrifices in order to maintain hegemonic equilibrium. When the hegemonic class is no longer able to generate leadership it resorts to repressive force, i.e., it shifts from ruling through "consent," to domination by "constraint" (Adamson 1980).

For Gramsci, ideology is the "cement" through which the "higher synthesis" of the hegemony is formed. And, clearly, he denied existing economistic conceptions of ideology as false consciousness, system of ideas, or mere appearances. The so-called "consciousness" that people develop is the ever-changing product of a continuous struggle between two hegemonic principles and is always the product of social practice (Mouffe 1981a: 226). Needless to say, consciousness for Gramsci refers to much more than conscious, rational thoughts. Here we see the roots of Althusser's theory of the subjectivity and the material nature of ideology (Mouffe 1981b). Certain institutions—schools, churches, the media, and architecture—elaborate and spread ideology. These "hegemonic apparatuses" or "civil society" (Buci-Glucksman 1980), become in Althusser's work the Ideological State Apparatuses.

Gramsci's notion of ideology is a nonreductionist one. Subjects are not class subjects, but inter-class subjects. Classes do not have their own paradigmatic ideologies, neither do all ideological elements have a necessary class belonging (Mouffe 1981a: 228). Rather, ideological elements are articulated by a hegemonic principle: "a system of values the realisation of which depends on the central role played by the fundamental class at the level of the relations of production" (Mouffe 1981a: 231). So, while ideologies and their elements are not class specific, in the end the articulating hegemonic principle is that of a fundamental class (Femia 1981). Ernesto Laclau and Mouffe (1985) have moved away from this privileging of class in their social analysis. I, too, want to assert not the ultimate primacy of the economic, but the indisputable benefits of such a sophisticated Marxist analysis.

Again and again Gramsci insisted that "all men are philosophers," and he did this for two reasons. First, he believed in the socially transformative power of philosophical, or critical, labor. Second, he was concerned to demonstrate the interconnectedness of different levels of consciousness. Everyone, for him, has a "spontaneous philosophy" that consists in "language itself," "good sense," "common sense," and "popular religion." It is worth trying to bring these levels into sharper focus.

The highest level of consciousness is philosophy, or reason, a "critical and coherent conception of the world" (Gramsci 1971: 324). There are many of these conceptions of the world. The common expression "to be philosophical about something" has, for Gramsci, the positive implication that "one should apply one's power of rational concentration and not let oneself be carried away by instinctive and violent impulses" (1971: 328).

Much of the thrust of my book is away from a heavy reliance on the possible authority of the free intellect, and it may seem odd in this connection to appeal to Gramsci. There does seem to be, however, some ambiguity in his writings about the exact nature of "philosophy": "philosophy in general does not in fact exist. Various philosophies or conceptions of the world exist, and one always makes a choice between them" (1971: 326). So while he continually advocates the revolutionary role of organic intellectuals, he does not suggest that the knowledge or philosophy they are able to forge is synonymous with Truth: "philosophy cannot be separated from the history of philosophy." "How," he asks, "is it possible to consider the present, and quite specific present, with a mode of thought elaborated for a past which is often remote and superseded?" Unless, he answers, the intellectual is aware of the "historicity" of the world, such a person is "a walking anachronism, a fossil, and not living in the modern world, or at least . . . he is strangely composite." Gramsci does not, then, advocate the possibility of philosophy as truth, but he does insist on "'knowing thyself' as a product of the historical process to date which has deposited in you an infinity of traces, without leaving an inventory" (324). Knowledge of ourselves as historical social products is true knowledge, it seems, but the traces of this production can never be fully undone. It does not stretch plausibility to point out that Freud's belief in the real but limited transformative power of analysis is in sync with Gramsci's notion of the extent of philosophy. While one can agree or disagree with Gramsci's faith in the power of rational critique, there are similarities within his understanding to repression, the repetition compulsion, and the therapeutic functions of psychoanalysis.

Gramsci speaks of the struggles of the intellectual "systemization" of fragmented thinking that "has been elaborated over the centuries" through "collective effort" and has "subsumed and absorbed all this past history, including all its follies" (1971: 327). But all philosophical thinking has a "sedimentation of 'common sense'" (326). "In philosophy the features of individual elaboration of thought are the most salient: in common sense on the other hand it is the diffuse, uncoordinated features of a generic form of thought common to a particular period and a particular popular environment" (330). Gramsci speaks of people having "two theoretical consciousnesses (or one contradictory consciousness)": one embodied in activity and "transformation of the real world," and one "superficially explicit or verbal," "inherited from the past and uncritically absorbed" (333). Common sense, thus, is a lower level of consciousness: it is the sediment of philosophy articulated with experience; pervasive but unsystematic. Common sense is not something immobile, but a "collective noun" (325), continually transforming itself, enriching itself with scientific ideas and with philosophical opinions that have entered ordinary life.

Common sense is the folklore of philosophy and exists always between folklore and the philosophy, science, and economics of the specialists. It is "the conception of the world which is uncritically absorbed by the various social and cultural environments in which the moral individuality of the average man is developed." "Common sense creates the folklore of the future, that is as a relatively rigid phase of popular knowledge at a given place and time" (1971: 326). Freud's notion of children identifying with their parents' super-egos and thus inheriting tradition comes to mind. Gramsci speaks of a philosophy becoming diffuse because of its connection with "practical life" and elaborated "so that it becomes a renewed common sense possessing the coherence and the sinew of individual philosophies" (330). The systems of thought of traditional intellectuals and high culture are "unknown to the multitude and have no direct influence on its thinking and acting. . . . These systems influence the popular masses as an external political force." This means that the masses become subordinate to philosophy without its "positive effect of a vital ferment of interior transformation" (419-20). Common sense is the "philosophy of non-philosophers." However, there is a "healthy nucleus" in common sense, namely the undeveloped ability of ordinary people to think critically about their world; "it is not possible to separate what is known as 'scientific' philosophy from the common and popular philosophy" (328). The place of intellectuals is crucial, he said; the relationship between common sense and the upper level of philosophy is assured by "politics" (331). Common sense is the "sub-stratum" of ideology, ideology being the more general term for the processes by which ideas and assumptions become material forces in society (Bennett et al. 1981a: 207).

There is often confusion about the pair of terms used by Gramsci for that region of consciousness beneath philosophy and above religion. An editor's note in *Selections from the Prison Notebooks* clarifies the difference between "common sense" and "good sense": the former "means the incoherent set of broadly held assumptions and beliefs common to any given society," while the latter refers to "practical empirical common sense in the English sense of the term" (Gramsci 1971: 323n).

The level of consciousness that exists below that of common sense is religion, "an element of fragmented common sense" (Gramsci 1971: 326). "The relationship between common sense and religion is much more intimate than that between common sense and the philosophical systems of the intellectuals." Religion and common sense "cannot constitute an intellectual order, because they cannot be reduced to unity and coherence even within an individual consciousness, let alone collective consciousness" (326); "philosophy is criticism and the superseding of religion and 'common sense'" (326). Below religion as such is "popular religion," "the entire system of beliefs, superstitions, opinions, ways of seeing things and of acting, which are collectively bundled together under the name of 'folklore.'" Popular religion involves faith and it unifies contradictions and ignores logic and differences in time in similar ways to the operation of deeper levels of consciousness in psychoanalysis.

The contents of these levels can move dynamically and determine each other in complex ways. Similarly to Freud's psychic structure of the mind, the lower the level of consciousness, the more implicitly accepted are its contents and the less accessible are they to rational inspection.

Gramsci emphasized the important role of "consciously and critically" working out "one's own conception of the world" and "refusing to accept passively and supinely from outside the moulding of one's personality" (324), political consciousness being an important part of cultural change. Nevertheless, he acknowledged that "creating a new culture does not only mean one's own individual 'original' discoveries. It also, and most particularly, means the diffusion in a critical form of truths already discovered, their 'socialisation' as it were" (325). "In acquiring one's conception of the world one always belongs to a particular grouping which is that of all the social elements which share the same mode of thinking and acting" (324). Without delving into the mechanisms involved, Gramsci took as a basic tenet the intimate connections between the personal and the social. He described a cultural movement as "a 'religion,' a 'faith.'" He was prepared to use the word "ideology" here "but on condition that the word is used in its highest sense of a conception of the world that is implicitly manifest in art, in law, in economic activity and in all manifestations of individual and collective life" (328). We have here a notion of ideology that is, on the one hand, the product of individual (social), rational choice, and, on the other, something *already in* social practices.

Gramsci distinguished between "organic ideologies," those structurally "necessary," and ideologies which are "arbitrary, rationalistic, or 'willed'":

> To the extent that ideologies are historically necessary they have a validity which is "psychological"; they "organise" human masses, and create the terrain on which men move, acquire consciousness of their position, struggle, etc. To the extent that they are arbitrary they only create individual "movements," polemics and so on. (1971: 377)

It will soon become clear that this distinction is identical in form with the distinction I propose between ideology-*in-general* and ideolog*ies*. Bennett et al. point out that, for Gramsci, organic ideology is historically a necessary material force that creates the social terrain of human action and at the same time "has an 'internal' psychological dimension . . . that is the way in which consciousness itself is structured" (1981a: 209). Clearly, the ideas of Freud, while not delved into by Gramsci, are relevant to this understanding of ideology. (While he only mentions Freud twice in his prison writings, Gramsci was sympathetic to the psychoanalytic treatment undertaken by his wife.) "The general social structure and the individual are brought together in this formulation in a complex relationship of dominance and subordination" (Bennett et al. 1981a: 209). In case there is any doubt that historically necessary ideologies are specific instances of what my book calls ideology-in-general, Gramsci has said that material forces are the content and ideologies the form—though this distinction between form and content has purely didactic value, since material forces would be inconceivable historically without form and the ideologies would be individual fancies without the material forces (1971: 377).

To summarize, then, for Gramsci, as for Freud, human socialization has an important depth-psychological character. Gramsci, while not by any means a psychologist, acknowledged the complexity of the mind: "the personality is strangely composite: it contains Stone Age elements and principles of a more advanced science, prejudices from all past phases of history at the local level and intuitions of a future philosophy which will be that of a human race united the world over" (1971: 324). And for him all these levels of consciousness operated in the dynamic arena of ideology. While intuiting the importance and complexity of what happens in people's minds, Gramsci did not integrate his thoughts into a coherent psychology. His allusions to "Stone Age elements" and "instinctive and violent impulses" are tantalizing, but he lacks a theory of the unconscious. Possible areas of overlap between Gramsci's work and some psychoanalytic principles have been sketched, however. Whether my fanciful speculation holds up, what follows describes the product of just such an amalgamation, Althusser's theory of ideology—a theory that at once owes a great deal to the work of Gramsci and to the psychoanalysis of Lacan.

ALTHUSSER AND IDEOLOGY

In his early work, as we have seen in the previous chapter, Althusser was dedicated to defending Marx's science of history (historical materialism) and to the elaboration of "another scientific discipline," Marxist philosophy (dialectical materialism). Marx had laid the foundation of this latter science in *The German Ideology* (with Engels), *The Poverty of Philosophy*, the unpublished 1857 "Introduction," and in some parts of *Capital*, notably the 1873 postface to the second German edition of Volume 1. According to Althusser, Engels' and Lenin's works remained "ideological," not displaying the "degree of elaboration or systematicity, hence scientificity, at all comparable to historical materialism and imparted by *Capital*" (1965c, quoted in Elliott 1987: 74).

It has been shown that Althusser's view of science is nonpositivistic. Science for him is a highly sophisticated system of counter-intuitive thought that operates and is evaluated largely by its own internal principles. Some distinctions are needed here. On the one hand, Lukács (1923), and other Marxists who returned to Hegel, categorized knowledge into the natural sciences, which are "bourgeois science," and historical materialism, which is "proletarian science." Althusser and Balibar (1965) reject this view whereby proletarian science is the expression of the subject of history (the proletariat) rather than knowledge of an object.

Humanist Marxism, Althusser objects, views Marxism not as an equal of the other sciences (1965e: 140-41), but as the view of a particular historical grouping. Althusser remembered the postwar years as a time when communist intellectuals were "slicing up the world with a single blade, arts, literature, philosophies, science with the pitiless demarcation of class" (1965e: 86).

For Stalinism, on the other hand, the dialectical materialism of Engels' later work was regarded as the science of "nature, society and thought." Compared to Hegelian Marxism's proletarian science which was to be distinguished from the natural sciences, Stalinism saw Marxist-Leninism *as* a natural science along positivistic lines. This manifested itself in Zhdanov in the cultural domain, and Lysenko in the scientific.

A major intention of this chapter is to demonstrate that Althusser's theory of ideology is quite distinct from both the humanist and Stalinist notions.

Various Meanings of "Ideology"

Raymond Williams (1976) has traced the development of the word "ideology," showing the origins of its several meanings. Elizabeth Frazer describes the "headache and disorientation" experienced by those who try to sort out this "row." In everyday language and in social theory, the term ideology is "confused to the point of Babel" (1989: 117-18). Dieter Guess (1981) narrows down three ways in which ideology has been used in critical theory: (a) "descriptive," the belief system of a group; (b) "pejorative," a form of "false consciousness" that can, by implication, be remedied by ideology critique; and (c) "positive," ideology as created by, for example, the Leninist vanguard. Smith points out that "Althusser's writing on ideology touches on each of these meanings" (1984: 129).

Althusser has used ideology in the sense of being descriptive, for example, when he says: "There is no practice except by and in *an* ideology (1970: 170, emphasis added). These "particular ideologies," of course, change through history; they "have to do with *shared presumptions about accepted realities*" (170). Even here, though, ideolo*gies* can be seen to be more than just a set of ideas. The psychoanalyst Vann Spriuell says:

> World views are partly derived from internalizations out of the deepest past, partly from what the person senses about him, and partly from what his peers believe or claim to believe are truths. Motives derived from perceptions and constructions of external reality interdigitate with the other great sets of intrapsychic motivations which underlie every personal psychic act: from the interests of the id, ego and super-ego. (1988: 172)

It is worth mentioning here that "ideological themes such as nationalism or democracy are in themselves neutral, and not the monopoly of one class" (Mouzelis 1978: 46).

Althusser also speaks of mystifying ideologies in the sense identified by Guess as pejorative. In class societies, he said, ideology's goal is not to provide "objective knowledge" of the social system, but rather "to furnish them with a mystified representation of it in order to keep them in their 'place' in the system of class exploitation" (1965c, quoted in Elliott 1987: 174).

This is Althusser at his most functionalist. Ideology is here anthropomorphized as something that has a "goal," namely to mystify people. Because of the revealing powers of ideology-critique, he suggests, while ideology is always "mythical" it will not always "mystify" (1965c, quoted in Elliott 1987: 174). Ideology for some writers continues to mean "a kind of 'false consciousness' which, although claiming to be all-embracing, is segmented and partial" (Hernandez 1988: 167). There are many in the Left who want to maintain the idea that "ideology is that set of social practices and meaning which conceal and/or attempt to conceal class contradictions" (Hayes 1989: 90). Within educational theory, Rachel Sharp has been adamant on this score: "ideology *is* a form of false consciousness and false practice, a distorted form of resolution to contradictions in reality." Abolish the "real contradictions," she says, and ideology is abolished (Sharp 1982: 73).

Althusser, unwilling to drop the tactic of the leadership role of the Leninist party, has also used his science/ideology split in the sense that Guess has labeled as "positive." Rejecting the left-wing humanism of the young Lukacs and Karl Korsch, which proposed bourgeois science and proletarian science, Althusser has argued that the proletariat is incapable of developing the science of society. This theoretical practice is to occur outside the proletariat and be "imported" into it (Althusser 1965e: 141). Marxism will produce "a *new* form of ideology in the masses (an ideology which will depend on a science this time—*which has never been the case before*)" (Althusser 1965e: 131), that science to be developed by the party.

Wexler, in a rather different way, has insisted on the "positive moment" of ideology, ideology as much more than a form of social control. The denial of this moment is "the denial of the role of sentiment, character, belief and 'the emotional, the subconscious and the irrational' in the individual actualization and collective mobilization of social action which can change the conditions of its own production" (Wexler 1982b: 55). The dominated can and do develop ideologies, and that is why we can speak of "ideological struggles" and "transformative practice" (Chisholm and Sole 1981: 115).

However, although he uses the term in various ways depending on the task at hand, Althusser's real contribution to the theorization of ideology comes from a position distinct from those outlined by Guess. For want of a better term it will be called "ideology-in-general"—ideology as "lived relation." Althusser's fullest account of this is to be found in the essay "Ideology and Ideological State Apparatuses: Notes towards an investigation" (1970, hereafter "the ISA paper"). McLennan, Molina, and Peters put it thus: "ideology in general represents only the abstraction of the common elements of any concrete ideology, the theoretical fixation of the general mechanism of every ideology." In other words, ideology-in-general is "a different conceptual terrain" from that of "concrete ideologies" (95). Ideology-in-general, says Althusser, is "*an organic part of every social totality*" because "human societies secrete ideology as the very element and atmosphere indispensable to their historical respiration and life" (1965g: 232). Ideology-in-general is indeed, then, as his critics claim, "ethereal" and a priori; it "stands prior to our experience" (Frazer 1989: 121). For Althusser, not even communist societies will be free of ideology; it is a form indispensable to the historical life of societies. It need hardly be pointed out the radical departure this represents from Stalinism, which construed communism as the time of the "end of ideology." Opposed to this orthodoxy, Althusser says that human beings are ideological animals.

> Ideology is present to such an extent in all the activities of individuals that it is *indistinguishable* from their "lived experience." [Ideology ensures] men's *bonds* with each other in all the forms of their existence, the *relation* of individuals to the tasks assigned them by the social structure. (1965c, quoted in Elliott 1987: 173-74)

Jacques Ranciere is both right and wrong to say that for Althusser "*false ideas come from social practice*" (quoted in Elliott 1987: 178). In the sense that social practices produce ideology that is a "representation" of the social relation, it is true that social practice can never produce *true* ideas. But is wrong to imply that Althusser is arguing here for ideology as false consciousness. Indeed, ideology-in-general should not be regarded as true or false, but as a transhistorical human condition—a condition that is necessarily mythical. It is "crucially to be located at the level of *individuality* (individual 'imaginary-lived' relations), and cannot be regarded, therefore, as simply false or 'distorted' ideas" (McLennan, Molina, and Peters 1977: 97).

Althusser himself acknowledges his early error of "theoreticism." In his "Elements of self-criticism" (1974), he says that he had earlier confused two meanings of the word ideology. The word can be a philosophical concept that distinguishes between the truth and error of ideas, or it can be a scientific concept referring to the formation of the superstructure (1974: 119); "not as possession, as ideas possessed, but as *social practices*" (Therborn 1980: vii). It is this latter use that Althusser affirmed and that is to be maintained and elaborated in this book.

Reproduction of the Social Formation

In the ISA paper, Althusser is trying to understand how it is that social formations are reproduced; he recalls Marx's famous statement in a letter to Kugelman of July 11 1865, that any social formation will only "last the year" unless it reproduces its conditions of production (Marx and Engels 1975: 196). This involves the reproduction of both the forces and the relations of production. Althusser notes that the forces of production consist not only of the means of production but also to labor power, which is reproduced by wages (physical reproduction) and the educational system. At school, he says, children learn both skills ("know-how") and the "rules of good behavior." "But this is to recognize the effective presence of a new reality: *ideology*" (Althusser 1970: 128). Before he can address the reproduction of the relations of production, Althusser first asks, What is a society? The answer to this question he finds in the base-superstructure metaphor, where the economic base (the forces and relations of production) is the level on which the superstructure rests. The superstructure itself consists of two "levels": the politico-legal and ideology. This is not the "primitive infantilism" of crude Marxism where "every fluctuation of politics and ideology" is "an immediate expression of the structure" (Gramsci 1971: 407). Rather, Althusser's conception of the social formation "constitutes an engaging and genuinely innovating intervention in the 'base/superstructure' debate" (McLennan, Molina, and Peters 1977: 82). Althusser explains the "respective indices of effectivity," by which he means the fact that the base determines the superstructure "in the last instance," while the superstructure's influence on the base is theorized by its "relative autonomy" from, and "reciprocal action" on, the base (1970: 129-130). Ideology is not "a single, homogenous substance"; it has specific properties "which define it as distinct from the other levels or instances" of the social formation (McLennan, Molina, and Peters 1977: 83). But while acknowledging its usefulness, Althusser wants to go beyond this spatial metaphor of base and superstructure as it remains "descriptive." This must be done, he says, "*from the point of view of reproduction*" (Althusser 1970: 131). To this end he turns to the Repressive and Ideological State Apparatuses (RSA and ISAs) of the superstructure.

The RSA includes the police, army, courts, and prisons and operates mainly by repression, although also by ideology. The ISAs, conversely, work principally via ideology and only secondarily though repression. The ISAs (churches, schools, the family, legal institutions, the political system, trade unions, cultural forms) are mainly "private." (Wexler wants to extend the ISAs to mass media and beyond—"the living room, the bus stop, the 'walk-man' cassette, and video-game machines" [1982b: 60].) But the private/public split is only a creation of bourgeois law, says Althusser—the ISAs function as state apparatuses. (Perry Anderson [1977] makes the point that Althusser's conflation of the state with all social relations makes it impossible to theorize about the private and public spheres, and it also precludes any discussion of different types of capitalist state. However, just as Althusser proposed ideology-in-general and particular ideologies, it may be useful to suggest a similar distinction: the state-in-general, and particular spheres and forms of states.)

ISAs are both the "stake" and the "site" of class struggle (Althusser 1970: 140). Now Althusser can return to find out how the reproduction of the relations of production is secured—"for the most part, it is secured by the legal-political and ideological superstructure," the ISAs and RSA (141). As with Gramsci's coercion versus consent, the RSA secures the political conditions for the actions of the ISAs—the dominant ISA being the "School/Family couple." Althusser argues that the relatively autonomous levels of base and superstructure are articulated via the operation of ideology.

As troublesome as the notion of the determination of the superstructure in the last instance by the base has been, without it Marxism surely ceases to make a distinct contribution. One is left only with historical eras, the generation of which remains mysterious. Muller and Crewe argue that while the criticisms of Althusser's anti-humanism and ahistoricism are misplaced, there remain two problems with his work: economistic reduction, "all discriminations are at root economic discriminations"; and class reduction, workers and capitalists as the "fundamental social division" (1981: 118). It seems to me that unless one is prepared to give up the insights into history provided by Marxism, one has to maintain some notion of economic determination. This does not limit one to simple economic and class reductions, however; rather, it is to say that in any particular era the forms of production, exchange, and consumption are in the final analysis different from those of any other era, and that such production, exchange, and consumption constitute the structure within which any number of cultural practices can occur. What is it that distinguishes the capitalist era from the feudal? One can talk, as Foucault does, of "classical," "modern," etc., "epistemes"—times of quite different knowledge/power forms. But, without wanting to discard his very important work by sleight of hand, it should be pointed out that these epistemes to a very large extent coincide with Marx's periodization of history. As long as one understands Marx to mean that beneath human cultures there are "deep economic structures" that set limits on possible action, there is much of explanatory value in a statement like this of Wexler's: "the deep structure of the ideological apparatus is simply the production of meaning for profit" (1982a: 61). This is not, of course, to deny that there remains an unresolved question: "What is the relation between the *nature* of ideology and *class* domination?" (McLennan, Molina, and Peters 1977: 94).

Ideology operates in the ISAs (and in the RSA) that reproduce the relations of production and in the reproduction of labor power. Education is necessary to the reproduction of both the relations of production and labor power.

The school, according to Althusser, "ejects" masses of children into different productive positions with the appropriate know-how and the ideology appropriate to class roles: the exploited, the agent of exploitation, the agent of repression, or the professional ideologist (1970: 147). Wexler, Whitson, and Moscowitz (1981) argue that schooling is lessening in social effect because of its growing inappropriateness, and along these lines Hall (1988) refers to the school/family/media nexus as the dominant ISA in capitalist society. Be that as it may, it is as a part of the principal ISA complex that education teaches know-how and the rules of good behavior, thereby reproducing both the forces and the relations of production.

A word on reproduction: reproduction is a "process" and not "mere repetition and maintenance" (McLennan, Molina, and Peters 1977: 94). Muller and Crewe (1981) put it thus: individuals/subjects are *produced* by ideology, and social relations of production are *reproduced* by this production.

Four Axioms

The ISA paper then proceeds to theorize the concept of ideology. Althusser presents four major axioms.

1. "*Ideology has no History*" (Althusser 1970: 150). "Ideolog*ies have a history of their own,*" but ideology *in general has no history* (151).

Elaine Lee (an opponent of Althusserianism) makes the point well: Althusser, she says, outlines "a theory of Ideology (capital 'I') in general—to find a scientific definition of ideology as a structure, in order to elucidate common factors and issues relating to particular ideologies (which referring back to Marx's concept, are always rooted in the class struggle)" (1983: 26).

2. "*Ideology is a 'Representation' of the Imaginary Relationship of Individuals to their Real Conditions of Existence*" (Althusser 1970: 152).

Here "imaginary," like Lacan's "Imaginary" of a unified self in the mirror stage (see the Chapter 6), is "of the image," not a false idea; "the 'imaginary' is simply the historically specific way in which historically real persons live their conditions of existence *as if they could experience reality cold*" (Muller and Crewe 1983: 5). The imaginary does not emphasize the phantasy aspect of life (although the Chapter 5 will show that even this has a materiality), but its "*active encounter*"—"we actively engage our social formation through structured paths" (6). It is important to be clear here: Althusser is not saying that in ideology people experience or interpret the relation between themselves and the world, what one might call the "real" relation, "but *the way* they live the relation between them and their conditions of existence," the "lived" relation. Ideology is not a representation of reality, it is "a representation of an (individual) relationship to reality" (McLennan, Molina, and Peters 1977: 95), what Althusser called "a relation of the second degree" (1965g: 233). It is "the expression of the relation between men and their 'world,' that is the (overdetermined) unity of the real relation and the imaginary relation between them and their real conditions of existence" (234). Ideologies are "*shared presumptions about accepted realities*" (Spruiell 1988: 172).

McLennan, Molina, and Peters, exceptionally astute readers of Althusser, make a strange inference here. They say: "If ideology is the way we live our relations to our real conditions of existence, it is therefore changeable and capable of being ended altogether" (1977: 99). One can agree with all but the final six words of this statement; ideology is an expression of the imaginary relation to the relations of existence, and this imaginary is *of necessity*, i.e., *always*, a misrecognition. As will be shown later, Althusser borrowed the notion of misrecognition and the imaginary from Lacan according to whom the very existence of language denies the possibility of access to the real. Indeed, a social world free of misrecognition would be an impossible world without desire or repression, a world where we would have ready and unmediated access to reality.

3. "Ideology has a material existence" (Althusser 1970: 155).

Ideas are material actions in material practices of material rituals shaped by material ideological apparatus (158). Or again, "every transformation (every practice) presupposes the transformation of a raw material into products by setting in motion determinate means of production" (Althusser 1965f: 184). Contra to those who assert that there is a lack of struggle in Althusser's theory of ideology, he says quite clearly that ideologies are "bodies of representations existing in institutions and practices: they feature in the super-structure and are based in the class struggle" (1972: 7).

4. "*Ideology Interpellates Individuals as Subjects*" (Althusser 1970: 158).

For example, when we recognize ourselves in a police officer's address—"Hey, you there!"—we have been interpellated into a particular subject position. What is common to all ideologies is their representation of concrete individuals as subjects who experience themselves as autonomous actors; this is the "practico-social function specific to ideology" (McLennan, Molina, and Peters 1977: 96). "This inversion, by which the determinate is falsely presented as the determinant, takes place through a process of 'hailing' or 'interpellating' individuals as subjects" (Mouzelis 1978: 47). At the very moment that the subject "recognizes" that s/he is "working by him/herself," s/he is "working by and in ideology" (McLennan, Molina, and Peters 1977: 42). Diane MacDonell objects that interpellation is a "single mechanism." This, she says, is too simple and does not allow for contestation, as ideologies are "simply effected identifications" (1986: 39-40). But identifications, certainly for psychoanalysis, are far from simple processes (for a review see Meissner 1970, 1971, 1972), and this book (especially the following chapter) sets out to show that the mechanism of interpellation should be understood as a complex, ambiguous, and conflictual set of material interactive processes.

Instead of paraphrasing Althusser, I will rather attempt to briefly state what is at stake here. Althusser is saying that individuals are not volitional agents; our experiences and practices are always in and through ideology. (Thus, ideology is not false consciousness because true consciousness is impossible.) Ideology is not simply "thoughts"—thoughts arise from practice and ideology is therefore grounded in reality (although this reality can never be fully disclosed). So ideology is a representation (not a reflection) of the imaginary relationship of individuals to the real world. Ideology-in-general is not a historical phenomenon, but it exists throughout history—it is a "structural limitation" (Jameson 1981: 285). And this structure places (interpellates) people in subject positions, i.e., people are not free individuals (ideology makes us experience this as true), but we are in fact subjects of ideological discourses.

Thompson versus Althusser

Theories of subjectivity have been readily adopted and developed in French Marxism, while they are either grudgingly incorporated or hotly contested in Britain and also the United States. In order to highlight the disjunctures between French structuralist Marxism and English culturalist Marxism it will be interesting to pit two of their most famous combatants against one another—Louis Althusser versus E.P. Thompson. The sparks that fly should illuminate their differences.

Thompson says of Althusser's ISA paper: "This is, perhaps, the ugliest thing he has ever done, the crisis of the idealist delirium" (1978: 174). An outline of Thompson's problems with structuralism in general, and Althusser in particular, will present the meat of the culturalist/humanist Marxist project in its opposition to structuralism.

Part I of the ISA paper, with its explication of the theoretical structure of the capitalist mode of production, is what Thompson calls a "system of closure." "It is the place where all Marx*isms*, conceived of as self-sufficient, self-validating, self-extrapolating theoretical systems must end" (Thompson 1978: 167). Thompson's point is that simply to accept Marx's categories as true is theology, not theory. And it is a fact that Marx, as a dialectician who profoundly understood historical change, would almost certainly himself have been opposed to any reification of his concepts. The end of Marxist analysis, Thompson says, "is not to discover a (reformed) finite conceptual system, Marx*ism*. There can never be such a finite system" (167).

Thompson's point is well taken—history has shown that any theory can be used to justify any number of practices. But at the same time he displays a rather convenient naïvety about the nature of theory. Theories are by their nature systems of explanation. Indeed, one of the ways that we evaluate theories is by their rigor and internal logic. A problem that often arises in intellectual work is that not all the components of a theory are made explicit, and it thus appears as a collection of hypotheses waiting to be tested in the world. Thompson's own historical work, for example, claims to start with almost no preconceived theory of extant classes.

> "Working classes" is a descriptive term, which evades as much as it defines. It ties loosely together a bundle of discrete phenomena. There were tailors here and weavers there, and together they make up the working class.
>   By class I understand an historical phenomenon, unifying a number of disparate and seemingly unconnected events, both in the raw material of experience and in consciousness. I do not see a class as a "structure," nor even as a "category" but as something which in fact happens . . . in human relationships. (1963: 9)

This is the positivism into which Thompson's theory-allergy has placed him. Althusser, as has been shown, does understand the nature of theoretical work. Even if one rejects his distinction between ideology and science, as I suggest one must, the sophistication of Althusser's notion of theoretical practice is impressive. Such practice must satisfy the criteria of epistemological break and of problematic, theoretical practice being counter-intuitive and coherent. And, it should be added, theoretical practice is aware of itself as theory. It is absurd, then, to criticize Althusser for having a "self-sufficient, self-validating, self-extrapolating theory," as if this is something he does behind our backs. Rather, Althusser has openly set up rigid standards that enable us to evaluate theories, including his own, from within. He has demonstrated the vision to realize that theories cannot be critiqued from without, theories being "incommensurable" (Feyerabend 1975).

If Thompson disagrees vehemently with Part I of the ISA paper, it is to be expected that he will have problems with Part II; he says:

> Althusser invents a (wholly imaginary) device of "interpellation" or "hailing" by which the State via its ideological apparatus . . . cries out to individuals: "Ahoy, there!" It is only necessary for the State to hail them, and they are "recruited" instantly to whatever "imaginary relationship" the State requires. (1978: 174)

There are three misreadings in this short passage. First, Thompson confuses the everyday meaning of "imaginary" as mystification and falsity, with imaginary as a representational image. Second, Thompson renders the State as "the government"—little wonder that he is incensed over the apparent claim that the government of the day has all the ISAs under its control! Third, therefore, the "imaginary relationship" is portrayed as a mystifying false consciousness that the government fools us into, whereas for Althusser the State is an inevitable societal superstructure. "Imaginary relationship" refers to the fact that we can never see things cold or as they are, but only as a representation of ourselves as unified subjects and of our perceptions of our relationships with the world. His misconceptions allow Thompson to portray ideology as follows:

> It is a touching scenario. . . . The wicked witch of State appears! The wand of ideology is flourished! Not only has the prince become a frog, but the entire coach-and-six of the reformist trade union movement (another ideological State apparatus) has become a match-box drawn by six white mice. (1978: 174)

It seems when considering this disagreement that "the symmetry of their opposition is virtually complete" (Anderson 1980). Subjects oppose agents, determination confronts dialectics, and reproduction encounters struggle. It is true, though, that now and then hints of similarities between Althusser and Thompson can be glimpsed. At the very end of the ISA paper Althusser says:

> If it is true that the ISAs represent the *form* in which the ideology of the ruling class must *necessarily* be realised, and the form in which the ideology of the ruling class must *necessarily* be measured and confronted, ideologies are not "born" in the ISAs but from the social classes at grips in the class struggle: from their conditions of existence, their practices, their experiences of struggle, etc. (1970: 172-73)

And Thompson speaks of "the crucial ambivalence of our human presence in our own history, part-subjects, part-objects, the voluntary agents of our own involuntary determinations" (1978: 280). In response to criticism, Thompson later claims that he has always meant by "experience" that "junction between culture and non-culture, lying half within social being, half within social consciousness. We might perhaps call these experience I—lived experience and II—perceived experience" (1981: 406). While this understanding is to be welcomed, it is not one that is explicated in "The Poverty of Theory." Indeed, Thompson's attack on Althusser would have collapsed with this new distinction, a distinction not incompatible with that between ideology-in-general and ideolog*ies*.

It is important to remind ourselves of their *raisons d'être*. Thompson rejects the notion of the inevitability of revolution. While contesting economic reduction, he wants a Marxism that relocates the human agent at its center. Althusser, on the other hand, also opposing economic reductionism as well as humanism, is attempting to understand why the inevitable world proletarian revolution has not happened. Why is it that the bourgeois social order is so tenacious? He finds the answer to this question in the (unconscious) structures of society. So it should come as no surprise that their tasks and methods differ: Althusser explains while Thompson describes. They are asking different questions: Althusser asks, Why are things so difficult to change? and Thompson wants to know, How have people changed their worlds?

THEORETICAL PROMISE

It was mentioned earlier that Althusser's work has largely fallen into disrepute. For some, the theory of ideology has become "monolithic" (Frazer 1989: 120-21) and "too broad," with "no beginning and no end" (Lee 1983: 38-39). (Chapter 6 shows with reference to Kristeva that it is possible to theorize an aspect of cultural practice that is indeed non ideological.) Before trying to extract some genuinely novel and useful concepts from his writing, it is worth reiterating the extent to which Althusser's name is anathema in so much of critical social theory.

> Explicit critical judgements have for the most part been going one way: Against Althusser. For some—a-political literary deconstructionists—he is too faithful to Marxism and, consequently, unworthy of a place in the theoretical adventure playground that is post-structuralism at its worst. For others—the post-Althusserians—he is to be praised for having prepared the way for their own "post-Marxist" paradigms. If, for the Nietzschean avant-garde, he is the Marxist Same, for humanist Marxism he is the Stalinist Other. As far as some anglophobe Marxists are concerned, on the other hand, he is simply all-too-French. (Elliott 1987: 327)

Now and then, of course, a major theorist like Terry Eagleton (1986), Stuart Hall (1985), or Slavoj Žižek (1989) acknowledges an intellectual debt to Althusser. Fredric Jameson, to give another example, says that Althusser has provided "the first new and as yet insufficiently developed conception of the nature of ideology since Marx and Nietzsche" (1977: 393-94).

What exactly have been the contributions of Althusser to Marxist social theory generally? And more specifically, What are the contributions from which a theoretically undeveloped discipline like CSOE can draw? It is hoped that the above section has gone some way to affirming Jameson's conclusion about the importance of Althusser's work, viz. that it is "antiempiricist" because it "drives the wedge of the concept of a 'text'" between the real relations and social experience; it "liberates us from the empirical object—whether institution, event, or individual work—by displacing our attention to its *constitution* as an object and its *relationship* to other objects thus constituted" (Jameson 1981: 296-97).

From all of Althusser's corpus and from the critiques one can extract the following theoretical contributions:

1. Althusser has returned western Marxism to the consideration of *Capital* as Marx's most important work.
2. He has produced a model of "theoretical practice" that, once separated from scientific pretensions, deals with counter-intuitive problematic intellectual labor.
3. He has provided a spark for renewed, theoretically sophisticated work in many disciplines (much of which does not acknowledge any debt to him).
4. He has engaged in theoretical anti-Stalinism, thereby rejuvenating classical Marxism.
5. He has reintroduced Mao's complex notion of the dialectic as an overdetermined relation.
6. He has reconceived the social structure as having relatively autonomous and irreducible political and ideological realms.
7. He has reintroduced psychoanalysis into Marxist analysis.
8. He has proposed a structural causality of economic determination, not dominance, in the last instance.
9. By theorizing the articulations of forces and relations of production, he has overturned the teleological notion of the inevitable succession of modes of production.
10. He has developed a theory of ideology-in-general, the inevitable state of human lived-relations.
11. He has countered humanism's agent with the theory of a split, decentered, and necessarily contradictory subject.
12. He has proposed how such subjects are positioned by interpellation.

This book attempts to remedy the pre-Freudian elements that linger in Althusser's notion of the subject. These tendencies are a result of his economistic hangovers, which lead him to suggest that "the imaginary *means* of ideological representation . . . are derived from, or subordinated to, *that which is represented*," the latter of which is "an economically defined goal or function . . . the place of which is filled by human agents" (McLennan, Molina, and Peters 1977: 102). In the process of developing a model of the psychic economy of subjectivity, I will deny the claim that "it is impossible to research ideology" (Frazer 1989: 121).

CONCLUSION

This chapter has attempted to elaborate a notion of ideology-in-general that is theoretically sophisticated and also highly relevant to those interested in the interconnections and workings of humanization and social institutions. This work of Althusser (derived as it is in large measure from Gramsci and Lacan) is readily aligned and articulated with basic psychoanalytic concepts. For example: the mental is much more than self-aware consciousness; there is a dynamic

LIBRARY OF MOUNT ST. MARY'S COLLEGE EMMITSBURG, MARYLAND

interaction of levels of consciousness; the super-ego and ego ideal is the psychic "location" of entrenched tradition, folklore and common sense; and the ego serves several masters.

Intending to develop Althusser's theory of ideology as far as possible, the next two chapters delve further into psychoanalysis in order to flesh out the other key term's of Althusser's organizing principle, "Ideology interpellates individuals as subjects."

5

THE DYNAMICS
OF INTERPELLATION

Passion, I see, is catching, for mine eyes,
Seeing those beads of sorrow stand in thine
Began to water.

—William Shakespeare
Julius Caesar

There is more than one way to tackle the microsociological mechanisms of socialization. This book borrows from psychoanalysis in order to theorize the ways the social and the personal relate. To elaborate on Althusser's theory of ideology-in-general, Freud's model of the unconscious psychic structure has been used to demonstrate the unseen forces that determine consciousness. And in the following chapter, Lacan's work will be used to show what is at stake in the notion of subjectivity. But before that, this chapter attempts to expand on Althusser's notion of "interpellation" by delving into object relations theory in order to propose and examine projective identification: or, how the intrapsychic/interpersonal relation operates. It can be said that this chapter, although meaningless in isolation from the others, is the most important of the book. Here it is suggested *how* the interpellation or positioning of subjects happens. It is unavoidably also a longer chapter, as I am concerned to give a detailed description of people's influence one another.

This chapter, in trying to specify what might happen during what Althusser calls "interpellation," first outlines Klein's developmental theory. This is outlined at some length in order to generate a feel for the dark sides of our selves. Second, it synthesizes the many psychoanalytic concepts of externalization and internalization. Third, it follows the career of the concept of projective identification. Fourth, Ogden's integrated model of object relations as well as his development of projective identification is outlined. Fifth, a brief demonstration is given of how the projective identificatory mechanisms elaborated in the chapter could be used to study group interactions particularly in educational settings.

KLEIN'S WORK

A writer of the stature of Melanie Klein could quite fruitfully be used to drive a host of research questions. As it does with Freud and Lacan, I will select some basic concepts from her corpus in order to develop my problematic, viz. socialization. Her notions will not be isolated from their original theoretical context; rather, some of Klein's relevant elementary concepts will be briefly described as they fit into her greater conceptualization of psychic development. At the same time, while not attempting the perhaps impossible task of formally uniting the work of Freud, Lacan, and Klein, significant areas of overlap, extension, and disagreement will be pointed out.

Like Freud's before her, Klein's theory of psychic development was accomplished in reverse order to the development in the individual. Hanna Segal (1974: 1) has divided Klein's "march backward" (Shapiro 1981) into three stages. First, Klein established child analysis as a legitimate enterprise, in the process discovering early, pregenital roots of the super-ego and the Oedipus complex (1932). Second, she conceptualized "the depressive position" and manic defence mechanisms (1935, 1940). Third, and developmentally most primary, she formulated "the paranoid-schizoid position" (1946, 1957).

Child Analysis

Freud (1920), as we know, took an interest in the play of infants, realizing that it could be understood as a representation of unconscious conflict. Similarly, Klein studied children at play. Children, analysts like Anna Freud insist, cannot free associate or form transference relationships and can thus not be psychoanalyzed. Klein, however, believes that play itself can be used by the analyst to uncover the anxieties and phantasies out of which it springs (1926). In this work she not only confirmed the existence of childhood sexuality, but she also found that the super-ego and the Oedipus complex exist at the level of phantasy much earlier than classical theory had supposed: in her view internal and external object relations start "from the beginning of life" (Rosenfeld 1983). Moreover, these phantasies contain genital tendencies (before the genital stage), and the primordial super-ego is, she says, particularly savage.

The child's object relationships she traced back to the earliest months, when its relationships are not yet to whole people (or to their internal representations of whole objects), but to part-objects like the breast or the penis. This early time is one of anxiety, which can influence later stages and the particular form of a child's Oedipus complex.

For Klein, the younger the child, the greater the extent to which he or she is dominated by omnipotent phantasies. For her the child gradually develops a more "realistic" relation with objects around it. (Of course, this is quite contrary to Lacan's theory, which argues that all post mirror stage representations are alienated, and which suggests, indeed, that the fragmented bodily experience of the earliest months of life is the more "Real" one. Juliet Mitchell, a follower of both these theorists makes a sensible compromise when she says that to endorse fragmentation, as Lacan-inspired French feminists have done, is to fragment. While not arguing for adaptation to reality, she sees both Lacan and Klein as talking about "*change* and the immense difficulty of change" [1988: 83]. It is my contention, the reader will know by now, that it is precisely this latter point which is missing from CSOE.)

The struggle between symbiosis with the mother and separation anxiety from her is one that dominates the life of the infant, and it is one whose traces are felt throughout life. There is a deep "golden fantasy" within each of us that is "a simple and familiar one: *it is the wish to have all one's needs met in a relationship hallowed by perfection*" (Smith 1977: 311). This phantasy is in conflict with the need to strike out in independence. There is consequently a constant blurring of boundaries between self and object; the break is never complete. Klaus Angel illustrates this when he says that in order for a bird that lives in biological symbiosis off the ticks on the back of a rhinoceros to have the psychoanalytic symbiosis we have with our internal objects, the bird "would need to have to develop object representations of the rhinoceros and subsequently be entirely unsure whether he is a bird or a rhinoceros" (1972: 541).

Infantile anxiety is a reaction more to aggression than to libido, for Klein, and it is against aggression and anxiety that defences are first built. So, long before repression is organized, the infant erects defences mainly through the mechanisms of denial, splitting of objects, projection of bad feelings, and introjection of good objects.

(Unavoidable) frustration and (insufficient) satisfaction with relation to the breast is the original source of ambivalence. The earliest stage of super-ego development occurs during the oral-sadistic phase when the child attacks the breast, attempting to destroy this persecuting part-object, thereby incorporating a cruel breast imago. During this stage the infant also incorporates a good and loving breast, the prototype of the ego ideal. The super-ego, then, is the product of a complex development, which culminates during the genital stage.

A word on object relations theory. The name refers, firstly to the psychic construction of the self and of other people in the external (object) world. The mind develops internal representations of external reality, "internal objects" (Sandler and Sandler 1978). Our initial object relations are formative, and future relations inevitably return to these prototypes. Throughout life, psychic representation of other people is a conglomeration of these actual others and our internal others. So, the person who exhibits an "Othello syndrome"—paranoid delusions of infidelity (West 1968)—and the suicide who wishes to kill and to punish another (Menninger 1938), both demonstrate patterns of relationships that exist as a "template" of early object relations "to some extent demonstrable in everyone" (Greenberg and Mitchell 1983). Object relations, it is generally agreed, are traces within the individual's mind of relationships with people important to that individual, and object relations theory is concerned with the fact that we all live in internal and external worlds simultaneously.

This much practically all schools of psychoanalysis would agree upon. Greenberg and Mitchell stress, however, the radical dissension that exists about what else object relations refers to, and of what importance it is to each particular viewpoint. Most fundamentally, there are those object relations theorists who agree with Freud that the object is the target of a drive (like the ego psychologists Edith Jacobson and Otto Kernberg), and those who totally reject drive theory (like W.R.D. Fairbairn and Harry Guntrip). It will serve us well here to simply neglect entering these arguments at this stage and to accept Greenberg and Mitchell's definition whereby object relations refers to the "individuals' interactions with external and internal (real and imagined) other people, and to the relationships between their internal and external object worlds" (1983: 13-14). This definition is sufficiently broad to evoke the dual inner and outer nature of interactions, and to point to the wide variability—"active or static, benign or malignant, alive or dead, and so on" (14)—of such objects. Also, it suggests the experientially tangible nature of objects, as well as their alterability. Such structures are both stable and dynamic (20). (Perhaps recklessly, I am avoiding being sidetracked by the famous internecine struggles in the British Psychoanalytic Society. It is enough to concentrate on the similarities between the Kleinians and the other object relations theorists.)

The child, then, builds a complex internal world in which objects stand not only in relation to the child's sense of self but also to each other (i.e., objects relating to other objects). For example, the infant's phantasies about parental sexuality when the parental couple becomes an internal object, are to be an important part of the structure of the infant's internal world.

Klein says that the child's desires and phantasies of the breast begin to extend to the whole of the mother's body which is phantasized as "containing all riches including new babies and the father's penis" (Segal 1974: 4). The mother's body is an orally loved and hated object. The infant both desires to scoop out and consume the phantasized objects inside the mother's body, or to bite and destroy them. Urethral sadistic phantasies of drowning, cutting, and burning, and anal sadism of exploding and poisoning, together with oral sadism turn the mother's body into a terrifying place full of destroyed and vengeful objects (Klein 1946).

During normal development, anxiety drives the child to extend to the environment through "symbolization," his or her fascination with the mother's body (Klein 1930). Psychotics, she discovered, have excessive anxiety with relation to the mother's body and consequently an inability to develop symbol formation. (Symbolization will be developed in the section on Ogden's work later in this chapter.)

As the child begins to conceive of the parents as distinct objects and as a couple, he or she ambivalently displaces desire and anxiety onto them. The child loves and fears not only the real parents but the internal parents too. Klein found that this construction of an internal world is the result of the highly active operation of introjection of good (and also, unavoidably, bad) objects, splitting of good imagoes and loving feelings from bad imagoes and feelings of hate, and expulsion of bad objects. The child's phantasy attacks on the parents may involve the child attacking them, or the parents attacking each other. Thus the sadistic and terrifying nature of the primal scene.

Some internal objects the ego identifies with through introjective identification. Others, like the super-ego, it incorporates as separate internal objects. All these internal objects are in relation to each other in a complex internal world.

The normal infant is occupied principally with sleeping, feeding, and experiencing pleasure, real and phantasized, however. The inevitable anxiety of frustration, for example, produces the defences of normal development. For Klein, the anxieties created by internal objects, together with the anxieties, sadism, and guilt of the oral and anal stages, lead the child to attempt to make reparation and to form a less sadistic genital relationship with the real parents, who are less fearsome than their internal imagoes. Thus, she says, the super-ego stimulates the development of the Oedipus complex. And no experience, as Freud also showed, is ever fully extinguished or superseded. For all of us, our most primary anxieties may be restimulated, reactivating the early defences.

The analysis of infants' play as a way of understanding the child's phantasies and of developing transference relationships led to Klein's belief that in fact all childhood activities "served to express, contain and canalise the child's unconscious phantasy by means of symbolization" (Segal 1974: 9). Unconscious phantasy and its symbolization, Klein realized, has an essential place in human development.

The "objects" of object relations psychoanalysis generally, and Kleinian theory in particular, then are not real objects but phantasies people have about what they possess internally. In trying to answer the question, What do we mean by phantasy? Anne Hayman defines it as imaginative wish fulfillment, as well as denoting "the primary content of the unconscious mental processes and corollary of instinctual urges" (1989: 113). Unconscious phantasy itself, then, is not a sign of pathology—it operates always in every person. For Klein it is the nature of phantasies and their relation to the world that is decisive (1959).

Phantasies are the psychic expression of wishes and fears (Isaacs 1952). "Phantasy is not merely an escape from reality, but a constant and unavoidable accompaniment of real experiences, constantly interacting with them" (Segal 1974: 14). As drives operate from birth, so phantasy begins then too. Hunger, for example, produces not only bodily pangs but also the phantasy of an object capable of satisfying that hunger. (See Chapter 6 for Lacan's similar distinction between need and desire.) Segal gives the example of the infant falling asleep contentedly sucking its fingers and phantasizing that it is incorporating the breast. On the other hand, a hungry infant phantasizes that it is attacking the breast and feels its own screams as the torn internal breast attacking from the inside. When such a child is then offered the breast it may reject and turn away from it; the bad breast has been attacked and destroyed in phantasy and the real breast is now seen, not as a good breast, but as a bad, avenging one. So, even people who have no trouble accurately perceiving reality may (perhaps one should say "will") attribute causes to this "reality" based upon unconscious phantasies.

There is a dialectical relationship between phantasy and reality. Phantasy constantly colors and affects one's interpretation of reality. However, reality also always influences phantasy by being experienced and incorporated in mediated ways. So, Klein says, exactly when a hungry child is fed—early on or after a long time—influences the development of good or bad internal objects. Crucially this means that it is not a bad environment per se that makes an experience a bad one, but whether the infant is simultaneously having aggressive phantasies. Such a coincidence establishes more firmly not only the felt badness of the environment, but also the child's own badness. In this respect, Klein is like Lacan (and Althusser) who insists that we never see things as they are, but only as representations of relations. Segal suggests that thought is not opposed to phantasy, but that thought, being at root the reality testing of phantasy, comes from phantasy (1974: 23).

For Klein, phantasy formation is an ego function. (Here she and Lacan differ enormously. For Lacan, we shall see, the ego is formed at the mirror stage, while for Klein it is naturally present at birth. She argues that by age six months the ego has a well-integrated ego. Prior to that it is disorganized but has a tendency to integration, and it already has the ability to experience anxiety, build defences, and form object relations. In this Klein also departs from Freud, for whom the ego develops out of the id and is thus surely not present at birth except as a potential.) Beside being the mental representatives of drives, phantasies are also defensive. Gratification gained from phantasy can be seen as a defence against either the bad external or internal worlds. The hungry infant who phantasizes possession of a good breast thereby avoids external frustration and defends itself against internal malevolence. Also, a manic phantasy may keep at bay a depressive phantasy. Mechanisms of defence are experienced as phantasies.

The Paranoid-Schizoid Position

The anxiety experienced from birth by the infant is for Klein primarily a product of conflict between the life and death drives. The infant is confronted simultaneously with an external environment that is both harsh and gentle. The anxiety of the death drive is converted into projections into the breast and into aggression. Thus fear of death becomes fear of the persecutor.

(This chapter speaks of projection "into" and not "onto" the object. Common in Kleinian language, "into" is justified if it is kept in mind that the "projection is a process that involves self- and object-*representations*" (Sandler 1987b: 20). Later usages of the notion of projective identification make the use of "into" more literally appropriate.)

As well as forming a persecuting object, the infant forms an ideal object, both by projecting libido into the breast and by forming a relationship with the internal ideal object. The primary object, the breast, is thus split into a persecuting breast and a good breast. These phantasies are consolidated by good and bad experiences with the real mother: gratification wards off persecution, and deprivation becomes the threat of persecution. The infant attempts to have and to hold the ideal object, and to keep at bay bad objects and parts of the self.

Klein called this the paranoid-schizoid position, because the dominant anxiety is a paranoid one, and because this is a time of schizoid splitting of good and bad objects (1946). A word on the term "position" is in order here. Klein chose to use this word over "stage" or "phase" because, although the paranoid-schizoid position precedes the depressive position developmentally, the latter does not fully integrate the former and so does not supersede it. Neither do either of these subdivisions of the oral stage ever cease to influence future development of and functioning of the personality.

To protect itself from the anxiety of persecution, the infant builds a set of externalizing and internalizing defences: introjection and projection of the good and the bad. In order to maintain the split between the ideal object and bad objects, overwhelming threat may be denied through the phantasy of the obliteration of the persecutors. Alternatively, the persecuting object may itself be idealized. An important defence mechanism here is projective identification where parts of the self are projected into the external object that is then identified with. Projective identification is the earliest form of empathy and symbol formation and this may be employed in order to make contact with the ideal object or to control a threat. Bad internal parts may be projected in order to cast them out and destroy the object, while good parts may be projected in order to protect them from bad internal objects.

While defence mechanisms deflect the fear of death, they produce further anxieties. Projection of bad feelings leads to feelings of external persecution, while projection of good parts causes depletion and further danger of persecution. For Klein projective identification produces anxiety that the assaulted object may retaliate and the fear of being in the control of the external object. We will see shortly that Klein's notion of projective identification has subsequently been developed and extended to the extent that many psychoanalytic theorists now consider it to be a normal and ubiquitous mechanism.

Defence mechanisms not only protect the ego; they are also part of development. But if the above defence mechanisms fail, then the ego may disintegrate to avoid anxiety, whereupon the fragmented bits are projected. This is pathological projective identification. In more normal development, parts of the self and internal objects are projected into the breast and into the mother. Relatively unchanged in form, these projections are then reintrojected and integrated into the ego. During times of aggression and envy, however, projective identification is pathological. The projected internal object is shattered into tiny bits and then projected into the external object, thereby splintering it. Both a persecutory object and an object of unbearable envious feelings can be disintegrated in this way. Instead of discriminating between good and bad objects, this pathological projective identification creates "bizarre objects," fragmented perceptions with some intense badness in each of the splinters of the projection. Thus, painful perception can lead, through this form of projective identification, to increasingly painful and persecutory perception and reduction of the ego's integration.

It is with the paranoid-schizoid position that the chaos of the first experiences and emotions are organized along lines of goodness and badness. Splitting is also the foundation for what developmentally later becomes repression. This basic channeling according to idealization and persecution continues to be operative throughout life.

During the paranoid-schizoid position the infant is not aware of whole persons but of part-objects; the first part-object being the breast. If there is a dominance of good over bad experiences, the paranoid-schizoid position advances smoothly on to its successor, the depressive position. But this depends on factors both internal and external. An internal factor like envy may adversely influence even a favorable external environment.

Envy is not the same as jealousy or greed (Klein 1957). Jealousy, founded on love, has the aims of possession of the loved object and the departure of the rival. Greed desires to have all the goodness that can be had from the object even if this means the destruction of that object. By contrast, envy aims at becoming as good as the object and, when this cannot be achieved, it tries to destroy the object's goodness in order to prevent the development of envious feelings. Strong envy prevents schizoid splitting between good and bad, as the ideal object itself causes envy and is consequently ruined. Thus no ideal object will be available to be built up and introjected. Intense envy produces feelings of persecution, despair for the possibility of love, and, later, guilt. Attempts may be made to retain the ideal object either by splitting it, thereby devaluing it and making it not worthy of envy, or by rigid idealization, whereby the increasingly perfect object intensifies envy. Both attempts fail in preventing envy and are roots of later pathology. In more favorable development, gratification toward the ideal breast supersedes and alters envy. Envy, then, can operate with guilt in an increasing spiral, or with gratitude in a diminishing spiral (Klein 1957).

In the paranoid-schizoid position, the manipulation of early anxieties begins organizing the internal world. Splitting, projection, and introjection aid the distinguishing between perception and emotion. Also, the infant manufactures an ideal object that it tries to identify with, and a bad object full of projected aggression. The bad object threatens the infant and its ideal object. During successful development, the ideal object is experienced as stronger than the bad object and bad impulses. The infant is less frightened and less likely to project these outwards. Thus the power of the bad object lessens as do paranoid fears.

Need fulfillment continues throughout life. "The four-month-old screams when mother leaves, the two-year-old screams when mother leaves, and the adult screams (sometimes) when the wife (or husband) leaves. Who has separation anxiety or symbiotic panic . . . ? The one who screams the loudest?" (Angel 1972, 541). There is a "complex interplay between the adult and the infantile neurosis" within the pathological family, with compulsions reproducing and re-creating neuroses (Calogeras and Alston 1985). Early identification with the primal object in the early years produces fixation points to which the patient keeps reverting. Edna O'Shaugnessy describes the case of a three-and-a-half-year-old boy who, despite quite lengthy treatment, maintained an "underlying melancholic identification" (1986: 178). The fixation points of psychosis are in the first phase of development, the paranoid-schizoid position; it is to this disturbed time that the psychotic returns.

When the mother is seen as a whole person, the depressive position starts. This is a time of integration, ambivalence, depressive anxiety, and guilt.

The Depressive Position

The depressive position begins as the ego becomes more integrated. This is when the infant recognizes and relates to a whole object: first the mother, then usually the father, and then others. Now the child sees that the good and bad, present and absent mother is the same mother. This recognition involves seeing her as an independent individual, an understanding this leads to a depressive experience of helplessness and total dependence as well as to jealousy of others. At the same time, according to Klein, the infant's ego becomes less split into good and bad parts, and more a whole object. There is less projection, greater integration of ego and object, and consequently less distorted perception. The distance between good and bad objects is diminished. Also, the integration of whole objects aids the integration of the ego.

As projection lessens, so repression rather than splitting of the ego begins to dominate: "psychotic mechanisms gradually give way to neurotic mechanisms, inhibitions, repression and displacement" (Segal 1974: 75). Gradually the infant understands that it is the same person, loving and hating the same mother. For the first time it is confronted with the conflicts associated with ambivalence. So while in the paranoid-schizoid position the dominant anxiety is with regard to the destruction of the ego by bad objects, in the depressive position the main anxiety is experienced that the infant's own impulses will destroy the loved object. This results in new feelings of mourning, longing, and guilt (Klein 1940). When the mother is unavailable, the infant feels depressive despair during which it believes that the loved object has been lost through the infant's own destructiveness. For the first time the infant suffers for the mother with whom it identifies. The infant tries to resolve this situation through the reparation of damaged objects. In other words, it experiences a constant seesawing of destructiveness and reparation.

During what D.W. Winnicott (1956) has called "good-enough-mothering," the mother's reappearance and her devoted attention to the infant serve to lessen its belief in the omnipotence of its destructive impulses, just as (necessarily) incomplete reparation lessens its faith in the omnipotence of love. The individual who has to a considerable degree worked through the depressive position later has neurotic, rather than psychotic, symptoms.

Segal (1952) has written on how, during the depressive position, symbol formation happens. The real breast has to be given up and supplanted by an object representation, and every giving up of a libidinal wish or object is a repetition of that primal relinquishment. If such a loss can be assimilated internally, she says, it becomes a symbol within the ego. So symbol formation is the creative product of the pain and labor of mourning. Once one has cleared away some terminological confusion, an overlap with Lacan is instructive here. Lacan, we will see, talks about the signifiers of language standing in the place of a lack, the signified which cannot be recovered. This begins to happen upon the entry of the infant into language, the Symbolic. One must not imagine that Segal means precisely the same with her "symbol formation" as Lacan does with "the Symbolic." But, nevertheless, it is apparent that both writers understand that the formation of symbols is the product of a painful process implicated in a tragic longing for what can no longer be.

The depressive position is never fully worked through. The anxieties pertaining to ambivalence and guilt, as well as situations of loss, which reawaken depressive experiences, are always with us. Good external objects in adult life always symbolize and contain aspects of the primary good object, internal and external, so that any loss in later life re-awakens the anxiety of losing the good internal object and, with this anxiety, all the anxieties experienced originally in the depressive position. (Segal 1974: 80)

There are two types of defences against depression: manic defences and reparation. The former can result in lessening of despair and development of reparative abilities. However, too-powerful manic defences initiate vicious cycles with points of fixation that hinder this development. Manic defences (splitting, idealization, projective identification, denial) work against the experience of dependence, ambivalence, and guilt that are at the root of the depressive position. The love object is normally dealt with in ambivalent ways but, when guilt and loss are unbearable, manic defences regard the object with contempt, control, and triumph. During such defensive activities reparation cannot take place; indeed these aggravated attacks increase the sense of guilt and loss, thereby increasing depressive anxieties.

Phantasies of reparation, on the other hand, lessen the depressive anxieties. Object loss is diminished by retrieval of the object. When the loving mother repeatedly returns after an absence, the infant begins to perceive its objects as more lasting, at the same time as the infant's own attacks are understood as less than omnipotent. It begins to accept the strength of its love and is then able to endure absences with less hatred for the object. (Klein also describes manic reparation, whereby the object is repaired in an omnipotent way—for example, where the recipients of one's charity are seen as unworthy and dangerous.)

A brief word on the Oedipus complex will conclude this summary of Klein's developmental theory. The Oedipus complex begins during the depressive position. Now the infant perceives people as individuals in relation to each other: the most basic external relation is the one between mother and father. The infant projects its own oral, urethral, anal, and genital needs into its parents, who are phantasized as being in almost constant intercourse. This results in feelings of acute deprivation, jealousy, and envy, which in turn leads to increased aggression against the parents in phantasy, and is immediately introjected as an internal destroyed parental couple.

Initially, the mother's breast is the loved object of both the boy and girl infant. For Klein, the persecution and depressive anxieties accompanying this relationship result in the father's penis becoming an alternative loved object for both boy and girl. For both the boy and the girl, these alternative oral objects are heterosexual and homosexual, the particular form of later genital development depending on the ways in which the oral, anal, urethral, and genital desires for the mother and the father develop into a genital situation. Again it needs to be said that nothing in individual development disappears; every Oedipal resolution contains its repressed shadow.

Perhaps this section appears to be too detailed. However it has been written in this way in order to give a reasonably full description of the internal interactions central to Klein's object relations theory. While Klein herself will largely now be left behind, her influence on the object relations work that follows persists. This despite the fact the British Independent theorists as well as North American object relations theorists distance themselves from some of her work.

EXTERNALIZATION AND INTERNALIZATION

Now we are in a position to consider projective identification, a psychic mechanism I want to use to understand interpellation. The concept of "projective identification," as has been noted, was introduced into psychoanalytic discourse by Klein in 1946. Since then it has become an important yet "blurred" concept, meaning "too many different things [to] too many different people under too many different circumstances" (Kernberg 1987: 93). Precisely because projective identification has come to be used in a fast and loose fashion, this chapter is devoted to clarifying the concept so that "if projective identification is used as an explanation, its specific meaning in the relevant context" (Sandler 1987b: 26) can be given.

Projective identification needs to be considered in the context of its theoretical forebears, the various concepts of expulsion out of and taking into the self. These overlapping concepts have included: appersonization, exteriorization, extrajection, extraspection, deegotization, objectivization, objectification, objectivation (Ornston 1978: 155-56), imitation, merger, fusion, idealization, and integration (Meissner 1981). This section briefly reviews the more notable and commonly used of the psychoanalytic concepts of outward- and inward-directed psychic actions: projection, externalization, internalization, identification, and incorporation. It builds upon Joseph Sandler and Meir Perlow's (1987) excellent summary.

Projection

Freud first mentioned projection in "Draft H" when he described it as the transposition of an intolerable idea outside of the self: in other words, attributing an internal conflict to an external cause. Projection is, he said, "a psychic mechanism that is very commonly employed an normal life" (Freud 1895: 109). In his comprehensive review of Freud's usage of the concept, Darius Ornston confirms that Freud always considered projective thinking to be ubiquitous and normal.

Freud proposed that from early infancy on, whenever we mentally attend or tentatively classify, whenever we orient or organize, whenever we anticipate or understand, we project. We always regard a puzzling predicament as similar to a past or familiar situation, or we think about our own mental activities as shared with, and complementary to, those of another person. . . . It is merely more evident when it does not work very well, as in phobias and paranoid disorders. In ordinary life, we can regress comfortably and altogether unconsciously because at the same time we mentally maintain certain differences. (Ornston 1978: 154-55)

Lacan says something similar when he describes knowledge as "paranoid" (1949: 2). Besides Freud's use of the concept projection to explain phobias (1926) and paranoia (1911a), he also wrote about projection in relation to jealousy (1922), defence (1895), masochism (1924), dreams (1917a), the formation of the external world (1912-1913), religion (1927), and space (1941).

Since Freud, the concept of projection has followed two main paths (Sandler and Perlow 1987: 3-4). First, Anna Freud (1936) understood projection as a defence mechanism. Second, Klein (1930, 1931) asserted that projection is the expulsion by the ego of its sadistic impulses into the world.

Projection may involve attributing qualities to others that they do not possess, diminishing a quality of one's own while greatly exaggerating it in others, or simply appealing to the imagined thoughts of others to justify one's inner state of mind. Nevertheless, all types of projection involve "a displacement of mental content from a self-representation to an external object representation, to a representation of an aspect of the world that is 'not-me'" (Sandler and Perlow 1987: 4).

Externalization

Freud used the term externalization as synonymous with projection as, for example, when he called the dream "a *projection*: an externalization of an internal process" (1917a: 223). Somewhat more specifically, Anna Freud called the transposition of conflict externalization. She considered externalization as both normal and pathological, although she tried to specify externalization as a subspecies of transference wherein the patient uses "the person of the analyst to represent one or other part of the patient's personality structure" (A. Freud 1965: 41). However, this distinction is not a clear one, as her ideas on externalization and object relations are not easily separated (Sandler and Perlow 1987: 6). Sandler and Sandler (1978) have isolated an aspect of transference that is different from the projection or externalization of a self-representation; during "dialogue with the introject," the patient externalizes an aspect of the introject into the analyst.

All in all, projection and externalization have not been successfully differentiated. Attempts to broaden the latter have made it coincide with projective identification.

Internalization

Processes of introjection, incorporation, and identification are often covered by the blanket term "internalization." Freud himself used the latter term in two related ways (Sandler and Perlow 1987: 7), both in reference to the development of the super-ego; he spoke of the internalization of external prohibitions, and the internalization of aggression. Subsequently, attempts have been made to extend the notion of internalization to include developmental processes of independence from the environment, like the development of thinking and of the super-ego, and mastery of internal danger (Hartmann 1939). Hans Loewald (1962) distinguishes between primary internalization (separating self and object) and secondary internalization (subsequent taking in), emphasizing that relationships with external objects are internalized as intrapsychic. The creative aspect of object formation is demonstrated by the fact that what one internalizes need not actually exist; Hawant Gill (1991) describes a case of a woman who had never met her father but who nevertheless constructed a father object from her own wishes and fears, from what she had been told, and from what she had discovered. David Rapaport (1967) limits internalization to those processes actually affecting the psychic structure, with incorporation, introjection and identification referring to those processes that only *involve* the psychic structure. Anna Freud (1965) spoke of the internalization of external as opposed to internal conflict. Given the disparate usage of the term, Sandler and Perlow (1987: 8) suggest that internalization be retained as a broad term referring to all "taking in."

Identification

While it has been acknowledged that identification is central to the formation of ego, super-ego, identity, and character, the term has been poorly defined, taking on whatever meaning each author has given it. All writers, though, would probably agree with Erich Simenauer's minimal description: "Identification is unconscious, partial and ambivalent" (1985: 182). This section will closely follow W.W. Meissner's work in order to bring some clarity to the matter, starting with his critical review of Freud's insights (Meissner 1970).

Before 1900, Freud addressed hysterical identification, the unconscious identification of one person with another based on a repressed wish. For example, he cited the case of hysterical identification with a dead person whereby the patient becomes immobile, mimicking the rigor mortis of the deceased (in Masson 1985). In *The Interpretation of Dreams* (1900) Freud became more specific, saying that identification is not simple imitation but that it represents an unconscious element common to both subject and object. In dreams, the mechanism whereby such commonality is already present he called identification (while the mechanism whereby commonality is constructed he called composition). By the process of identification, several people likened in the unconscious by a shared element may be represented in the dream by a single figure. Or the dreamer may dream of another person because of a wished-for mutuality.

What is common in hysterical identification and identification in dreams, then, is the unconscious recognition of common elements. The mechanism eludes repression and is a vehicle for the expression of libidinal impulses. Although identification was at this stage of Freud's work regarded as a pathological process, it already contained the possibility of one person taking on the qualities of another based on a perceived common element.

Between 1900 and 1915 Freud elaborated rather than developed his libidinal theory. In the case of slips of the tongue, for example, addressing someone by another's name is evidence that the two have been identified with each other in the mind of the speaker (1901: 80). And a theater audience may, via identification with a character, experience an emotion with they might not have in everyday life. Identifications, Freud now suggested, can influence personality development and life history, as when a person becomes a doctor after having identified as a child with the family doctor (1901: 196-97).

By the time Freud's thinking on narcissism flowered, his notion of identification had moved beyond being simply a neurotic function to playing a developmental and structural role. Thus, not only can a person temporarily adopt the characteristics of another, he or she could take in and preserve objects as part of his or her psychic structure. For example, Freud said that the oral phase has as its sexual aim the "incorporation" of the object (1905b: 198). In "Instincts and Their Vicissitudes," he used Sandor Ferenczi's term "introjection" to describe the process whereby the ego takes into itself pleasure-giving objects and "projects" objects that cause it pain (1915a: 129-32). "Mourning and Melancholia" (1917b) discusses depression, during which attacks on the self in fact represent hostility to a lost object. Upon the (real or imagined) loss of a loved object, the ego identifies with that object and libido flows toward the new narcissistic object. The original ambivalent ego/object relation becomes an inner relation between the "critical agency" (later the super-ego) and the ego. Ambivalence can be seen in the oral nature of identification, whereby love for the object also involves the destructive devouring of it. Hate for the substitute and internal object and the consequent internal torment satisfy both the subject's sadism and masochism. The projection of the object onto the ego throws light upon a split in the ego which involves little internal modification, and which allows the person to put him or herself in the place of the lost object. Narcissistic identification, deriving from an object relation, regresses from it to a more primitive relation to the object. Hysterical identification, on the other hand, is based on an unconscious wish to replace someone else, and not on an object relation. To illustrate this we may consider Freud's example of young women who "catch" the hysterical fit of a friend who has lost her suitor, without themselves having had any relation to the object (the friend's suitor) (1921: 107). Narcissistic identification, then, differs from hysterical identification: while both derive from attachment to an object, in the case of hysterical identification the object cathexis is maintained and the person takes on some of the qualities of the object, while in narcissistic identification the object cathexis is abandoned and the person does not adopt the object's qualities.

In *Group Psychology and the Analysis of the Ego* (1921) Freud compared identification to love. "Partial identification" here refers to the recognition of a common quality with a person who is not a sexual object. So, in partial identification the ego is enriched by the introjection of the object (the object is lost then regained, thereby partially altering the ego), while in love the ego surrenders itself to the object and substitutes the object for its own ego ideal (the object is taken in at the expense of the ego). Groups, as we have seen, are united by a double tie: partial identification, and the substitution of the object for the ego ideal. Members identify with each other and they take the leader as an ideal—the former identification being the result of a perceived shared characteristic, namely the tie to the leader. "To identify with . . ." is always an object relationship that fulfills a wish and is itself a drive goal, says Daniel Widlocher (1985), attempting to unite drive theory and object relations theory. But identification need not be motivated by admiration. Identification based on envy is an "identification with a vengeance," "analogizing" and destroying the link between subject and object (Boris 1990: 139). With *The Ego and the Id* (1923) and the formulation of the structural ego/super-ego/id model of the mind, Freud's notion of identification "acquired an explicit structuralizing function which had until then been more or less implicit" (Meissner 1970: 578).

Sandler and Rosenblatt (1962) have made a useful distinction with regard to identification. Primary identification refers to the time before self and object have been differentiated. Later regression to this stage occurs in severe psychotic states, although "fleeting primary identification" is a normal phenomenon (Sandler 1961). Secondary identification occurs when the subject takes into his or her self-representation a real or phantasized aspect of the object without erasing the boundary between self and object.

Introjection

Introduced by Ferenczi (1909), introjection is a concept generally used to describe all internalization, "*every sort of object love* (or *transference*) both in normal and neurotic people" (Ferenczi 1912: 316). Sandler and Perlow (1987: 10-11), however, do make the following differentiations: introjection as perception of the external world; introjection as the construction of a comforting introject in the child's fantasy world; and introjection of the parental objects as super-ego. Further, they differentiate between identification (modification of self-representation) and introjection of internal "phantom" companions (internal, yet not part of self-representation). Thus we can make sense of "identification with the introject" whereby, for example, one identifies with one's super-ego and so takes up a moral stance.

Incorporation

Often used as a synonym for all internalization, incorporation has also been used in several other ways. Freud (1933) used it to mean the aim of the oral instinct. Some have argued that incorporation should be limited to the physical taking into an orifice, especially the mouth (Fenichel 1925; Sandler and Dare 1970), while others have applied it to the incorporation of a wish or fantasy (Meissner 1981; Schafer 1968). Kleinians use incorporation to refer to both oral taking in and as a synonym for all internalization. Adding some clarity, Sandler and Perlow (1987: 11) distinguish between the physical act of incorporation and fantasies or thoughts of incorporation.

We have seen that theorizing processes of "putting into" another and "taking in" to the self has not been settled in the psychoanalytic literature. Projection, externalization, internalization, identification, introjection, and incorporation overlap and are often used as synonyms for general processes of externalization and internalization. However, it is also true that some of these terms are used more often than others. For example, compare the frequencies with which the terms outlined above were cited as key words in the psychoanalytic literature in the late 1980s with the frequencies of the term projective identification (see Table 1). These figures are an indication of the relative centrality of the latter concept in recent psychoanalysis.

PROJECTIVE IDENTIFICATION: KLEIN AND BEYOND

As we have seen, processes of externalization and internalization are fundamental in the psychoanalytic view. A concept that combines these processes is the Kleinian notion of projective identification. What follows is a brief review of the literature on projective identification and an attempt to formulate a clear description of it for making sense of the larger interpersonal concerns of this book.

As in the above section on externalization and internalization, this review will be built around a previously existing attempt by Joseph Sandler. This is for

Table 1
Frequencies of Terms of Internalizing and Externalizing

	1985	1986	1987-1988
projection	47	33	65
externalization	0	0	0
internalization	70	54	94
identification	26	45	61
incorporation	4	7	5
introjection	42	33	58
projective identification	53	43	96

Source: Chicago Psychoanalytic Literature Index, 1985-1988.

two reasons. First, as a follower more of Anna Freud than of Klein, Sandler does not slavishly follow (nor does he reject) every Kleinian assumption. Second, his review "The Concept of Projective Identification" (1987a) is structured in a useful historical fashion that specifies three stages.

The First Stage

Klein's notion of projective identification is a development of her earlier theory of projection (1929) and that of Freud. Following Freud's theory of the death instinct (1920), Klein argued that, as has been said, from the beginning of its life the infant is tormented by inner destructive urges from which it tries to escape by pushing the bad affect outward and into objects. Also, defences are employed against the nonexternalized traces of the death instinct, these defences being the seeds of the developing super-ego. The projection and introjection of the death instinct produces in the child a fear of persecuting objects, Klein's paranoid-schizoid position. Additionally, the infant mourns for loved objects attacked by internal objects and fears losing them, the depressive position. These normal developmental positions may be pathologically mobilized as obsession, mania, or paranoia.

Normal development or analytic treatment, according to this view, involve moving from the paranoid-schizoid to the depressive position. During this development, "these projections lessen [and the child] becomes more able to tolerate his ambivalence, his love and hate and dependence on objects" (Joseph 1987: 66). Movement toward the depressive position produces increased concern for the object and decreased desire to dominate the object. While never completely abandoned, projection "will no longer involve the complete splitting off and disowning of parts of the self, but will be less absolute, more temporary, and more able to be drawn back into the individual's personality—and thus be the basis of empathy"—i.e, projective identification.

For Klein, projection is more than a defence against internal anxiety or a device for attributing internal disharmony to external forces. Projection is a necessary process and the point of origin of object relations. In "Notes on Some Schizoid Mechanisms" (1946), she first introduced projective identification, and it is to that paper that we now turn. (Segal 1974, tells how Klein actually dealt very irregularly and briefly with projective identification, and that she immediately regretted it.) Klein reiterated her belief that object relations exist from the beginning of life, the first object being the breast. The gratifying good breast and the frustrating bad breast are the sources of love and hate. "I have further suggested that the relation to the first object implies its introjection and projection, and thus from the beginning object-relations are moulded by an interaction between introjection and projection, between internal and external objects and situations" (Klein 1946: 2). The early unintegrated ego experiences anxiety because of a combination of frustration of needs, birth trauma, and the death instinct, and in order to deal with this anxiety the ego develops fundamental mechanisms and defences (4-5). Some of the infant's anxiety is projected outward and attaches itself to the first external object—the breast—and the rest of the anxiety is "bound by the libido within the organism." However, the anxiety of "being destroyed from within remains" (5), and the ego's response of falling to pieces or splitting underlies the pathological condition of schizophrenia. Splitting, then, is a primary ego defence mechanism, and projection and identification are used to accomplish it.

Klein goes on to describe "a confluence of oral, urethral and anal desires, both libidinal and aggressive" (1946: 7-8), in the infant's onslaughts on the mother's breast. During this onslaught, we have seen, the oral impulses are to suck dry, bite, scoop out, and rob the breast of its good contents, while the urethral and anal impulses are to expel substances out of the self into the mother. It is here that Klein proposes the term projective identification. Hatred against part of the self (anxiety of internal destruction) is projected into the mother, and she is then felt to be a persecutor. Similarly, good parts of the self may also be projected into the mother.

The place where this process is most obvious is in the analytic situation where the analyst may have an object projected by the patient (transference) so strongly into him or her—identifying with that projection—that the analyst's own feelings, thoughts, and behavior may be affected. At times of such countertransference it becomes obvious that analysis is more than a simple interplay between analyst and patient. Herbert Rosenfeld (1983) shows how it is necessary to distinguish between the analyst's confusion and that projected into the analyst by the patient. Sydney Smith provides an example of an analyst feeling "compelled" to hold a patient's hand, an action running counter to standard psychoanalytic practice. "What one sees in this incident is the power of the patient's fantasy in controlling relationships" (Smith 1977: 322).

The following description of an analytic session with a four-year-old girl demonstrates projective identification (as understood in this first stage of the concept's development) in action. Near the end of a Friday session the girl, C, announced her intention of making a candle. The analyst interpreted that C wished to take a warm Mrs. Barros (the analyst) home with her, and her fear of running out of time. "C started to scream, saying that she would have some spare candles; she then started to stare through the window with a vacant, lost expression" (Joseph 1987: 68). The analyst interpreted that C wished to let the analyst know the awfulness of ending the session while expressing the wish for the analyst's warmth for the weekend. "The child screamed: 'Bastard! Take off your clothes and jump outside.'" The analyst returned to the child's fear of being sent off into the cold.

> C replied: "Stop your talking, take off your clothes. You are cold. I'm not cold."
> The feeling in the session was extremely moving. Here the words carry the concrete meaning, to the child, of the separation of the weekend—the awful coldness. This she tries to force into the analyst, and it is felt to have been concretely achieved. "You are cold; I am not cold." (Joseph 1987: 68)

Joseph sees the child's vacant expression as indicating her loss of contact with reality during powerful projective identification, and the screaming as further "emptying out." Altogether, these process enable C temporarily to get rid of her feeling of loss and the attendant emotions. Projective identification here is a fantasy of taking control of the object by expelling into it bad parts of the self and identifying with the internal object thereby modified. The aims of projective identification include splitting off and expelling unwanted parts of the self; controlling an object by projecting parts of the self into the object, thereby avoiding feelings of being separate; entering an object and making its capabilities one's own; and invading an object to damage or destroy it. The object is thus not regarded as separate, but as part of the self (Klein 1963). Joseph emphasizes that these processes of splitting off and projecting parts of the self are vital for both normal and abnormal development and object relations. A person who continues to employ powerful projective identification "can avoid any awareness of separateness, dependence, or admiration or of the concomitant sense of loss, anger, envy, etc." But this is at the price of establishing "persecutory anxieties, claustrophobia, panics and the like" (Joseph 1987: 65-66).

Although Klein (1959) insisted that adult psychological processes are rooted in early infantile development, Sandler (1987a: 19) makes the point that it is possible to accept projective identification as an important concept without having to assume the Kleinian theory of development. It may also seem that Klein's language is too concrete; Sandler stresses, though, that projective identification here consists of processes that are "*imagined* as concrete, i.e. involving images of literal incorporation or of 'forcing' something into an object" (1987a: 14); Sandler interprets Klein as referring to changes within the representational world (Sandler and Rosenblatt 1962). Projective identification is a mechanism involving splitting off of parts of the self- or the object-representation. In contrast, identification with the object involves taking into the self-representation aspects of the object-representation, while projection involves displacement of the self-representation into an object-representation. D.S. Jaffe (1968) has noted the dualistic nature of projective identification. The wish to destroy the threatening object is in conflict with the desire to preserve the object with which one has identified. Projective identification is, one can say, persistently ambivalent.

For Kleinians, projective identification has an important element of illusory control. By putting into an object unwanted parts of the self, and by controlling the internalized object, one gains "the unconscious illusion that one is controlling the unwanted and projected aspect of the self" (Sandler 1987a: 20). In this regard Sandler cites the examples of "altruistic surrender" (A. Freud 1936), and of the person "attacked by an internal persecutor." By projecting a bad part and identifying with the persecutor, the person identifies with the super-ego introject and gets rid of the unwanted part. But this does not mean that externalizing processes produce distorted perception. It is more useful to consider that "this distortion [of reality] has to do with what the perception means" (Meissner 1987: 32), depending on one's convictions and needs. Projective identification, then, is an interpretive distortion of reality.

A self-object boundary is necessary for a person to feel dissociated from split-off parts. The fact that massive projective identification is seen to occur in psychotics does not contradict this fact. Although to the observer psychotics cannot maintain such boundaries, for the psychotic the existence of voices is evidence of a type of self-object boundary (Sandler 1987a: 21). However, projective identification does involve "confusion where something belonging to the subject is passed on to the object, resulting in the former losing his individuality and the latter being invested with what in fact does not belong to him" (Etchegoyen 1985: 12).

There is considerable conflict between ego psychologists and object-relations psychologists about how early such ego defence mechanisms can occur. A problem, for instance, faces Kleinians who on the one hand credit projective identification with a role in the infant's ability to distinguish a boundary between self and object; but a self-object boundary is needed for projective identification to be able to occur. Sandler proposes a way of avoiding this classic chicken-and-egg situation. He proposes infantile *attempts* at projection and identification, "or, perhaps better, identification and disidentification" (Sandler 1987a: 21), while the infant tries to organize the state of primary confusion. These attempts slowly lead to self/object boundary formation.

It is impossible to know, according to Meissner (1987b), whether externalizing and internalizing processes are originally defensive, as Klein claims, or differentiating and developmental. Meissner's description is a good one, however.

> The structuring of the inner world begins from the very first. Incorporative aspects of the infant's global and undifferentiated experience precede the capacity to distinguish between self and object, but contribute a qualitative modification to the global experience. The experience is good or bad, or perhaps both, and to the degree that it is unpleasurable leads to primary attempts at externalization, which organize the emerging lines of differentiation. As these lines begin to form, introjection becomes possible and the continuing structuralization of the inner world takes place through introjective mechanisms. The quality of the introjects is derivative from and constituted by elements from both the inner and the outer worlds. (Meissner 1987b: 30)

Projective identification is accompanied by regression and dependency. It is generally the adult, governing, or understanding part of the self that is split off to experience pain.

> Once that has happened, the individual has to some extent infantalized himself, made himself childlike, but that is not all. Once that part of the self is lodged in somebody else it must be attended to in that other person, so the individual becomes dependant on the other. (Sandler 1987b: 61)

Michael Conran (in Sandler 1987b) gives as an analogy a "derelict, empty, silent" individual in court, a person whose feelings and argument reside in others—the judge, counsel, the police, witnesses.

To summarize, for Klein projective identification does not affect the objects involved—"the parts of the self put into the object are put into the fantasy object, the 'internal' object, not the external object" (Sandler 1987b: 17). For example, transference is regarded by Klein as a reflection of infantile object relations principally involving projective identification, which is a distortion of the patient's perception of the analyst. Countertransference, on the other hand, is seen by Klein as a sign of pathology in the analyst and as a technical obstacle to analysis. (Segal argues that while Klein intuitively used in her clinical practice what is today understood as countertransference, Klein avoided talking about countertransference, concerned as she was that it could be used as an excuse by the analyst [in Hunter 1994: 54].)

The Second Stage

While for Klein projective identification is limited to the phantasy life of the child and the patient, for other writers the analyst's countertransference, produced by the patient's projective identifications, is an important analytic tool. H. Racker (1968) described, for example, how through projective identification the patient unconsciously intends for the analyst to feel guilty, sad, or depressed. Another example would be a psychiatrist unwittingly enacting one of the patient's dreams (Nash and McGehee 1986). Identification of the analyst with the patient's self- or object-representations is one type of countertransference.

There is considerable disagreement in the literature here. Some assert that there are four fundamental aspects of the analytic relationship: realistic, working, transference, primary (de Jonghe, Rijnierse, and Janssen 1991). Joseph calls transference "a living relationship in which there is constant movement and change," and where everything in the patient's psychic organization will be "lived out in some way." Often countertransference is the only way to detect the patient's communications (1985: 453-54). When the analyst identifies with the patient's phantasies, the analyst has access to what is happening in the patient as the analyst's countertransference "is the patient's *creation*, it is part of the patient's personality" (Heimann 1950: 83). It is, then, becoming increasingly difficult to speak of a "non-transference relationship in the psychoanalytic situation" (Greenson and Wexler 1969).

Charles Chediak has tried to differentiate out all the levels of reactions in the analyst during countertransference. He comes up with five: intellectual understanding; the general response to the patient as a person; the analyst's transference to the patient; the analyst's countertransference; and empathic identification (Chediak 1979: 117). According to Racker there are two basic ways in which countertransference can happen (1968): "concordant identification" happens when the analyst identifies with the patient's own self-representation; "complementary identification" occurs when the analyst identifies with the object-representation in the patient's transference fantasy. Ogden (1983), it will be shown, develops this notion further.

Unsatisfied with saying that the internal phantasy object is simply "put into" the analyst, Sandler explains countertransference as follows. First, the patient creates a wishful phantasy involving the analyst. Second, the patient tries to make actual these unconscious wishes, "to make them real, to experience them (either overtly or in disguised form) as part of reality" (1987a: 22). The fantasy includes self- and object-representation and their interaction, not simply a wish toward an object. The wished-for response of the object is as important as the actions of the subject in the wish. "It is not a great step to say that the striving towards actualization is part of the wish-fulfilling aspect of all object relationships" (22). The patient's attempts at actualization may evoke a countertransference response in the analyst that in some way reflects the patient's wishful object-role. The question of how exactly the patient causes affect changes in the analyst is one that has not received enough attention. Projective identification has very subtle behavioral components that are verbal and nonverbal. Freud alluded to this when he said of the communications of patients: "If their lips are silent, they gossip with their fingertips" (1905a: 77-78). There is an awareness among psychoanalysts that the countertransference evinced by the patient needs extremely careful working through by the analyst. Joseph argues that even patients who are not very sick can subtly make the analyst feel "too comfortable or too good or too friendly or too nice" (in Sandler 1987a: 85). John E. Gedo (1989) uses Heisenberg's Uncertainty Principle of the effects of the observer on the observed to illustrate transference interactions. Different analytic techniques produce different reactions. He also says that the analyst's age, sex, sociocultural background and language affect the nature of the transference. Transference is therefore codetermined by the analyst's particular technique and personal characteristics. There is a reciprocal, or intersubjective, relationship between the patient's transference neurosis and the analyst's countertransference (Ulman and Stolorow 1985). This relationship is ambiguous in essence because "it is unclear to both participants how much of the current difficulty is related to the past, how much to the present, how much is transference, and how much is the real relationship" (Adler 1989: 101).

The Third Stage

Wilfred Bion saw projective identification as one of the most important types of interaction in individual as well as in group analysis (1959a, 1959b). He described projective identification as a concrete and not a phantasy process. Or one could say with Neville Symington that "phantasy does not just inhabit a mental realm within the individual" (1985: 356). During this process, Bion (1962, 1963) said, parts of the self-representation or of the internal object are actually projected directly into the external object, thus modifying the latter. The object acts as a "container." For example, the child projects bad parts into the breast of the mother. Having a capacity for "reverie," the mother changes the feelings attached to the bad breast. The infant then takes in this transformed and mitigated object, thus gaining relief. This process is Winnicott's "holding" function of the good-enough mother.

The introject too does not merely act on the level of phantasy. The quality of the introject is determined both by the characteristics of the real object and by its attributes, which come from the inner world (Meissner 1987: 30). "Phantasy is itself an active agent, so that the image within the phantasy is brought into effect through a subtle stimulation of the social environment" (Symington 1985: 356-57). The person does not, therefore, create images that are simply (distorted) reflections of his or her own inner world. Instead, following Macherey (1966), we can rather say that the person *produces* images out of internal and external material, and that these images have a material existence via projective identification.

To return to Bion's container model, projective identification can be a mutually beneficial process. It is also a process that occurs in any relational setting. Operating pathologically, projective identification is, according to Bion, psychosis with heightened splitting and projection. Thus the psychotic experiences fragmented, bizarre, persecutory objects and a diminution of the ego.

Important for the sociological questions of this book is the increasingly popular notion in psychoanalysis of projective identification: activation of internal objects in the recipient as "basic to all human interaction from the beginning of life" (de Bea 1989: 265).

Bion described how projective identification can be used as a form of communication. Undigested parts are put into the object as a way of having them understood and returned in a more manageable fashion. In fact, projective identification as described by Ogden is a container/contained facility (Hamilton 1990: 451). Joseph (1987: 67) goes further, saying that by its very nature projective identification is communication. This is most apparent in countertransference. Describing a case where a patient invaded her with despair (73), Joseph shows the concrete quality of projective identification.

Following Bion, Eulalia Torras de Bea says that projective identification has two functions: communicative, which involves differentiation and linking, but where contact with the projected objects is maintained; and defensive, through splitting or dissociation, and where the parts are cut off and kept separate. The former is "the primary mechanism of healthy psychological evolution," while the latter is "characteristic of psychopathological evolution" (1989: 265). "The best service an analyst can do for a patient is, I believe, to differentiate where the patient dissociates" (271).

Projective identification is a "transactional process," and internal change is the result of this interpersonal interchange (Knapp 1989). One can describe projective identificatory communication as a bridge, and, as Lars Sjögren has pointed out, a bridge has two bridgeheads (in Sandler 1987b: 78). "The phantasy does not exist just in the patient or just in the analyst but is in the communication system between the two" (Symington 1985: 353). The analyst is faced with the vexing question of discriminating between what the patient has projected into the analyst, and what the patient has provoked that is part of the analyst's own pathology (Joseph, in Sandler 1987b: 80).

According to Bion's container model, the mother (or the analyst) is attentive and tolerant of the infant's (or the patient's) needs, distress, anger, and love. The mother reassures the child that she can contain these feelings, and she responds at an appropriate time in an appropriate way. The infant thereby learns that his or her anxiety is not disastrous. In the same way, a "we" rather than an "I and you" alliance will be formed in the analytic situation only if the analyst is "strong enough to withstand the vehemence and anxiety" of the patient's projections (de Folch 1983: 318). If the analyst tolerates and contains these projections, they can be transformed and returned and, as manageable versions of previously threatening parts of the self, accepted by the patient.

Michael Porder has an interesting perspective on projective identification. He says that consciously the patient usually experiences the analyst as "the powerful parent within the transference." Through projective identification, however, "there is an *unconscious reversal* which casts the analyst in the role of the bad child and the patient as the powerful, demanding, critical, sadistic, or masochistic parent. . . . Such patients not only speak, they enact" (Porder 1987: 439). This understanding reproblematizes the question asked by Harriet Knapp: What is the direction of the projection? While she says that there are several factors that will affect this direction—the vulnerability of the recipient, the intensity of the interaction, and the status or power of the projector—it is to the latter that she accords the determining ability as to "the extent to which the projection becomes accepted as an aspect of identity" (Knapp 1989: 54). "As a transactional process we can predict that its greatest effect will be in the direction flowing from the most powerful to the least" (56). Now, the very fact that the patient can project into the analyst denies Knapp's assertion, unless by the most powerful she means the one who is able to project into the other (in which case her argument is circular). It cannot be stressed strongly enough that if psychoanalytic concepts are going to be of any use in matters sociological, the deadend assumptions of sociology (e.g., how power operates) cannot be allowed to prematurely affect concepts of psychoanalysis. So, if we are serious about trying to understand the intra- and interpersonal interactions that constitute society, we cannot assume that preconceptions about societal processes are correct and simply in need of some psychoanalytical sophistication.

To recap, there is a broad groundswell of opinion in psychoanalysis that emphasizes "*a change within the analyst*" (Green 1975: 2). In 1988, as an example, the journal *Psychoanalytic Inquiry* published a special issue on the topic of transference as the interface between the intrapsychic and the interpersonal. David Scharff is just one writer arguing that we have now reached a time of such a theoretical synthesis (1988). Countertransference, a material interpersonal phenomenon as opposed to purely intrapsychic transference, is found by many analysts to be crucial in their work (even though one still reads of countertransference as "those feelings that inhibit the work of the therapy" [Campbell 1995: 53]). "One can even speak of a swing from the transference to the countertransference without which no elaboration of what is transmitted by the patient could take place" (Scharff 1988). Andre Green points out that today countertransference is generally understood as being much more than the feelings aroused by the transference; it includes "the whole mental functioning of the analyst as it is influenced, not only by the patient's material, but also by his reading or his discussions with his colleagues" (Green 1975: 3).

An analogy from literary criticism is Norman Holland's proposed "identity theory," which asserts that we read texts with combinations of "defence, expectation, fantasy, and transformation"—DEFT. But what is more, we also DEFT people. Identity is "action, representation, and consequence"—ARC. We ARC DEFTly. "Identity theory says we take in the other—literature, society, politics, culture, even our own genders and selves—through our identities, which are themselves representations" (Holland 1985: 287).

The moment we engage with the objective world it moves into a transitional area, neither subjective nor objective: "Is it I or is it you? Is this now or was it then? Did I do this or was it done to me?" (Adler 1989: 85). Here we externalize parts of ourselves into the world and introject aspects of it, sometimes, in the case of projective identification, actually changing the external object itself. "Phantasy has an active force which effects that which it imagines or represents," says Neville Symington (1985: 354). Or to use the language of structuralism and poststructuralism, we are spoken.

Contra Projective Identification

Some authors disagree with any sharp distinctions between projection, identification, and projective identification. Malin and Grotstein (1966) have argued that all projection involves identification. Also, identification involves projection as we project content in order to receive it back. Other writers want to maintain a distinction between projection and projective identification. Jaffe (1968) mentions a difference in the degree of splitting involved. Otto Kernberg (1965) points to the greater regression of projective identification, especially in the blurring of ego boundaries. Projective identification is for him a more primitive mechanism than projection (Kernberg 1987). Projective identification is characterized by projection of unwanted aspects, continued empathy with the projection, attempts to control the projection, and unconsciously inducing the projected parts into the real object; projection consists of repression of unwanted aspects, projection, lack of empathy with the object, and distancing from the object. Kernberg suggests that there is a developmental line between projective identification (based on splitting) and projection (based on repression). Projective identification predominates in the psychoses with the loss of both reality testing and self/object boundaries. In borderline conditions, projective identification occurs, but reality testing is maintained. In the neuroses, projective identification is largely superseded by projection, he says.

In his argument against the wide application of the concept of projective identification, Meissner distinguishes between projective identification in a "one-body context and a two-body context" (1987: 43-44). In a one-body context, projective identification affects the individual's object-representation and occurs entirely internally. In a two-or-more-body context, he says, identification takes place in others. These are, he insists, "separate processes taking place in different heads" (44). Meissner also wants to limit projective identification to the psychotic process, which he understands Klein as having intended. According to this conception, part of the self is projected into the object-*representation*, and the self loses its sense of independent existence. Meissner argues that we do not yet have evidence to show whether projective identification is "a mental process as a part of the operative structure of the mind" (43), or whether it is merely the phantasy that one can put thoughts into another's mind, thereby controlling them. He also believes that the concept of projective identification obscures more than it makes clear (1980). He disagrees with the assertion that in projective identification there is an actualizing reaction within the recipient of the projection. Rather, he says, these are two separate, but affectively connected, processes (1987: 49). In interpersonal relations, Meissner argues, there are "inevitable . . . emotional pressures to draw the object into compliance with the projection and to reinforce it" (44). We should rather, then, speak of processes of projection and of introjection, he says.

It is fascinating, however, to note that when in the process of making the above case at a conference in Israel on projective identification, Meissner gave three clinical examples. One of these was the case of a masochistic woman who was dominated by her husband. During the discussion of the paper (in Sandler 1987b: 54), Paulina Kernberg pointed out that far from disproving projective identification, Meissner had shown, by the high feeling with which he, Meissner, had denounced the husband, evidence for externalization by one person into another. Also in response to Meissner, Otto Kernberg (in Sandler 1987a: 58) said that *any* term in psychoanalysis becomes unspecific, and a return to projection and introjection does not relieve us of the task of specifying what exactly it is that we mean.

There are many unresolved questions with regard to the concept of projective identification:

> Should it refer only to the patient's phantasy, or should it be used only in cases in which the object is affected by what is projected into him? Should it be used

only in cases where the patient has lost conscious awareness of the quality and part of the self he has projected, or does it also apply in cases in which such awareness is retained? What about the projection of good qualities and good parts of the self: should the concept be used for these as well, as Klein thought, or should it be reserved for the projection of bad qualities, which has been the dominant tendency? Should a distinction be made between projection and projective identification? Should the term projection be reserved for the mechanism and projective identification for the phantasy? Should one always be specific about the bodily phantasy involved in the projection, or is it enough to speak of it in mental terms? (Spillius 1983: 322)

The work of Ogden and others will help to clear up some of these problems.

OGDEN'S OBJECT RELATIONS

Thomas H. Ogden has actively attempted both to synthesize object relations theory and to move conceptualization forward. In this he is not alone. Stephen A. Mitchell, for example, is an object relations theorist who argues strenuously for a relational rather than a drive model for psychoanalysis. In tune with Ogden and others, Mitchell views "psychological reality as operating within a relationship matrix which encompasses both intrapsychic and interpersonal realms" (1988: 9), the drive model being impossible without "some relational field within which the drive seeks discharge or expression" (53). Thus, he says, "the innate drops into the background" (61), and it is here that, I believe, writers like Ogden part company with Mitchell. It is true, says André Lussier, that as we grow older "the less noticeable will be that original source, the libido, but it can never be fully extinguished" (1988: 545). "All in all, libido and object are there from the very start in a closed unit" (544). Without himself belonging to any of the theoretical camps of object relations theory, Ogden sees his work as "an outgrowth of the work of Freud, Abraham, Melanie Klein, Fairbairn, Winnicott and Bion" (1983: 227). In a similar vein, without claiming that they have been satisfactorily amalgamated, Vann Spruiell asserts the "indivisibility of Freudian object relations and drive theories" (1988). It is obvious that this matter is far from settled in psychoanalytic theory. Ogden's is an attempt at a nonpartisan overview.

Ogden speaks of four "spheres of reality": physiological capacities; psychological representations ("thoughts, feelings, fantasies, memories, perceptions, and so forth, often in diffuse, inchoate, and archaic forms"); psychological capacities ("in Freud's structural theory referred to as the id, ego, and super-ego functions and psychological structures"); and "people existing outside of oneself" (Ogden 1982: 174). Psychoanalysis, he argues, lacks the theory to bridge the intrapsychic with external reality and interpersonal relations (1979: 357). For him, object relations theory is not "an exclusively intrapersonal theory," but instead "fundamentally a theory of unconscious internal object relations in dynamic interplay with current interpersonal experience" (1983: 227). Projective identification for him, we shall see, addresses and conceptualizes the dynamic interplay between the four spheres of reality.

Ogden proposes a developmental position antedating both Klein's paranoid-schizoid position, which "generates a good deal of immediacy and vitality of concretely symbolized experience," and the depressive position, which "allows for the creation of an historical, interpreting self." This "autistic-contiguous" position, "the primitive edge of experience" (Ogden 1989), "provides much of the 'sensory floor' of experience" (1991: 595-96). This is a "presymbolic core" based predominantly on physical contact and preverbal bodily sensation. While these three positions follow each other developmentally, they are related synchronically as well as diachronically; they have "a relationship of interactive simultaneity in that all three modes of experience represent dimensions of every human experience" (1988: 596). (The point cannot be elaborated upon here, but there appears to be potential conceptual overlap between these three positions and Lacan's Real, Imaginary, and Symbolic orders of experience, as outlined in Chapter 6.)

Experience in general, not only the transference-countertransference experience, says Ogden, is the product of an interplay between the "three modes of creating psychological meaning": the autistic-contiguous, the paranoid-schizoid, and the depressive (1991: 593). The dynamic interplay of these constitute the "background state of being," the "psychological matrix" "within which one is living at any given moment" (593).

Meissner (1970) suggests that the introject functions like what Winnicott has called a transitional object. Winnicott spoke of the inanimate objects to which babies become attached and which are constant sources of comfort; "the first not-me possessions, or transitional objects" (1951). For the first time the infant is able to acknowledge that the absent mother "is alive, is not a physical part of the baby nor yet its external possession" (Elmhirst 1980: 367). This is an important stage in the infant's task of constructing its individuality. When the mother is absent for extended periods, the transitional object begins to lose its comforting quality. An analyst like Susanna Elmhirst (1980), it must be said, objects to widening the original notion of transitional object (soft toy or suck-rag) to cover what she feels is an ego function of relating the internal and the external.

Arnold Modell argues that the growing understanding of the importance of the environment on development has led to modifications of Freud's view of the relationship between the ego and the environment. These are no longer viewed as distinct, but rather "the external object, that is the environment, is in part subjectively created by the subject." Modell shows how Winnicott's notion of the transitional object is in fact an argument for a "transitional intermediate area of shared subjectivity" between psychic and external reality (Modell 1975: 66). Attachment to the transitional object happens in the second half of the first year of the infant's life, the parents becoming aware of this attachment once it is fairly intense. Usually the transitional object is a soft, malleable object—clothing, cloth, or soft toy—in the infant's crib. The infant bites on, chews, and sucks the transitional object, thereby orally "recreating the symbiotic tie to the mother" (Busch and McKnight 1977: 479). Throughout life we continue quite normally to use certain objects and activities as transitional objects standing in for absent objects. Charles Brandes speaks, for example, of "the meaning of work as transitional phenomenon for men at mid-life" (1986). Gerald Adler argues that in a "good enough holding environment," projective identification and transitional phenomena can be different labels for almost the same experience. The quality of the introjects depends upon the qualities attributed to the object, i.e., projections, and the qualities of the object itself. If destructive or loving impulses are projected into the object, it becomes threatening or loving respectively. This, however, is mitigated by the object's response. A loving object can absorb aggressive impulses, thus producing an ambivalent introject. Or a hostile object can intensify the projected aggression, producing an introject of greater destruction (Meissner 1987b: 30). So, for Meissner, externalizing and internalizing mechanisms are not only defensive but also play a crucial part in the development of self/object differentiation and of the quality of self- and object-representation.

A prominent mainstream analyst who conceives of the importance of the interpersonal, Ogden's work is of direct relevance to the proposals of this book.

Ogden and Internal Object Relations

In Ogden's "integrated conception," he argues that the formation of internal object relations involves the splitting of the ego into "a pair of dynamically unconscious suborganizations of personality, one identified with the self and the other with the object in the original early object relationship" (1983: 237). "This internal relationship is shaped by the nature of the original object relationship, but does not by any means bear a one-to-one correspondence with it, as is in addition potentially modifiable by subsequent experience" (227). Each of the self- and object-parts of the internal object relation "has the capacity to generate experience (e.g., to think, feel, and perceive) semi-autonomously and yet in relation to one another" (237). The importance of the first introjections remains central in this conception, as does their necessarily split structure. They "are radically different from the others. The have nothing to do with mourning but rather with primitive mechanisms which question the subject/object polarity and . . . spring from envy" (Etchegoyen 1985: 16). "Adult 'internalizations' are built upon existing splits in the ego and do not involve the creation of new ones"

(Ogden 1983: 234). In this connection, the reader will see, Lacan speaks of early channeling of desire, the unsatisfiability of and otherness of desire, and the perpetual chain of signifiers emanating from primary lack.

Donald Meltzer (1986) explains our first emotional impressions of people, e.g., instant love or instant hate, with reference to primitive internal object relations. When we first encounter a stranger, the id fits him or her into "a pre-existing dream," testing the stranger's suitability for a particular role. The mind, he says, is full of characters in search of parts to play. Or, as Jay Martin says: "It is a central fact of human life that each person invents a reality in which we live. We do not discover reality, we construct it" (1988: 26). His book *Who Am I This Time?* elaborates on the pathological form of this normal capacity. The "fictive personality" is a condition that arises when the self or the world are experienced as "inauthentic, fragmentary, or unavailable, so that only ready-made fictions seem whole and complete" (78). Martin leaves us with a dilemma here as to how to distinguish the normal from the pathological. He acknowledges that it is not possible to do away with fictions, but he says that "however many roles we play for others, we must play as few as possible for ourselves" (255). But given the deep unconscious nature of many of our fictions, they are not roles in and out of which we can consciously climb.

Continuing in a similar vein, Christopher Bollas stresses that the object is a process, as opposed to an inanimate thing that is incorporated; "the baby does not internalise an object, but does internalise a process derived from an object" (1987: 60). Whenever we experience the uncanny moment of aesthetic rapport, for example, the relationship with the original, maternal object is reexperienced as a "sense of being reminded of something never cognitively apprehended, but existentially known" (1979: 99). The first object he calls "the transformational object . . . linking our notion of the object with the infant's subjective knowing of it" (105). Winnicott once said that there is no such thing as a baby without a mother. Bollas adds that there is no adult who, "in relation to himself as an object . . . is not existentially . . . managing aspects of himself as a mother does a baby" (1982: 347). The experience of the process of the transformational object, "remains as an unconscious memory in the adult who relives it through his adamant quest for a transformational object: a new partner, a different form of work, a new material acquisition, an ideology or a belief" (1979: 106).

Writing about "the relation to the self as an object," Bollas says that "our external world evokes unconscious elements of the self as object relation, and our relation to reality is therefore influenced by those unconscious associations elicited by environmental conditions" (1982: 350).

If Mary marries Jim whom she insists is ideal and he in turn idealises her, he is projectively identified with a role which he must fulfil or incur Mary's extreme displeasure. In this relationship it is questionable whether Mary is really relating to Jim or to Jim as a split off fragment of her own self; in this way the relationship simply lives out her unconscious relation to herself as object. (351)

Bollas goes further: "Intersubjective relations always imply a relation to the self as an object" (358). In other words, there are only degrees of variation to the dilemma we face in the case of Mary above. (Chapters 6 and 7 deal to a greater degree with the relation to the Other as a relation to an aspect of oneself.) In any social interaction, "each individual transfers elements of that maternal care system that handled them as an object in infancy and childhood by relocating this parental care system into the person's own way of managing themselves as an object" (358).

Ogden and Potential Space

Ogden has done much to elaborate what Winnicott meant by his idea of potential space, the area of experience that lies between phantasy and reality. Winnicott said that potential space serves to both link and separate the infant and the mother. This is a psychic state created by a to-ing and fro-ing between phantasy and reality, I and thou, the symbol and the symbolized. The symbol is the bridge between inner and outer experience (Levine 1982). "The development of the capacity for symbol formation frees one from the prison of the realm of the thing in itself" (Ogden 1985: 135). Ogden notes here that Lacan has also spoken of the entry into language as an escape from the prison of unmediated sensory experience only for this to be followed by the entry into the prison of the Symbolic. The ability to produce symbols developmentally allows the "invisible oneness" of mother-infant to become the subjective "threeness" of the mother-and-infant as objects and the infant as "interpreting subject" (139) in a dynamic interplay. In geometrical terms, the mother-infant unity can be thought of as a point, while symbol, symbolized, and subject create the "possibility of triangularity within which space is created" (133). This is Winnicott's potential space, the area in which we exist as human beings rather than as reactive animals (133).

Some forms of potential space are: the areas of play, transitional object and phenomena, analytic space, cultural experience, and creativity (Ogden 1985: 129). Ogden speaks of "a psychological dialectic" between a "fantasy pole" and a "reality pole." Indeed, given the general belief in mainstream psychoanalysis in an accessible reality, his views here are noteworthy. "Reality" should not be thought of as independent of "one's processing of perception." Rather, "the term *reality* is used here to refer to that which is experienced as outside of the realm of the subject's omnipotence" (134).

Ogden and Projective Identification

Ogden (1991) emphasizes the role of projective identification in dialectically linking the internal and external and in producing countertransference phantasies that are, he says, the main source of information about the patient's inner life. One of the recommendations for a close reading of Ogden's writings here is their ability to be straightforward about projective identification's mechanics while at the same time giving a sense of the complexity, subtlety, and rapidity of this "single psychological event" (1979: 358).

It is interesting that Ogden asserts that projective identification is somehow separate from existing psychoanalytic dogmas. Projective identification is not, he says, a metaphorical construct, a piece of imagery, or an idea compatible with other theoretical notions. It is "a clinical-level conceptualization" comprising three phases that are each observable and verifiable (1982: 9). He thus attempts to dissociate himself from Kleinianism (although his work does borrow from her theories). While looking askance at his assertions of scientific and theoretical neutrality, the reader can take seriously Ogden's elaboration of an ubiquitous analytic experience, and one which seems to have affinities with all psychoanalytic schools. It is not necessary when considering projective identification for us to become sidetracked by disputes over, for example, the Kleinian developmental timetable.

Although Winnicott seldom uses the term projective identification, Ogden aligns himself with his work, which Ogden sees as "a study of the role of maternal projective identifications in early development and the implications of that form of object relatedness for both normal and pathological development" (1979: 365). In short, projective identification is "a group of fantasies and accompanying object relations having to do with ridding the self of unwanted aspects of the self; the depositing of those unwanted 'parts' into another person; and finally, with the 'recovery' of a modified version of what was extended" (357). All that is necessary for the occurrence of projective identification are the following: the projector must be capable of "projective fantasy and specific types of object-relatedness"; and the object of the projection must be capable of the type of object-relatedness involved in "receiving a projection, and some form of 'processing' of the projection" (364).

Although Ogden speaks of "reverberating circuits of projective identifications" (1982: 8), projective identification can be conceptualized as consisting of three stages. First, there is "the fantasy of projecting a part of oneself into another person and of that part taking over the person from within" (1979: 358). This is like ordinary projection in that a part of the self that either threatens the self from within, or which is itself threatened by other parts of the self, must be stored in another person. It is experientially quite distinct from ordinary projection, though. In projection one feels psychological distance from the object, while "in projective identification, one feels profoundly connected with the object" (359). Still, one must not draw distinctions that are too hard and fast: "projection and projective identification should be viewed as two ends of a gradient in which there is increasing preponderance of interplay between the projective and introjective processes as one moves toward the projective identification end of the gradient" (369). During the first phase of projective identification, the projector feels that the recipient is feeling the projector's own feeling, not one like it. The projector feels "at one with" the recipient, not, as in projection, "estranged from, threatened by, bewildered by, or out of touch with the object of the projection" (358).

Second, "there is pressure exerted via the interpersonal interaction such that the 'recipient' of the projection experiences pressure to think, feel, and behave in a manner congruent with the projection." During this phase of "induction" or "actualization" (Ogden 1982: 176), there is a pressure on the recipient to respond emotionally and behaviorally in accordance with the projective fantasy. Ogden quotes Harold Searles, who says that in the analytic situation the analyst "feels a genuine sense of deep participation," or "feeling-participation," with the patient (1979: 366). For example, shortly before a patient's suicide the analyst may feel a lack of concern for the patient—the patient's lack of caring for his or her own self having been induced in the analyst. Or, one member of a family might manipulate reality, thereby inducing a verification from another family member; "reality that is not useful in confirming a projection is treated as if it did not exist" (360).

And in the third stage of projective identification, "the projected feelings, after being 'psychologically processed' by the recipient, are reinternalized by the projector" (Ogden 1979: 358). On its own, this is like regular identification, the difference here being that what is internalized is a modified form of what has previously been projected. During this third stage there is psychological processing of the projection by the recipient, and reinternalization by the projector.

As we are concerned in this book with the nature of interpellation, it is worth quoting at length Ogden's description of what happens within the recipient of the projection.

> [He] experiences himself in part as he is pictured in the projective fantasy. The reality is that the recipient's experience is a new set of feelings experienced by a person different from the projector. The recipient's feelings may be close to those of the projector, but those feelings are not transplanted feelings. The recipient is author of his own feelings albeit feelings elicited under a very specific kind of pressure from the projector. The elicited feelings are the product of a different personality system with different strengths and weaknesses. This fact opens the door to the possibility that the projected feelings (more accurately, the congruent set of feelings elicited in the recipient) will be handled differently

from the manner in which the projector has been able to handle them. (Ogden 1979: 360)

So, the recipient, instead of simply reflecting the feelings directly back at the projector, or acting on them, can contain or process them by integrating them into aspects of his or her own personality, trying to control them through interpretation, or through sublimation. Thus "a new set of feelings is generated." It must be repeated that the feelings actualized in the recipient are not identical with those projected, but rather are congruent with them. Indeed, "all processing will be incomplete and contaminated by the pathology of the recipient" (361). The recipient is not an inert receptacle, but a human being with unconscious conflicts. One is reminded here of Morley's (1980) notion of intertextuality, which asserts that the text is never read as is, but always becomes part of the texts that have constituted the reader and the textual context in which he or she lives. This is what Derrida means with his famous phrase: "There is nothing outside of the text" (1976: 163). Why is it that there is any connection at all between projector and recipient? "The feelings that patients are struggling with are, by their nature, highly charged, painful, conflict-laden areas of human experience for the therapist as well as for the patient" (Ogden 1979: 367). The fully interactional nature of this communication is defined by Sandler as "a *compromise* between [the analyst's] own tendencies or propensities and the role-relationship which the patient is unconsciously seeking to establish" (1976: 47).

For the analyst, the fact that projections can be processed and thus modified is crucial to therapeutic work and the possibility for the patient's psychological change. "The metabolized projection offers the projector the potential for attaining new ways of handling a set of feelings that he could only wish to get rid of in the past" (Ogden 1979: 361).

It will be remembered that Althusser asserts that ideology has a materiality. Ogden's understanding of projective identification matches this and provides some elaboration: "*This is not an imaginary pressure.* This is *real* pressure exerted by means of a multitude of interactions between the projector and the recipient" (Ogden 1979: 359, emphasis added). The "or else" of projective identification—the "muscle" behind the demand for compliance (acknowledging that at least the first and third stages are unconscious)—is something like: "If you are not what I need you to be, you don't exist for me," or "I can only see in you what I put there, and so if I don't see that in you, I see nothing" (360). An illustration of this in everyday life is the common experience already cited of entering a room filled with strangers and immediately making a (love or hate) connection with some, while at first not really seeing or noticing the others. Even though the phantasized control of the projector over the recipient is rather less than absolute, projective identification is indeed "an external pressure exerted by means of interpersonal interaction" (360).

So in response to the queries raised by those who cannot see the need for this concept, what distinguishes projective identification from other mechanisms of externalization and introjection (although these can occur simultaneously in various mixtures) are (1) the blurring of boundaries between self and object representations, and (2) Ogden's second stage of induction. And this is also what makes projective identification a very useful way of thinking about interpellation: it is a psychological process that is material. Quite obviously too, projective identification can only happen in a social interaction, whereas projection only requires the projector (the paranoid, for example, may project persecutory feelings into inanimate or even nonexistent objects), and identification can also be a one-body experience (we may identify with a fictional character). Ogden says it clearly: "*Projective identification does not exist where there is no interaction between projector and recipient*" (1982: 14).

Being "the dynamic interplay of . . . the intrapsychic and the interpersonal" (Ogden 1982: 3), "when projective identification goes into action, the distance between symbol and what is symbolized is shortened or lost" (Etchegoyen 1985: 12). Ogden says that "potential space lies between the symbol and the symbolized" (1985: 137). He relies on Winnicott when he describes the projection as a transitional phenomenon: "As with any transitional phenomenon, it is both reality and fantasy, subjective and objective" (Ogden 1979: 367).

Again, this is not the place to go into extensive detail regarding potential space. But as this chapter is concerned to provide some idea about the intimate workings of our internal worlds in relation to the external, it may be worth being a little more explicit. Potential space no longer exists when any one of symbol, symbolized, or subject disappears, the condition for triangular space having been removed (Ogden 1985: 137). Empathy, for Ogden, occurs within potential space; one person plays at being another, the existence of the opposite pole of the psychological dialectic lessening the danger of losing oneself completely in the other. Projective identification, however, occurs outside of potential space: "it is the negative of playing" (1985: 138). The subject-object merger of projective identification reduces the distances between symbol, symbolized, and observing subject. When the analyst processes a projective identification, this can be seen as the re-creation of a psychological dialectical process whereby a provoked affective state can be "experienced, thought about, and understood by an interpreting subject" (138). Ogden describes the case of a suicidal in-patient who communicated to him that she was afraid of not doing well in the consultation. She proceeded to tell him several things about herself that it later transpired were only previous interpretations made by her therapist. He decribed the "routine feel" of the interview; its lack of a "sense of discovery, surprise, humor, originality on either of our parts." The patient easily fed the analyst what she thought he wanted to hear. Ogden describes feeling an overwhelming need to talk to someone, to anyone and about anything, after this interview. "Her communication was not in words, but by means of an induction of a feeling of loneliness in me" (138-39). This incident is mentioned here both to illustrate the limitations within projector and recipient to generate symbolic meanings, and also to suggest the kind of considerations a psychoanalytic study could generate of routine and alienating classroom events like students regurgitating what they believe the teacher wants from them.

Certainly an area for further theoretical work is the possible connection between object relation theory's nonsymbolic projective identification, and the Lacanian presymbolic Imaginary to be discussed in Chapter 6. It will have to suffice for now merely to suggest that perhaps the weakness of ideology-critique is precisely that it tends to concentrate on symbolic (and conscious) communication.

It is probably true that writers in the analytic literature have concentrated too much on the projection of unwanted parts and too little on the projection of good parts. Gregory Hamilton recommends distinguishing between positive and negative projective identifications, although he acknowledges that these "can be found in complex combinations and permutations" (1986: 494). He suggests, nevertheless, that positive projective identification is good and negative projective identification is bad. This seems an unnecessary and flawed notion. Projecting bad parts and reincorporating these bits in modified form surely helps to build "good" internal objects, the paradigmatic example being the analyst's interpretations in the transference situation.

Incidentally, projective identification should not be seen as being synonymous with transference. The latter may be wholly an intrapsychic projection, while the former also involves the evocation of countertransference feelings in the analyst (Ogden 1982: 2-3). Projective identification is a ubiquitous characteristic of externalizing an internal object relation, "i.e. of transference. What is variable is the degree to which the external object is enlisted as a participant in the externalization of the internal object relation" (Ogden 1983: 236).

Ogden uses theater as a metaphor for the "interpersonal enactment" of an internal object relationship via projective identification in the analytic situation. The patient in this analogy is both the director and one of the principal actors, and the analyst is a nonvoluntary and "unwitting actor." Projective identification is the mechanism whereby the analyst is given stage directions. Only retrospectively does the analyst realize that he or she "has been playing a role in the patient's enactment of an aspect of his inner world" (1982: 4).

Pere Folch Mateu says that projective identification has come to include a "complex simultaneity of clinical facts." Mateu feels that "to name all this complex group of functions by the brief and fragmentary term of projective identification is to name the whole by one of its parts." Projective identification is "a Gestalt, an integrative figure, which contains all the moments of the interaction between self and the internal and external objects" (Mateu 1986:

209). Mateu (see Figure 1) ably expresses this fluctuating "projective-introjective identificatory circuit" (210), the vertical axis being spatial and representing "the structural interchanges between self and objects," and the horizontal axis being temporal and representing "the dynamic of affects—impulses and anxieties—that produce and in turn are produced by those interchanges." The vertical line indicates the "dual circular process (projection-reintrojection-reprojection . . .) in the interaction and interchange of self and objects." The anxiety horizontal vector also has a dual direction; "anxiety can be a starting point of an interchange between self and object, leading to another anxiety." The oblique lines "point out the progressive differentiation (with possible regressions) between self and objects" (210).

How does the recipient of projective identification "pick up" the unspoken messages of the projector? Symington sees a relationship between the somatic, the psychic, and the external.

> I do not think that even the most abstract thought takes place independently of bodily registration. Therefore the most secret thought is picked up or is capable of being picked up, even though unconsciously, by someone attuned to the person who executes the so-called inner act. . . . So it is not only that the mental does not exist as a solitary realm but also that the psychic acts of one individual cross the boundaries of his own personal space to that of another. (Symington 1985: 351)

Ogden says that the interaction of projective identification is like that between mother and infant. He uses René Spitz's terms "quasi-telepathic" and "cones-thetic" "wherein sensing is visceral and stimuli are 'received' as opposed to being 'perceived'" (Ogden 1979: 363). As Freud said, "Betrayal forces its way through every pore" (1905a: 78).

It may be that the concept of projective identification is beginning to be used in the literature in too wide and loose a way. If so, this is something to be thrashed out by practicing analysts. Nevertheless, it has proven to be clinically useful and it has rich theoretical implications for social analysis. To end this section, what is crucial here for this book's argument is that, far from being limited to the transformation of representations of external objects, projective identification "attempts to, and often succeeds in, effecting specific alterations in the feeling state and self-representations of *another person*" (Ogden 1979: 369).

INTERPERSONAL RELATIONS

"All patients," says Ogden, (although it becomes clear that he sees projective identification as ubiquitous and not limited to pathology), "in an interpersonal setting are almost continually involved in the unconscious process of enlisting

Figure 1
The Projective-Introjective Identificatory Circuit

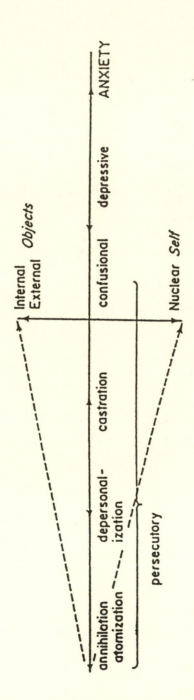

Source: Pere Folch Mateu, Identification and its vicissitudes, as observed in the neuroses, *International Journal of Psycho-Analysis* 1986, p. 210.

others to enact with them scenes from their internal world" (1982: 3). It is manifestly true that we do not understand well enough the interrelationships between group psychology, the functioning of institutions, and individual psychology: between "the stubborn self" and "indispensable and stifling culture" (Gay 1985). Nevertheless, projective identification is a promising conceptual bridge; "our awareness of the mechanisms permits us to understand specific interactions *among* persons in terms of specific dynamic conflicts *within* individuals" (Zinner and Shapiro 1972: 523).

While some writers have attempted to limit the extent of projective identification, others have extrapolated the concept to link the intrapsychic and the interpersonal. For example, "Family interaction consists of an intricately coordinated flow (both simultaneous and serial) of shared and complementary behaviors and perceptions the sequencing of which resists characterization by discursive prose." "Role allocations for the collusive playing out of these fantasies are communicated and evoked in family members by the mechanism of projective identification" (Zinner and Shapiro 1972: 529). For Robert Langs (1975, 1976), the therapeutic interaction's basic element is projective identification. Bollas points to the collective search of adults "for an object that is identified with the metamorphosis of the self" (1979: 98). Advertising, he points out, "makes its living on the *trace* of this object": the ad promising to change the outside world, and thus also the inner feeling. de Bea is another who uses the notion of projective identification broadly (neglecting to make a conceptual distinction): "projection, or projective identification, consists of the activation of internal objects in the recipient and is the operative mechanism basic to *all human interaction* from the beginning of life" (1989: 265, emphasis added). Ogden, too, says that projection and projective identification "generate" transference and countertransference phenomena of analysis "*and all other interpersonal interactions*" (1983: 227, emphasis added).

As Robert Bak has said, though, we must, of course, beware of "grandiose fantasies of social application" (1973: 7). Grahame Hayes (1990) has the same reservations. Psychoanalysts generally would be against attempts to reduce human experience to the social, and social theorists are dismissive of what they see as the "psychologizing" of human life. While taking cognizance of both these positions, I argue, with psychoanalysis, we can better understand the social through understanding how the individual becomes and remains a social being. Projective identification is a concept that can aid the development of what Hans Gerth and C. Wright Mills call "social psychology." For them "the structural and historical features of modern society must be connected with the most intimate features of man's self" (1954: xxiii). Without hoping to fully describe what such an enterprise might involve, what follows are a few ideas on projective identification and an old psychoanalytical concern, viz. group psychology.

The Group Leader and the Central Person

Freud, as we have seen earlier, said that groups are formed by libidinal ties between members and to the leader (1921). Subsequently, Fritz Redl (1942) has shown that in fact the group leader is but one kind of significant catalyzing "central person" in the group situation. He describes several others, including the patriarchal sovereign, the tyrant, the organizer, the hero, and the good example, to name a few. From his observations, Redl draws two theoretical principles on group formation. First, the guilt-and-fear-assuaging effect of the initiatory act; and, second, the infectiousness of the unconflicted personality on the conflicted.

It has now become a truism of psychoanalytic group therapy that one member of a group may unconsciously give voice to or enact the feelings of the entire group (Hinshelwood 1987). This phenomenon is crucial to the study of the operation of ideology-in-general. But what exactly, Ogden asks, is meant by this common event? "How has the given group member ceased to speak or behave as an individual, and instead come to function as the vehicle for the expression of collective feelings?" It is, he says, through projective identifications within a group setting. "Pressure is exerted on the recipient to behave and experience himself only in a manner that is congruent with the shared projective fantasy" (1982: 129).

Chapter 7 will speculate further on how the assertions made in these pages might be applied in future educational work.

SUMMARY

Since Freud's original and fairly straightforward definition of projection as a defence mechanism, psychoanalysis has witnessed a proliferation of notions of related mechanisms of psychic pushing out of and taking into the self. As these concepts have become broader, so have they become more diffuse. Klein's concept of projective identification, which conjoined externalizing and internalizing processes, extended these mechanisms far beyond defence to apply to psychic development and object relations. The ensuing discussion in psychoanalysis has progressed from the role of psychotic fantasies and the boundaries of the self- and object-representations to normal functioning and interpersonal interactions.

Sandler ends his overview of projective identification by noting that we cannot clearly distinguish what belongs to the patient and what belongs to the analyst in the analytic situation.

> I would suggest that in all forms of defensive projection there is a constant to-and-fro, an alternation between the momentary state of "oneness," of primary identification or primary confusion, and the . . . "sorting out". . . . This would

allow one to feel that what is projected is fleetingly "mine," but then, reassuringly, "not mine." (Sandler 1987a: 26)

This can be related to what he and Joffe (1967) called the "tendency to persistence." There is, they argue, always a perseverance of the primary, boundary-less state of confusion whenever an object is perceived or its representation recalled. A common experience, for example, is physically righting ourselves when we see another stumble: before the self/object boundary is reimposed and the ego disidentifies with the object—"this is I and that is he." The persistence of this earlier confusion and the repeated disidentification, sorting out, and boundary formation, are the basis of empathy, aesthetic appreciation, and transference and countertransference.

This chapter has attempted to flesh out what is involved in interpellation. Projective identification, it suggests, describes what is involved in this positioning process. De Bea provides a description of the experience of being actualized or interpellated.

> Our attention might be completely captivated by these activated inner experiences. We become temporarily blind to the rest of the world; dissociated, it remains inaccessible and useless. We lose perspective and a sense of proportion about what is happening within us and the inner experience tends to dominate us. We have "identified" with the inner objects this experience entails, or we have been "invaded." (1989: 266)

She recalls how once a patient's projective identification affected her: "I was momentarily blind to the remainder of my inner objects and experiences so that I was unable to make use of them. The object activated in me overwhelmed me" (268). Ogden's work is again instructive here. The effect of projective identification on the recipient is to "threaten his ability to experience his subjective state as psychic reality." What is a personal creation is experienced as reality; there is a powerful sense of inevitability. Neither party can conceive of himself or of the other any differently or less intensely than he does at present" (Ogden 1985: 138).

Despite the fact that Symington sees phantasy as completely negative—"to muffle truth and throttle development" (1985: 352)—he has some interesting things to say about it. Phantasy, he says, is but should not be contrasted with reality. "Phantasy coheres in a communication system between people and derives its power from the fact that it draws its sustaining energy from a source deep in the personality structure of two people (or more than two) in communication with each other" (351). "To keep on being, a phantasy has to find in each person an area susceptible to its stimulation. These stimulations which emanate from the phantasy and find their source in it are very subtle and are usually below the threshold of awareness" (352). Substitute "ideology-in-general" for "phantasy" and one is well on the way to understanding Althusser's troublesome notion. And substituting "subject" for "person," it becomes necessary to turn to the work of Lacan.

6

SUBJECTIVITY

Her feeling of horror suddenly communicated itself to him: exactly the same expression of terror appeared on his face; he, too, stared at her in the same way, and almost with the same *child-like* smile.

—Fyodor Dostoyevsky
Crime and Punishment

In order to flesh out the idea of the interpellated ideological subject, it is necessary to turn to the source of Althusser's own ideas about humanization, the earlier work of Lacan. This chapter proceeds by systematically outlining Lacan's theory of subject formation, en route suggesting which elements are crucial to a theory of subjectivity. In particular, the chapter develops recent attempts by others to speak about subject positioning in educational settings.

LACAN'S PROJECT

Jacques Lacan undertook a very ambitious endeavour; and Lacanian social theory continues to try to account for the humanization of biological individuals, the role of language and representation in positioning these subjects, and their interpellation in specific ideological discourses (Hall 1980: 159).

The writing of Lacan is notoriously and purposely difficult. He wanted not only to persuade intellectually but to affect the reader emotionally, and he did this by writing in an allusive and punning way, thereby giving a feel for what, he argued, is the way the unconscious "speaks." His early attraction to surrealism is evident in his use of language. Deeply interested in poetry and in mathematics, Lacan's writing is both lyrical and highly logical and complex in construction. It is easy to see why Stanley Leavy, for example, describes Lacan's work as "phenomenological," but he is wrong to call it "descriptive" (1990: 438)—Lacan's work is nothing if not theoretical. The elements of his work are articulated with one another in a complicated system, although it should be pointed out before embarking on this journey that Lacan's work is impossible to recount in a linear fashion. Because he is "a builder of loosely moored conceptual mobiles" (Bowie 1979: 122), his corpus should be considered whole. Unavoidably, therefore, concepts will be mentioned (signification, the Other, lack, desire) in what follows without proper introduction, only to be circled back upon later.

This chapter will not spend time considering the development of Lacan's career, except to say that within psychoanalysis Lacan disputed the largely American version—ego psychology—with its principle of a core, biologically given ego, and the attendant therapeutic attempts to strengthen the ego in order to enable people to become well-adjusted citizens (Roudinesco 1990). Like Freud (Appel 1992b), as well as the early analysts, and later social commentators such as Jessica Benjamin, Christopher Lasch, and Joel Kovel, Lacan saw human beings in permanent conflict with their environment, and with themselves. In French intellectual culture generally, of course, Lacan was part of the project of the "critique of the subject." To avoid confusion it should be noted that the critique of the subject refers to a critique of the humanist, volitional agent: for Continental philosophy, the critical engagement with the Hegelian subject. When, for example, Agnes Heller (1990) speaks of the "death of the subject," she alludes to the fact that notions of both the transcendental Subject and the individual have been found wanting. Ernesto Laclau explains that "the death of *the* Subject (with a capital S) has been the main precondition of [the] renewed interest in the question of subjectivity" (1993: 1). The critique of the subject is perhaps better rendered for our purposes as the critique of subjectivism or identity. Things are, of course, never settled in philosophy—there is something of a backlash in France against antihumanism and the critique of identity (see Descombes 1991; M. Peters 1993).

Probably the most basic notion in Lacan's reading of Freud is that the subject is decentered. Rejecting traditional ideas of the self as a unified locus of thoughts and emotions, Lacan insisted that the human subject is split, without a center, and characterized by lack. Freud noted several times that poets and artists have intuitively known that the "I" of a sentence is split from the "I" who emits it. However, most of us most of the time accept as obvious and commonsensical that we each have an identity. Lacan's view is a counter-intuitive one. It posits that, despite what we experience and what we like to believe, the common-sense self-image is *méconnaisance*, a misrecognition of ourselves. We are not to trust the ego, or conscious "I," as it "neglects, scotomizes, misconstrues" (Lacan 1948: 22). "The ego for Lacan is thus formed on the basis of an *imaginary* relationship of the subject with his own body. The ego has the illusion of autonomy, but it is only an illusion, and the subject moves from fragmentation and insufficiency to illusory unity" (Benvenuto and

Kennedy 1986: 56). (It is worth noting again here the sense in which Freud used the word "illusion" as being a belief motivated by an unconscious wish.) This imaginary relationship was to become an important element in Althusser's theory of ideology-in-general, as has been seen. Clearly Althusser was deeply influenced by Lacan. He invited Lacan to hold his public seminar series at the École normale supérieure, attended the psychoanalyst's famous seminar, and wrote specifically and admiringly about Lacan's work in a well-known essay "Freud and Lacan": "It may be that, like everyone else, he errs in the detail or even the choice of his philosophical bearings; but we owe him the *essential*" (Althusser 1971b: 195n).

SUBJECTIVITY

Lacan's central concerns can be put as follows: "*Who* are we talking to in the psychoanalytic situation?; and how does *speech* (and desire) function in this field?" (Hayes 1990: 35). The first point to make about the human subject is that it is not the same as the ego. In contradistinction to Descartes, Lacan did not say "I think, therefore I am"; rather, he said, "I think where I am not by thought, therefore I am where I do not think." "Furthermore," Anika Lemaire points out, "this formula leads us to see that I 'am' more surely there where 'I' do not 'think'" (1970: 123-24). Lacan is principally concerned with the subject who comes into being in the impossible attempt to express desire. As we shall see, the "I" exists in a "primordial form" (Lacan 1968: 72), which at the mirror stage is constructed as the ego, and which upon the entry into language becomes the human subject; "a psycho-social history" of "that tutelage of desire which we commonly call growing up" (Muller 1985: 39). For Lacan there was no final way to distinguish between biology, self, and society. The human subject always makes sense of, lives, and interprets biology. It is language that makes us social; or, rather, we become social when we enter language.

Desire

Psychoanalysis, for Lacan, is not a biological determinism. It is true that biological realities support the unconscious and its "basic category," desire, "(exactly as biological existence supports historical existence) but neither *constitute*, nor *determine* it" (Althusser 1971b: 213n). Biology is always and only to be conceived of through the effects of drives, desire; psychoanalysis for Lacan deals with the configurational arrangements of desire.

Need, desire, and demand are related, but not synonymous. Need refers to biological needs like hunger, thirst, and sexual urges. Need, then, is nonrelational—it exists outside of any social relationship. Desire emerges out of need; in order to exist it requires the self-awareness involved in thinking, for example,

"I am hungry." Unlike need, "desire aims not so much toward gratification as towards *recognition*" (Leavy 1990: 442). With Hegel, Lacan said that when one desires not a specific thing (food) but the desire of another, one has become human. Hegel saw human consciousness as being relational: the consciousness of the master being structured by the meaning he has for the slave, and vice versa. Similarly for Lacan, the subject is structured in an intersubjective relationship with the Other. The Lacanian subject/Other relation should, however, not be thought of in the same terms as the upward spiral of the Hegelian dialectic. Bowie makes this clear in his exegesis of the following of Lacan's ambivalent considerations of Hegel: "This is our personal *Aufhebung*, which transforms that of Hegel, which was his personal illusion, into an opportunity to pick out, instead and in place of the leaps of an ideal progress, the avatars of lack" (cited in Bowie 1991: 97). (For a stimulating discussion of Lacan, Hegel, and dialectics, see Slavoj Žižek [1991a].)

The Other has several meanings in Lacan's work. It is the Other that creates an unfillable lack in the subject, thereby ensuring that desire will remain unsatisfied, as its aims are perpetually out of its reach. The Other sometimes refers to the whole domain of subject-Other interaction, sometimes it refers only to the latter term. Lacan's term means variously: "a father, a place, a point, any dialectical partner, a horizon within the subject, a horizon beyond the subject, the unconscious, language, the signifier" (Bowie 1979: 136). This seeming pot-pourri can be made sense of if it is understood that for Lacan the abyss between desire and its object is introduced by the name of the father, language, the original Other. All of the inevitable alienations throughout life are manifestations of the "otherness" first put in place by the proto-Other. Language, "the complete tease" (Bowie 1991: 83), is the medium through which the subject is constituted:

> The function of language is not to inform but to evoke.
> What I seek in speech is the response of the other. What constitutes me as a subject is my question. . . .
> I identify myself in language, but only by losing myself in it like an object.
> (Lacan 1953: 86)

So desire is understood by Lacan in more than one way. First, desire is not directed toward a thing (*objet petit a*) but toward yet another lacking desire, the desire of another. Second, objects are only loved if they appear to promise the filling in of the subject's lack; desire is, thus, narcissistic, the unachievable struggle for wholeness. Demand is the address to a specific other person for a specific thing—it is a signification of desire. Desire, of course, cannot be specific; it is precisely what cannot be articulated by particularistic demand. The subject wants not only to have the object but to be the object of another's desire—to be desired or recognized. Because we have (biological) needs *and* desire (for love), every intersubjective act is ambiguous: is it aimed at satisfying a need or at displaying love? As the reaction of the Other is always ambiguous, demand is perpetually repeated, forever incompletely addressed. Žižek uses the Hegelian phrase "loss of loss" with regard to *jouissance,* or pleasure-driven desire and its ever-changing goals: "by obtaining the object, we lose the fascinating dimension of loss as that which captivates our desire" (Žižek 1991b: 86).

Desire, then, exists chronologically between need and demand. At (indeed before) birth the infant has certain biological needs. Later, the child realizes the incompleteness of the mother and of him or herself, and so desires what is missing. (The influence of the early Heidegger on Lacan is apparent here. The subject is intentional in that he or she wishes to speak but, because his or her desire is always deflected, cannot.) This desire is expressed as demand or repression. Desire is analogous to Freud's term *Wunsch,* which refers to directed drives as opposed to libido, the elemental energy as yet unconnected to specific images. Desire, though, does not refer only to specific acts of wishing, but more to a "continuous force" (Sheridan 1977: viii). All our demands are symbolic representations of our desire to be whole; our lack is in regard to an original state of oneness, of undifferentiated bliss. The subject/Other relationship is constituted by desire. In the encounter with the Other, the subject is continually remade; it is from the Other that the subject "receives even the message that he emits" (Bowie 1979: 135).

So it is lack—the deficit between need and its articulation as demand—that brings desire into being. Lack is also formed in the process of differentiation from the mother when the very channelling of libido is prescribed to the drives and the infant loses the original contact with his or her own libido. At the entry into language the infant becomes a subject, alienated from him/herself—yet another lack. The model of desire and lack can be applied to make sense of the larger social scene.

It has been necessary to expand upon desire at some length here, as it is the "unspoken" (Macherey 1966) of poststructuralist accounts of education. Lacan's theorization of deep affective formation and form can be contrasted with Bronwyn Davies' ideas about desire. Acknowledging that "desire is spoken into existence," Davies explicitly turns her back on psychoanalysis: "I find psychoanalysis one more individualistic discourse" (1990: 504). In so doing, she loses the dynamic capacity of Lacan's theory of subjects constituting each other through the evocation of necessary lack. If desire is a factor in social life, but it is not conceived of via psychoanalysis, what is it, what part does it play in subjectivity, and where does it come from? To show exactly how deep (or otherwise) "desire" is in her work, Davies says: "As a feminist I desire a world in which anyone's sex/gender is made relevant only in the process of biological reproduction" (1990: 501). Desire is "implicated in storyline," we are told; "it is through story that children can learn the patterns of desire appropriate for their gender" (Davies and Banks 1992: 5). Clearly, what is called "desire" here is little more than learned preferences. It follows, then, that such likes and dislikes can be *un*learned; thus the exhortations to "write and speak utopias" (Davies 1990: 515). "Positions" (Davies and Harré 1990) thereby become personae or social character parts that we play in stories. Without the motivational trajectories of deeper, unsatisfiable desire, social life becomes no more than bad and good narratives, stories that we are at liberty to rewrite.

Real, Imaginary, Symbolic

In The Rome Discourse ("The Function and Field of Speech and Language in Psychoanalysis," 1953), Lacan proposed three orders or planes of existence: the Real, the Symbolic, and the Imaginary. Again, their precise meaning is not easy to pin down. Lacan argued that psychoanalysis has not taken language seriously enough, thus getting lost in symbols. Not only is language the principle medium of psychoanalytic therapy; the unconscious itself, he said in a famous aphorism, is structured like a language. As usual, Lacan's startling formulation is precise here. Language, he meant, is *prior* to the unconscious. When the human subject enters language (*langue*, not *parole*), he or she is fitting into an extant Symbolic order that mediates the desire of said subject; drives are channeled by language. "The psychoanalytic experience has rediscovered in man the imperative of the Word as the law that has formed him in its image"; it is by way of "the gift of language" that "all reality has come to man and it is by his continued act that he maintains it" (Lacan 1953: 106). Truly, and at the risk of trivializing the issues here, for Lacan in the beginning was the Word.

The Real is that which is neither Imaginary nor Symbolic. Lying beyond language, it is the reality that we cannot have direct access to, although we must assume that it exists. Our experience of it is only via the mediation of the Imaginary and the Symbolic. Fredric Jameson (1977) says that the Real is History itself. One should read this as: History plus Nature plus the Unconscious, our relation to which is always characterized by lack; desire is both historical and transhistorical. The Real is that which is unspeakable, "the ineliminable residue of all articulation" (Sheridan 1977: x).

Lacan described the realm of the Imaginary as a preverbal (and later developmentally, nonverbal) realm of alienated phantasy. The Imaginary is characterized by identification and duality; it is narcissistic and fusionary. Early on, the child's experience is disorganized, fragmentary, and it is unable to distinguish between the inner and outer world. The infant thinks essentially visually, in the Imaginary order; i.e., Imaginary for Lacan derives from "image," not from "imagine." After entry into language, as we shall see, the child functions mainly in the Symbolic order of language, although "the imaginary remains the enduring treasury of images" (Leavy 1990: 439).

The Imaginary includes phantasies, images and nonlinguistic structures. By contrast, the Symbolic is not narcissistic, it is social; not a duality, but a triangularity. The Symbolic refers to language, the means through which desire is expressed; it is the domain of the signifier that continually restructures the subject. "A main intuition" of Lacan was that psychic functioning and structure "could be reorganized around a relatively small number of linguistic concepts" (Bowie 1979: 124). (It is also important to realize that, though Lacan borrowed from structural linguistics, he was not a linguistic psychoanalyst. Grahame Hayes [1990: 36-39] makes the point that it is the structural forms of Lévi-Strauss that were fundamental to Lacan's work, linguistics merely being used to demonstrate these forms.) Coherent speech can only occur if the infant fully occupies a place in the Symbolic system of conventions. This involves, for example, being positioned by certain terms, e.g., "boy," "girl," "son," "daughter." These terms are signifiers standing in particular relationships with a central signifier, the phallus, or the desire for the Other.

Without suggesting that the orders are coterminous with developmental stages, the entry of the child into language is the culmination of the journey from being a biological entity to a human subject. This transition is achieved within "the Law of Culture," which has the same "formal essence" as language (Althusser 1971b: 209). To simplify a complex theory of an unstable manifestation: the Real, necessarily inaccessible to the subject, is represented by the ever-*shifting* Symbolic (language) and experienced in the constantly *stabilizing* Imaginary (images and illusion). The orders are not distinct concepts or zones; all three are ever-present in shifting arrangements. Lacan's mathematical interest emerges in his attempts to illustrate the relationship between the Real, the Imaginary, the Symbolic, and the symptom with various Borromean knots (Turkle 1979: 25). The pertinent character of the knot is that untying any of the three rings undoes the other two.

For Lacan, the psychical developmental sequence is as follows: drives (need), desire (lack), unconscious (repression). Clearly this is all subsumed under the workings of the id. The unconscious is continually voluble, demanding to be heard. But the content of the unconscious is unacceptable to the subject and to the social order; when it reveals its existence in dreams, slips, symptoms, jokes, or phantasies, it is rejected as foolish, repugnant, or of little importance. The unconscious itself, that region of repressed tendencies and thoughts, is, to use another linguistic notion, the signifying chain along which desire passes—it is "the discourse of the Other." And language is an "endless tautology."

Symbolization

Language not only represents desire, it constitutes the subject. Moreover, it is not only the human mind that operates in and through language, human culture itself is representational; and these representational structures precede us and determine our fates.

> Symbols in fact envelop the life of man in a network so total that they join together, *before he comes into the world*, those who are going to engender him "by flesh and blood," so total that they *bring to his birth*, along with the gifts of the stars, if not with the gifts of the fairies, *the shape of his destiny*; so total that they give the words that will make him faithful or renegade, the law of the acts that will follow him right to the very place *where he is not yet* and even beyond his death. (Lacan 1953: 68, emphasis added)

Freud described in *Beyond the Pleasure Principle* (1920) a game played by his nephew. Holding onto a piece of string, the child would throw an attached cotton reel over the edge of his cot, uttering as he did so what sounded like the German word *fort* ("gone" or "away"). He would then pull back the cotton reel, joyfully saying what Freud understood to be *da* ("there"). The game, according to Freud, was an attempt by the infant to cope with the anxiety raised by the absence of his mother, the cotton reel acting as what Winnicott would come to call a "transitional object" for the mother. Lacan used this story to describe how language, at its very inception (or rather, at the child's entry into language), and symbols remove the human subject from the Real. In this example, first the cotton reel and then language become substitutes for the mother. The story is, then, about self-alienation. The infant is both split off from his drives and subordinated to the Symbolic. From then on, the identity and the desire of the child are determined by the Symbolic. Again, it is important to keep in mind that subjectivity is not delusional (false consciousness) but illusional, "a *necessary* illusion whereby one lives, as it were, a story of one's life, of who one is" (Mitchell 1988: 83).

Lacan spoke here of "the letter." The letter refers firstly to the actualization of language: text, *parole*, be it in spoken words or symptoms. The second area to which the letter refers is the structure of language that preexists and determines the subject (*langue*). Thus the essay title, "The Agency of the Letter in the Unconscious or Reason since Freud" (1957). In an instance of his playfulness with language he writes, "*lettre-l'être-l'autre*" (the letter implies being implies the Other). The subject is a "non-unitary . . . field of effects produced by discourse; in other words . . . a by-product of meaning" (Muller 1985: 34).

Sometimes it appears that structuralist/poststructuralist texts are unavoidably or, worse, deliberately vague and mystifying, terms coming to mean whatever the authors choose them to mean. This may well be the case in some confused and confusing accounts, but it is greatly to Lacan's credit that his notion of the empty, lacking, slipping, desiring subject should be "at once cogent and precise" (Bowie 1979: 132).

Lacanian Psychoanalysis

Importantly, for Lacan the task of the psychoanalyst is not to somehow bring the patient in tune with reality. This is impossible, as the above pages suggest. Of course the patient wants or desires *the answer* from the analyst, but it is the task of the analyst to guide the patient to acknowledgment of his or her lack. The change required in the patient involves an awareness of the necessity of our incompleteness. "That is why the question *of* the Other, which comes back to the subject from the place from which he expects an oracular reply in some such form as '*Che vuoi?*,' 'What do you want?,' is the one that best leads him to the path of his own desire" (Lacan 1960: 312). In the same way as Wilfred Bion's (1959a) analyst acts as a container, the analyst for Lacan reworks the patient's anxiety and projects back the question that indicates (in the sense of points to) the subject's lack. Although it is easy and almost overwhelmingly tempting to accept and cherish the ego, an image of unity, the patient's more difficult task is to come into contact with the discourse of desire. The conscious ego of the patient speaks "empty speech" (*la parole vide*). Empty speech is the expression by the patient of his or her desire without the patient knowing what it is that is being expressed. The patient talks about him/herself as an object; free associations are addressed to the Other, the psychoanalyst. It is the task of the analyst to direct the patient to what lies beneath, namely his or her impossible desire for wholeness. The analyst "takes the description of an everyday event for a fable addressed to whoever hath ears to hear, a long tirade for a direct interjection, or on the other hand a simple *lapsus* for a highly complex statement, or even the sigh of a momentary silence for the whole lyrical development it replaces" (Lacan 1953: 44). Lacan rejected either optimism or pessimism and, like Freud, confronted "the irremediable" (Bowie 1979: 151). The subject must come to know that "whatever his appetites may be, whatever his needs may be, none of them will find satisfaction in analysis, and that the most that he can expect of it is to organize his menu" (Lacan 1964: 269).

Can anything be learned here about the teacher/student relationship? If we leave aside the skills and overt knowledge taught, and concentrate upon the areas of particular concern to critical sociology of education—the hidden curriculum, cultural capital, and socialization—it is clear that there is a realm of overlap with Lacan's notions of psychoanalysis. While not the student's therapist, the teacher is involved in deep or transcendent change of students, and vice versa; schooling does make a difference. However, in the literature we see an exaggerated and ingrained trust in the possibility of insight leading to wholeness. Capitalism/patriarchy/racism have cut us off from ourselves, the story goes, but it is possible, through consciousness-raising and social solidarity, to realize full selfhood and community, i.e., democracy: "a space where the self and other can conjoin in a discourse of mutuality and respect" (McLaren 1991: 34). Sydney Smith (1977) has called such "regressive reaction to separation anxiety," "The Golden Fantasy."

THE FORMATION OF THE *I*

> If what Freud discovered and rediscovers with a perpetually increasing sense of shock has a meaning, it is that the displacement of the signifier determines the subjects in their acts, in their destiny, in their refusals, their blind spots, their end and fate, their innate gifts and social acquisitions . . . without regard for character or sex, and that willingly or not, everything that might be considered the stuff of psychology, kit and caboodle, will follow the path of the signifier.
>
> —Jacques Lacan
> "The Seminar on Poe's 'Purloined Letter'"

So far the outlines of Lacan's theoretical apparatus have been laid out. How, though, do the I and the subject come into existence? In "The Mirror Stage as Formative of the Function of the I as Revealed in Psychoanalytic Experience," Lacan (1949) can be said to follow Freud, who had said that the ego is a mental projection; a later construction, and not a hereditary entity (1923: 26).

The Mirror Stage

In the first months of life, the infant is largely auto-erotic. Unable to distinguish between what is internal and what is external to its body, the infant does not perceive itself as a distinct or as a unified being. Rather, it experiences itself as fragmented parts among surrounding objects. This imagery of a piecemeal body continues to manifest itself throughout life in dreams and in schizoid phantasy; the paintings of Hieronymus Bosch recreate it. Infancy is a time dominated by satisfied and frustrated needs. The infant experiences its helplessness and fragmentation. Not present from birth, the ego develops following a formative event in the early months of life, said Lacan. This is when, for the first time, the infant recognizes itself in a mirror. Of course this does not necessarily have to occur literally before a mirror—the infant may recognize itself as reflected in the look or gaze of a person, typically the mother. Between six to eighteen months, then, the child perceives itself, paradigmatically in the image in a mirror, as a whole and complete person and no longer as a fragmented collection of sensation, limbs, and affects. The infant experiences triumph when it perceives that it controls its body—every movement being reproduced in its reflected image, the "Ideal-I." Compared to the previous auto-erotic stage during which the child had an erotic relationship with its fragmented body, now it falls in love with the image of a *Gestalt*, a complete and autonomous image. However, this is in anticipation of the mastery yet to be achieved: "The mirror stage is a drama whose internal thrust is precipitated from insufficiency to anticipation" (Leavy 1990: 442). Although the infant has poor control over its own body, it is able via the mirror stage to (mis)conceive itself as whole and self-controlled.

It is here that the self-alienation of the subject begins—alienation being fundamental to identification, because for identification to occur there must be a perceiving self and a perceived self. Or to put it in more accurate Lacanian terms, every act of identification constitutes, i.e., brings into existence, the I and its Other. From the time of the mirror stage onward reality is perceived as an image—an image, what is more, that tends towards completeness. Thus are unconscious desires enmeshed with the Imaginary phantasies. This moment of self-identification is vital, as it is the original instance of a lifelong tendency to strive for and to cherish a unitary sense of self. "Alienating identity . . . will mark with its rigid structure the subject's entire mental development" (Lacan 1949: 4) as well as all future social and cultural life. The relationship between the infant and the image is indeed an estranged one where the child, not in control of its own movements, experiences as mastery what is in fact mastery of an image. This image has a double existence: as the actual image reflected on the surface of the mirror, and as an I with "mental permanence," "it prefigures its alienating destination" (Lacan 1949: 2).

It is crucial to remember that while the I is certainly not in control of identification, the content of the subject is put into place by this identification. The mirror stage, in other words, is not something done by another to the infant, but something the infant does—albeit not at all fully consciously—in the active formation of the self. This activity is a form of human labor. All relationships with external objects will have an incongruous nature, this as a result of the imaginary and alienated experience of the ur-identification of the mirror stage. All identifications are, for Lacan, not only illusory, they are also ambivalent, aggressive, and narcissistic, being linked in a "correlative tension" in the "coming-into-being of the subject" (Lacan 1948: 22). The infant has an ambivalent relation with his or her mirror image: it loves the complete oneness of the image, while it hates the fact that the image is external to it. It is unlikely that the experience of subjectivity has been better and more concisely described than in Edgar Allen Poe's story "William Wilson," where the narrator talks about his relationship with his alter ego:

It is difficult, indeed, to define or even to describe, my real feelings towards him. They formed a motley and heterogeneous admixture;—some petulant animosity, which was not yet hatred, some esteem, more respect, much fear, with a world of uneasy curiousity. To the moralist it will be unnecessary to say, in addition, that Wilson and myself were the most inseparable companions. (1839: 8)

Like Klein (1946), Lacan saw aggression at work very early on in development. Pre-Oedipal identifications are characterized by anxiety and aggression, while post-Oedipal identifications are troubled by aggression and guilt toward paternal authority. It is a crucial feature of identification that aggression is released "in any relation to the other, even in a relation involving the most Samaritan of aid" (Lacan 1949: 6). Contrast this vacillation with the unalloyed altruism portrayed in the phantasies of critical pedagogy; McLaren, for example, wonders "as a critical educator . . . what love might mean at the level of the whole society" (1991: 34). If identification is, as Lacan portrays it, alienated and ambivalent, it is also conflicted in another way; it stabilizes (by constituting the individual's I) at the same time as it fragments (alienating the subject from its desire). At the mirror stage the infant comes to "see" both itself and the Other, to see itself *as* an Other. As the self is composed over the years of many such internalizations of misapprehensions, it is highly complex and conflictual. Although the "intersubjective dialectic" exists from the beginning, there is no possibility of the recognition necessary for full mutuality. (Indeed, Lacan said that his dog Justine was unique in that she was the only one who did not take him for someone else [Schneiderman 1983: 130].)

Althusser, as we know, spoke of the interpellation of the subject. Although Lacan did not explain the mechanisms at work in interpellation, he did provide a fuller theoretical account of subject formation, or positioning, than did Althusser in the incomplete example of the policeman's hailing, "Hey, you there!" (1971a: 174). The pre-Oedipal child lives in a dyadic, symbiotic relation with the mother; this is a time of the Imaginary. This relation is upset at the Oedipus stage with the entry of a third person, the father. The Oedipus complex positions the infant in language, in the family, and in gender. For Lacan this did not mean the actual presence of the person of the father, but rather the introduction of the father's *name* establishing his absent presence. The father here is not this or that particular father, but the symbolic father who powers the signifying chain of desire. The introduction of his name, the Law, is the introduction of the Symbolic; the entry of the child into language marks the birth of the subject.

The Path of the Signifier

To illustrate how subjectivity fixes and shifts, Lacan (1956) used Poe's story "The Purloined Letter," in which the Prefect of Police in Paris approaches Dupin for assistance in recovering a compromising letter apparently written to the Queen and then stolen from her by Minister D. The Queen had witnessed the theft but could not react for fear of implicating herself before the King. Although the police have thoroughly searched the minister's apartment they have been unable to find the letter. Dupin discovers the letter which lies, as he has reasoned, in full view. He steals the letter back, replacing it with a dummy letter. The story, Lacan argued, is structured in triads: the third person, the robber, and the loser. This structure is repeated with different characters filling the three positions. What is it that determines which position characters will occupy in the triad? The location of the letter. The letter moves along "a signifying chain." The robber (the minister and then Dupin) sees that the third person (the King and then the minister) has not detected the letter and has power as long as he possesses the letter. The place of the letter, and knowledge of that place, determines the possible actions of the subjects.

What does the letter signify? Pointedly, the contents of the letter are never revealed in Poe's story; we can never grasp the transcendant signifier. The letter, speech, the signifier, demand—these all refer to the positioning function of the Symbolic, to interpellation, and to the impossibility of grasping Kant's "thing-in-itself." The signifier determines the place of the subject without any need to invoke meaning or signification.

It is crucial to keep in mind that Lacan was not saying that *anyone* who comes into contact with the letter is automatically positioned in a particular way. Rather, he showed how positioning works in an overdetermined way: when one stands in a *particular relation* to the letter, one will be positioned by that letter. The reading of the letter, in other words, the specific meaning for, and effect on, the subject that the letter will have, is variable and unpredictable. This is, first, because the subject is already a subject of other letters, and, second, because the letter or instance of interpellation itself has many possible meanings.

Lacan employed what structural linguistics says are the basic binary elements of all symbolic systems, signifier and signified. He found it useful here to use and to extend Saussure's (1915) classic formulation of the sign, S/s, where the signifier is not only arbitrarily and conventionally related to the concept or signified, as Saussure would have it. Rather, Lacan saw the two parts of the sign being related not in a stable and predictable way, but where the signified (lower case letter, italic script, bottom position) is separated from the signifier (upper case letter, roman type, top position) by the bar that indicates disjunction, repression. The autonomy of the signifier is dependant on the resistance of the bar. So the concept and its name belong to different orders. Instead of a unity of signifier and signified (which Saussure indicated by placing the above formulaic expression in an ellipse), Lacan postulated constant signification along a signifying chain, each signified capable of behaving as a signifier. Furthermore, a signifier always signifies another signifier in relation to other signifiers. The signifier "dog" only has meaning in relation to like signifiers, e.g., "canine," "quadruped," "animal" and "pet," and to unlike signifiers, e.g., "cat." Language is a system of differences, and it is nonrepresentational; there is no natural connection between concept and name. Lacan insisted upon the *glissement* or slippage between signifiers along the signifying chain. Even an emotion is a signifier as it is an effect of desire. But it is not the case that there is *no* relationship between signified and signifier or between signifiers; rather, the precise nature of the relationship is finally indecipherable.

The subject has no history in that it is a "subject-for-discourse" (Morley 1980: 169), but each instance of positioning or interpellation occurs in a particular way at a particular social-historical moment. Signifiers are not free-floating, they are linked in some way to each other and to the signified. The bar, in other words, is permeable. It is true, though, that we can never "get at" the signified. The only possible object of study, Lacan said, is the signifying chain itself. As Žižek puts it: "If we look for the 'deeper, hidden meaning' of the figures appearing in a dream, we *blind* ourselves to the latent 'dream-thought' articulated in it" (1991b: 51). The subject is represented by the signifier, and this process can only provide representation for another signifier; "the signifier represents the subject for another signifier." This movement is not only linear. Over time we construct a proliferation of chains of signification, continually substituting signifiers. Each instance of the letter has attached to it "a whole articulation of relevant contexts" (Lacan 1957: 154): "In its symbolizing function speech is moving towards nothing less than a transformation of the subject to whom it is addressed by means of the link that it establishes with the one who emits it—in other words, by introducing the effect of a signifier" (Lacan 1953: 83). *Point de capiton* is the term Lacan used to describe the mechanisms of this articulation. It is wrong, then, to assume that Lacan was a textualist, one who believed that nothing exists *but* language. Rather, nothing *for the subject* exists *separate from* language. If Imaginary (mis)identification is an estrangement of the self, the Symbolic is a further alienation of the subject. This distinguishes Lacan from "many more facile celebrations of the primacy of language" (Jameson 1980: 359).

Lacan produced a model of intersubjective relationships (see Benvenuto and Kennedy 1986: 100) whereby the subject's movement toward the Other (or Real) is continuously diverted by the axis o—o', the relationship between the ego and its mirror image; we experience the social world through the Imaginary. And whenever the subject attempts to speak it is frozen and functions as a signifier. "The truth is thus always being 'purloined,' and the subject is constantly drawn to the four corners of the scheme. This duality of symbolic Other and imaginary other is basic to the structure of the subject" (Benvenuto and Kennedy 1986: 101).

Metaphor and Metonymy

Although what is ultimately signified is desire, meaning cannot be more than the movement from one instance of signification to another.

> Slips, failures, jokes and symptoms, like the elements of dreams themselves, became *signifiers*, inscribed in the chain of an unconscious discourse, doubling silently, i.e. deafeningly, in the misrecognition of "repression," the chain of the human subject's verbal discourse. (Althusser 1971b: 207-208)

Lacan again found it useful here to use linguistic concepts in order to theorize representations of the unconscious. Of course, because he saw language as constitutive of human subjectivity (or rather, saw language and subjectivity as being similarly structured), he intended for certain structural linguistic terminology to be more than just convenient ways of making his point. But as opposed to the "purely formalist textualism" (Wexler 1987: 152) of many critical theorists, it must be reemphasized that signification is not simply a closed complex of cross-referenced signs; signification is always the ultimately unsuccessful attempt to give expression to desire.

Signification, and thus also subject positioning, operates in one of two ways, ways analogous to the unconscious mechanisms of displacement and condensation that Freud postulated in *The Interpretation of Dreams* (1900). All signification operates, Lacan argued, like the linguistic tropes of metaphor and metonymy. Here he delved into the structural linguistics of Roman Jakobson (1956), who asserted that all connections between signifiers, all contiguity along the signifying chain, operate by these two linguistic tropes. Metonymy is the linguistic form where words follow one another linearly, one element being conflated into another (e.g., "Moscow said . . ."). This is like the splitting of the subject where desire is always for that which is lacking. If metonymy is the desire for something else, then metaphor, the substitution of one word for another, from one signifier to another (e.g., "the Iron Curtain"), is the mechanism by which that desire can be expressed. The object of desire is *le désir de l'Autre*, said Lacan. Benvenuto and Kennedy point out that this French expression can be translated into English as both the desire *of* the Other (metonymy) and desire *for* the Other (metaphor) (1986: 130).

Because the infant's desire is unknown to it, it seeks to satisfy its lack in the Other by trying to identify with the mother's desire, thereby becoming the mother's object of desire. At the same time, the infant has possessive desires for her. Desire, in Lacanian theory, operates according to rules analogous to the linguistic rules of the signifier. Neurotic symptoms, being psychical condensations, are metaphorical; fetishism, by contrast, being a stoppage in the displacement functions of unconscious desire, is metonymic.

CONCLUSION

A recent critical study of schooling has overtly made the realm of the psyche relevant to sociological analysis. Wexler has theorized that social relations in the school are premised on *"emotional dynamics of identification, attachment and caring"* (1992: 36), and he has described three permutations of these relations: lack of care and withdrawal from interaction; desocialisation and withdrawal from public life; and unintended assault on the self. The work covered in Chapters 3, 4, 5, and 6 of this book can be used to illuminate why and how these kinds of dynamics come to be.

To sum up, the ego, formed by imaginary identifications, is the alienated outcome of the desire for unity and oneness. It is fostered throughout life as whole, stable and coherent. Like the subject, the ego is relational, existing only with the development of the distinction between inner and outer, "me" and "you." The subject, by contrast, is not experienced as any one thing. It is the continuously changing field of tensions caused by the sense of loss and incompleteness that are inevitable in human life. The subject is "subject to" the Symbolic order. So, for example, in Lacanian theory "he" and "she" only apply to subjects as sexual identity is established in the Symbolic.

This chapter ends with the double point that (1) meaning and subjectivity are never final, rather it is sliding signification; and that (2) this drifting search for meaning is but demand, the impossible attempt to express desire. All this in order to throw a psychoanalytic light on Derrida's aphorism about nothing existing outside of the text.

If Lacanian theory of subjectivity is valuable to social analysis and if it is to be useful in the study of education, it becomes necessary to grasp what is entailed in the study of the subject/Other relation. While an emphasis on interpretation and signification is an advance, the focus on particular texts per se may produce readings that are asocial in that they take little account of the discursive context of each subject/text interaction. The "productivity of the text" must not come to refer only to the "capacity of the text to set the viewer 'in place' in a position of unproblematic identification/knowledge" (Hall 1980: 159). The reader or subject of any text is always *already* constituted as a subject of various and changing positions in several intersecting chains of signification. This preconstituted subject is not freely available for interpellation by any discourse that happens along. He or she bears the marks of previous interpellations that play a part in whether and how interpellation will occur. (Chapter

5 has theorized how this might happen.)

Extrapolating from Lacan's model of signification and subjectivity, one can say that no text has only one possible message. What any particular text can mean does not refer in any direct way to particular signifieds; rather, what a text signifies changes in the process of being read. There is, therefore, no moment when the text constitutes a subject in a way that could have been predicted. Other texts and discourses constantly act on subjects; Michel Pêcheux (1983) has introduced the term "interdiscourse" in this regard. The human subject *is* an interdiscourse, he says, marked throughout its life by several ideological discourses. Or, to use Freud's term again, the subject is "overdetermined." Accordingly, the appropriate object of study is not text/subject, but *multiplicity of* texts/subjects (Morley 1980: 166). All depends, thus, on how reader and text, or subject and signifier, each in its complex historical and multiplicitous context, combine at a particular moment.

We must not try to deduce subject position from the text. The educational literature is replete with examples of subject positions being ascribed reductively from educational activities and texts. Svi Shapiro says, for example: "People whose time is spent in the often mindless tasks of the classroom will be prepared for the mindless activities of the office or shop floor" (1987: 145); and Jean Anyon says that the hidden curriculum provides a "tacit preparation for relating to the process of production in a particular way," a way qualitatively different for each social class (1987: 225). The nonreductive nature of subjectivity does not therefore mean that we have to be content with a vision of a society as a systemic agglomeration of individually constituted subjects. Rather, every text has "preferred readings," and all readers and writers, "implicated as desiring bodies" (Wright 1984: 5), are "preferred readers." Far from static ideology-critique, Lacan's conceptualization of *glissement* of significations, which are in turn the demands of desire, is a dynamic, complex, theoretically coherent model of explanation. CSOE is replete with ideology-critique. For example, Heather Cathcart and Geoff Esland, after reviewing the "ideological substance of educational initiatives" for fourteen-to-sixteen year olds, advocate remedying the distortions by a "fuller discussion in the context of a more rigorous and *less biased* social and political education" (1985: 191, emphasis added). Many neo-Marxists find it extremely difficult to transcend ideology-critique; in the field of aesthetics, Terry Eagleton (1990) too quickly reduces movements in art and art theory to the historical state of economic production. Whether or not it is made explicit in each instance, ideology-critique is underpinned by a notion of false consciousness. It should not be necessary to point out the untenability of this position. Believing in false consciousness assumes the existence, or at least the possibility, of a true consciousness—held, no doubt, by the author.

There is an important distinction to be made between the constitution of the subject as an original potential space and the latter moments when this subject-in-general is interpellated into specific subject positions. As Morley (1980) says, we need to focus not on "the politics of the signifier" but on the moment when the constituted subject meets specific signification—the moment of interpellation. This book can do no more than suggest that psychoanalysis has conceptual tools for coming to grips with the actual processes of interpellation.

All human practices, poststructuralist educational analysis accepts, are discursive. For Foucault (1977a, 1977b), discourses are sets of signifying practices whereby knowledge is always suffused with power. Discourse can then be understood both in the generic sense in which this book has spoken of ideology-in-general, and also in the sense of specific discourses like, say, nationalism, patriarchy, etc. Discourses have the effect of closure, establishing bodies of knowledge that appear natural and commonsensical; and discourse analysis is concerned to expose the necessary incompleteness and normalizations of texts. If words like Critique, Crisis, Culture, Nature, and Civilization "become problematic, then the absolute claims of set methods of knowledge come into dispute: also their mechanisms of teaching learning and representing truth" (Stanton 1983: 19). Literary deconstruction "always has for its target to reveal the existence of hidden articulations and fragmentations within assumedly monadic totalities" (de Man 1979: 249). On its own, however, this textualism can become the mechanical searching for, and inevitable finding of, "a mind-boggling 'aporia'" (Lehman 1991: 129). (See Chapter 7 for a more promising theory than the spurious "resistance" through textual deconstruction: a theory of constitutive antagonisms found in the work of Laclau and Mouffe and Žižek.)

Johan Muller warns against letting the agency of subjects slip into the agency of discourse ("Clare uses her 'femininity' to ensnare Phil" 1985: 40). This is a useful reminder that any theory of the subject has as a basic postulate the notion that agency is the operation of subjects *of* and *in* ideological discourse. "Discourse," "ideology"—these are concepts that refer to the totalizing function of the Symbolic tendency toward mystificatory closure, and to the identifications of the Imaginary where the lacking subject sees itself as complete.

So far this book has spoken of the ubiquity of ideology-in-general, or ideological discourse, and may have suggested that in human cultural life there is nothing apart from ideology and its unconscious functioning. This implies a model of the world, or Nature, that we may accept does exist "out there," but that human beings can only approach through the mediation of culture. True, this notion of culture is a multileveled and complex one, but nevertheless it is one that might seem to suppose that there is no human practice outside of ideology, no such thing as a nondiscursive human practice. We need not be satisfied with this view. In a "jab" at Marxism, Lacan suggested that its fundamental dualism of nature/culture be replaced by nature/society/culture, "the last term of which could well be reduced to language, or to that which essentially distinguishes human societies from natural societies" (1957: 148). "Society" here refers to historical practice; it includes the pathways (Freud's *Bähnungen*) into which the drives are channeled *before* the entry into language. These persist in the form of rhythms, intonations, etc. The triple formulation, then, refers respectively to nature, actual social practices and directed drives, and the linguistic structures determining social life.

So, although Lacan is best known for his work on language and the Symbolic, an indispensable part of his theory is the (Freudian *pre*-Oedipal) *non*-Symbolic realm of the Imaginary. If cultural practices are all those interactive practices of the human being with his or her environment, then the very first practices of the infant are also cultural and therefore (a particular crucial to theory) there are cultural practices that *precede* language. While this point may not seem controversial at first glance, on reflection its implications for a theory of the subject and ideology-in-general become profound. Indeed, by in effect foregrounding the Symbolic and backgrounding the Imaginary, educational analysis tends to revert to a model of individuals adapting to society. CSOE is unable to theorize about the "structural resistance to identity . . . , the splitting of the ego and the inevitable mismatch of subject and culture"—it cannot account for "those aspects of subjectivity 'beyond interpellation'" (Donald 1991: 6). This resistance is, of course, not to be conflated with the conscious, rational, resistance of actors so overstated in critical sociology of education. Rather, it is a resistance to closure that is inherent to all human practices, i.e., it is structural.

Probably because Lacan himself was fascinated with the Symbolic order, and because of the place of the written word in the university, Lacanian cultural analysts have largely followed the tracks of signification and meaning. However, it is clear that the Imaginary, even if undeveloped theoretically, is a nondiscursive domain of culture that is usually ignored by word-drunk academia. There *is*, then, an aspect of human culture that is nonideological, nondiscursive. For example, the work of Foucault demonstrates that social power can act upon the body without being first mediated by consciousness. And we have noted Ogden's (1989) theorization of "the primitive edge of experience" based largely on physical contact and preverbal bodily sensation. A writer who has developed the pre/nonverbal part of Lacan's work is Julia Kristeva (1980, 1986). Repression is necessary for signifying practice, "*signifiance*," and, says Kristeva, the "semiotic order" of channeled energy continues to challenge language and is thus kept at arm's length at the edges of discourse. The semiotic order has the force of "negativity" and reappears as rhythms, tone, and linguistic transformations. The playful fluidity of semiotic and symbolic constitute the field of human life, interpellations being temporary moments of anchorage within that unstable field. Perhaps Kristeva's work provides a way to transcend the fixation on ideology-critique in educational studies.

While acknowledging a debt to Althusser, the theory postulated here is post-Althusserian: the starting point of inquiries are to be the *necessary failures* of ideology. The necessary failure of ideology is, it can be argued, the result of the nature of desire, the missing link of educational theory.

Freud (1937) spoke of three impossible professions: psychoanalysis, government, and education. James Donald suggests, in line with the above pages, that "this 'impossibility' is less a malfunction than a sign of the *necessary* failure of identity in the psyche and of closure in the social" (1991: 8).

From Lacan we learn about the unavoidably fragmentary nature of subjectivity, how the subject lives with the alienated confrontation with his or her lack. Not only is the subject lacking, so is the Other. The unconscious attempts to speak of what is forbidden—*jouissance* and death; but langauge, intonation, symptoms, dreams, etc., can only indirectly represent what is in the end inexpressible—desire.

NOTE

This chapter has been reprinted from the 1995 article "The Unconscious Subject of Education," *Discourse*, 16 (2), pp. 167-89.

EDUCATION AND CHANGE

We are not simply positioned, like a butterfly being pinned to a display board. We struggle from one position to another and, indeed, to break free—but to what?

—Valerie Walkerdine
Schoolgirl Fictions

It is customary at the end of a book to recap what has gone before, and to recommend directions for future study. This concluding chapter is no exception, but in order to do the latter task I have taken the liberty of speculating on how the psychoanalytically rooted theoretical work of the book may amalgamate with other suggestive social theories of social antagonism.

This book has followed this form: Chapter 1 provides a critical review of CSOE, showing the theoretical gap in the discipline, namely around the intricacies of socialization. I suggest that psychoanalysis needs to be looked to in order to consider questions of identity formation. Chapter 2 is a broad review of the work of Freud on social matters. Basic principles of psychoanalysis as well as the field's relevance to questions of "civilization" are demonstrated. The next four chapters constitute the body of the book where it is proposed that the work of Louis Althusser provides a model (the ideological interpellation of subjects) around which a sophisticated theory of identity formation or subjectivity can be built. Chapter 3 argues that the work of Althusser has been largely misread, and that his theory of ideology-in-general is wholly amenable to psychoanalytic development. Chapter 4 expands on the notion of ideology, showing the affinity of Althusser's and Gramsci's concepts of ideology with Freud's psychic model. Ideology-in-general is shown to be a useful way to conceive what is ubiquitous about human culture, the power of ideology lying in its largely unconscious character. Chapter 5 is an expansion of Althusser's notion of interpellation. I suggest that interpellative interactions are like those of the transference-countertransference relationship of analysis. Accordingly, the concept projective identification is traced from Melanie Klein's first usage of the term to the work of Thomas Ogden, the latter of whom shows that projective identification involves actual material change in both subject and object. Chapter 6 focuses on subjectivity, retracing Althusser's steps to Lacan's decentered, lacking subject and its necessarily alienated formation. Althusser's axiom can now be written as follows: ideology-in-general is the field of the social where the split, lacking, alienated, desiring subject is constituted as a coherent, volitional agent by the unconscious externalizing and internalizing interpsychic mechanism projective identification.

The body of the book having filled out Althusser's basic model of ideology-in-general, showing in some detail how identity is formed, this final chapter considers how changes in identity and social changes occur; how "social and economic contradictions are translated into class consciousness or banished therefrom" (Schneider 1973: 59). It also considers the question, What is the place of education in social change? Where the previous chapters walk somewhat doggedly through vast areas of psychoanalysis, this is something of a theoretical fight of fancy, and should be treated as such.

On an everyday level, it is important not to be naïve about the immediate benefits, in the classroom or for research, of the theory of social life extrapolated in this book. When asked why, despite trying to use the insights of psychoanalysis, cultural analysts still know so little about how, say, teenage femininity is acquired, the psychoanalyst Juliet Mitchell replies: "I agree, but with the important proviso that such a usage seems invariably to look for more rapid change than is actually possible." She cites Freud's example of the child breastfed until the age of two but who as an adult still feels deprived of the breast. No matter what happens socially, there is no simple shift across to the realm of psychic absences and frustrations. "The problem is that sociology cannot be made to match the very different structures of the unconscious. Sociology and psychoanalysis operate at completely different levels" (1988: 87). It is important to realise, then, that, although the objects of study are related, there is no simple or even necessary transfer between these disciplines. Any connections must be worked out historically and theoretically. It may be that the concepts built on in this book will contribute to the latter task.

This chapter first describes how the theory of ideology-in-general articulates internally and externally. Second, drawing on the work of Joel Kovel and Allen Wheelis, it proposes a schematic chain of intentional, organized change. Third, it introduces Chantal Mouffe and Ernesto Laclau's discourse theory of social antagonism, as elaborated by the Lacanian Slavoj Žižek, to point toward how the theory of the psychic economy of subjectivity might be developed. Fourth, with regard to the usability of the work of the book, the chapter suggests two possible directions for "the social analysis of education" (Wexler 1987) to pursue with the psychodynamic tools at hand.

ARTICULATION

Dennis Wrong has argued that social theory must be seen primarily as a set of answers to questions about social reality. Important among these are questions that seek transhistorical, universalistic answers: questions about how we are able to form societies, questions about the extent and sources of social change, and questions about how society domesticates our "animal nature." Furthermore, social theory cannot help but make assumptions about human nature, and if these assumptions are left implicit, "we will inevitably presuppose a view of man that is tailor-made to our special needs" (Wrong 1961: 193). CSOE, we have seen, has fallen precisely into the trap of not theorizing about human nature, thereby insinuating very simplistic and inconsistent ideas about society, human motivation, and change in schools. Structuralism and poststructuralism have retheorized the nature of the subject and the social, but, without some notion of drive, nonpsychoanalytic versions of these theories cannot deal with the questions of the "dialectic of selfhood" (Wexler 1981b: 159). Umberto Eco, for example, has spoken of the "world of unlimited semiosis" operating in "a sort of spiral movement, actual objects never being touched as such, but always transformed into significant forms." While this book affirms Eco's point that "in culture any entity becomes a semiotic phenomenon" (1973: 71), it argues that social life is not *only* linguistic. Lacan's work on the pre-Symbolic helps us here. Also, I deny that the Real is never "touched as such"; developments of Klein's term "projective identification" are followed in this regard. In both these cases, the centrality of a notion of drive and desire should be clear.

It is necessary to show how the theory of ideology-in-general is internally articulated, how it joins with the elements borrowed from various theoretical fields, and how the new theory links with other social theory. First, the theory of ideology-in-general has three principal concepts (ideology, interpellation, and subjectivity), and these are linked according to the logic of Althusser's axiom: ideology interpellates individuals as subjects. Second, it has been shown how Althusser himself was influenced by psychoanalysis, and much of the book has been spent trying to spell out psychoanalytic extensions of his formula. Of course, there is a truly perplexing array of schools, mainstream and alternative, making up this loose field of psychoanalytic schools whose theories may or may not eventually be "intertranslatable" (Wertheimer 1988). I have not even attempted to address this problem of commensurability. Instead, I have juxtaposed some of the most interesting and relevant concepts from the psychoanalytic corpus in an attempt to develop CSOE thinking about social dynamics. While not remaining committed to earlier physical/energy metaphors of Freudian instinct theory, a notion of drives is maintained, as it provides an elemental concept with which to consider the innate versus the social. Although Kleinian and object relations theories by and large ignore wider social forces, their constructivism opens the way for considering these forces by highlighting the interpersonal. And while Lacan may appear to have little in the way of therapeutic skills to teach his readers, he provides the theoretical tools needed to address questions of ideology and the subject.

Common notions have been indicated throughout. As unsatisfying as it may ultimately be, this author takes the advice of Stephen Frosh: let these ill-fitting parts be—they cannot be smoothly amalgamated (1987: 272). The theoretical work of this book is an attempt at "theory knitting": integration of the best aspects of a set of theories with one's own ideas about the question under view (Kalmar and Sternberg 1988), setting aside for the present the possible infiltration of unwanted aspects across perspectives (Appel 1992a). As Arthur Stinchcombe (1991) has argued, the criterion for whether lower-level theorizing about mechanisms is fruitful is not that of philosophical fit but whether it improves higher-level theorizing. So the problems, say, of integrating the object relations mechanism of projective identification with the Lacanian notion of misidentification can legitimately be shelved as long as these concepts make the higher-level theory of ideology-in-general more supple, more accurate, or more general. I do feel, however, that Winnicott and Lacan can to a large degree be integrated through the work of Ogden, Bollas, and Kristeva. But this is an idea that remains a wish for now.

The third level of theory articulation to be discussed is that with other social theories. Besides the awkward business of weaving together diverse strands of psychoanalysis, this book has continually concentrated on perhaps the major theoretical macro-micro problem of the century: making Marx and Freud compatible. For psychoanalysis is a theory of social life. "Do you think Adler is the only one, then, who believes that social conflict is important?" asked Freud. "Psychoanalysis has always recognized that denial of one sort or another is the cause of every neurosis" (Wortis 1954: 130). Psychoanalysis is "the body of theories that deals with the unconscious, and *hence* how the social and personal worlds interpenetrate" (Frosh 1987: 270, emphasis added). By only considering the adult in direct relation to the social structures, Marxism has tended to treat the child only as a small adult. Psychoanalysis, through its preoccupation with childhood, has tended to regard the adult as a big child. For Igor Caruso, psychoanalytical theory "can only become truly social when it realizes that, within its own perspectives, it is analyzing social exchanges. . . . The great psychic mechanisms like identification, projection, introjection, repression, sublimation, rationalization . . . exist only because they function, and they function because they are, in reality, historical and inter-psychic" (1965,

25). David Riesman makes this constitutive interdependence of the self and the social clear when he speaks of "the walking delegate from economics: the ego," (1950: 173) and "the walking delegate from ideology: the superego" (174).

Caruso suggests ways forward in the integration of micro- and macro-sociology. He enumerates some of the characteristics of the "psycho-social climate" of capitalism: alienation of work and concomitant anguish; amelioration of anguish by social ideals and certain forms of pleasure; aggression directed into social, racial and political hate, militarism, and criminality; and avoidance of conscious awareness alongside a "sordid materialism." "The family, which is the conscious and above all the unconscious educator of the child, lives, develops, works and disintegrates in this specific climate of insecurity and underlying despair." Adaptation of the family immersed in this psychosocial climate to "the demands of an oppressive and aggressive society" produces reactions of "defence, conformism, fear and insecurity." Thus, "before even coming into contact with the wider ambient society, the family and the child may have fallen victim to the neurotic triad: anguish, aggression, guilt" (1965: 30).

Group psychology, which does straddle the macro-micro divide, has not made an impact on Marxist studies. This is unfortunate, as there are valuable lessons to be learned; the family group provides the "basic pattern" for all other groups. The "emotional drives of the group" have as their source a fundamental ambivalence: "all groups stimulate and at the same time frustrate the individuals composing them; for the individual is impelled to seek the satisfaction of his needs in his group and is at the same time inhibited in this aim by the primitive fears which the group arouses" (Bion 1957: 475).

While the analysis of group psychology is a potentially rich direction for CSOE, it is important to theorize how the small group relates to both broader social relations and to the psychology of the group's members. It is not good enough to confuse an antagonistic social order with either an individual or a social psychogenic disorder. Social factors create particular climates that "increase or diminish the psycho-biological resistance of the person, without for all that 'creating' neuroses" (Caruso 1965: 28). At the level of the family, cultural institutions mediate between historical forces and individual psychology in three ways, according to Igor Caruso. First, particular organizations may increase a predisposition to neurosis. Second, organizations manifest the typical frustrations of individual development. Third, institutional organizations determine the form of expression of these neuroses. The historical situation determines the family, and the familial experience determines the child's fate. It may be necessary to reassert that determination is not being used here in a "hard" sense, which involves predictability (Loptson 1991). If a thing is caused, this does not mean that it is rigidly determined. Saying this does not mean, however, that we have to settle for a theory of randomness: we should rather think in terms of probabilities, but not equal probabilities. If *langue* is the realm of possibility of what might be said, and *parole* is what is actually said, then the freedom to make an utterance within the system remains a relative freedom: "The pressure of current clichés upon our current choice of combinations is considerable" (Jakobson 1956). Not explicitly, but by showing the child how surface rules can be made sense of and made to work in daily life, "the parent is helping the child to develop a 'sense of the social structure,' of what can be taken-for-granted and what can be discussed and questioned" (Cook 1973: 332).

The theory developed here is precisely aimed at addressing questions of how the individual being, through the channeling of desire by social influences, becomes a social subject. The way through the antinomy of structure and agency that dogs CSOE is to focus on the "important tension between subjectivity and collective action as working within historical conditions" (Wexler, Martusewicz, and Kern 1987: 238). This book has concentrated on the first part of this formula; it has theorized the tension at the heart of the complex of interactions "collective/self/collective" in general (Wexler 1991)—what Gilbert Rose (1978), following Winnicott, calls the "transitional process of everyday life." The task now for social analysis of education is to study particular ideologies or discursive practices while employing the concept of ideology-in-general.

Althusser has made a major intervention in the potential overlap of Marxism and psychoanalysis. I have regarded him as a Trojan Horse of radical social theory; a means of smuggling antihumanism, antiidealism, and antihistoricism into CSOE. The theory of ideology-in-general developed from his introductory model of ideology may be useful in the present conjunction of postmodernity, postindustrial production, and poststructural theory. Industrial production is rapidly giving way to the information age, or the semiotic society, where information becomes the primary product, and where the forces of production are less factory machines and more information technologies. In such an age, a "textualist study of discourse may at once also be a study of production" (Wexler 1987: 186). However, current social theories, collectively known as postmodernist, have elevated "to slogans the denial of both self and society, and so [make] it impossible to understand how self and social transformation interact": "a dynamic that begins and ends in collective social life, through the revolution in individual lives" (Wexler 1991: 247). This should be a "post-structuralism suitably leavened by history" (Muller 1989: 75). Textualism will have to accept that lived human experience is "psychological via the social, but first it is social via the psychological" (Caruso 1965: 31).

CSOE, because it is also largely ignorant of macro, international changes in society, cannot understand schools today. For instance, CSOE cannot understand that organized social change does not come about easily, nor can it understand why. The implied shift of many radical educational proposals—from depth to breadth in schooling, from mechanical to organic solidarity, from closed to open schools—arouses great anxiety, abhorrence, and insecurity. It is likely that students, by seeking their own age group as the "source of belief, relation and identity" may produce not an "open society" but a "closed society of the age group" (Bernstein 1967: 353). In other words, it may be that a reason for the disaffection of high school students is that, while the students are "already relating to future organizational and productive forms," schools are modeled on an older pattern (Wexler 1985a: 222). The task after CSOE, says Wexler, is precisely to work out the intricacies of an "immersion in the collective symbolic text, and a systematic understanding of its relation to both the forces of production and the individual unconscious" (227).

WORKING THROUGH, LABOR, AND CHANGE

All writers in CSOE are concerned with the issue of change, and especially the place of schooling in social change. Some, as we have seen, argue that schooling mitigates against change by reproducing the status quo; others emphasize the importance of social resistance in and out of schools and the possibilities for change. Let us get some clarity here—social change happens. Irrespective of what theorists believe about reproduction and resistance, change happens anyway. Indeed, Wexler says that the reason that so much of CSOE is "obsolete, even quaint" is that it has not considered the multilevel change around us. Corporatism has resulted in fundamental changes in social organization (especially in economic production), changes in culture, and changes in personal psychology (Wexler 1985b: 390). When CSOE discusses the possibilities of change, it is not so much concerned about change that happens, however, but with changes that can be organized and effected for the social good. It deals with the kind of changes that can be implemented in and by education—intended social change. This is a discourse of educational activism: what is that can be done via schooling to make the kinds of progressive societal changes we envisage? (If it is true that change can be forced on a person—say, through the physiological changes of adolescence, or by throwing him or her into prison—it is also true that CSOE often implies, and may even lead to, change similarly based on compulsion.) The lack of practical success of critical pedagogy is partly due to societal changes and inertia, and partly due to internal resistances to change in teachers, students, and communities. Radical teachers may wonder why students oppose social changes that are supposedly in the interest of students. But such imposed change is likely to be resisted because it does not take account of the use of institutions by individuals as a defence against persecuting and depressive anxiety (Jaques 1957).

Now, while one must sympathize and align oneself with the admirable intentions of wanting to make society more equitable, it is no doubt true that unless writers understand the nature of change, their strategies will have only a slim chance of success. This is because, it is argued here, social change is in the end a matter of depth psychology, "body and soul" (Wexler 1981a), and is thus more often than not counter-intuitive. Rational analyses and explanations are unlikely to do the job. Wexler, considering collective change, sketches a sequence of the processes of change that psychoanalysis can then elaborate. First, he says, a personal and shared experience of dissatisfaction and frustration is required. Second, knowledge of and belief in alternatives make existing conditions even more intolerable. Third, there is a long period of "cultural distortion" during which limited, regressive, self-destructive solutions are pursued. Fourth, a new cultural vision leads—if the movement succeeds—to reorganized social relations that better satisfy unmet needs. Fifth, changed social arrangements are routinized and institutionalized. CSOE often wants to bypass such a sequence and talks about class struggle as if classes are preexisting entities: in other words, without realizing that "the path from that initial identity politics to the struggle over society's stakes is precisely the path of class formation" (Wexler 1983: 29). A Marxism that imputes particular ideologies to particular classes attributes to the beginning what is the end result of politics; "politics must construct the meanings and deliver the group to the slogans, not assume that the group always 'really' knew the slogans and believed in them. They didn't!" (Hall 1988: 60).

This book tries to throw some light on a crucial moment of psychic change, the moment of interpellation. There is not the space here to elaborate a full theory of change, but the following pages will suggest the parameters of such a theory. In the process it indicates an overlap between the macro-social theories of Marx and the psychical theories of Freud.

Common cause in Left circles asserts that there is no such thing as human nature; everything that appears to be universal about us is in fact the product of social construction. However, Norman Geras (1983) has shown that Marx did have a basic notion of human nature, and Joel Kovel has pursued this matter further: "The core feature of human nature, its most central and essential aspect, is to create and express the self through transformation of the world" (1988b: 386), i.e., labor, or praxis. While Marx may have accepted labor as basic, psychoanalysis can say much about the why and wherefore of labor: it is "dialectically intertwined with desire," it cannot be either purely rationalist or fully biological. "Praxis enables us to eat, but also to prepare our own food as we wish." External, transformable reality and internal awareness of that reality both "contain" desire. "Desire is part of reality, and praxis transforms desire as much as it does the external world" (390). Kovel goes on to make a point which a major part of this book has been spent elaborating: "From the standpoint of praxis there is no purely external world. Because of desire, the subject and object always contain aspects of each other" (390-91).

What is "natural" in human nature is only the willingness to make, and the necessity for the "ensemble of social relations." The needs and the powers are mutually created in the making. It is this broader image of Man the Maker, *Homo faber*, which constitutes the heart of the Labour process. (Kovel 1988a: 170-71)

For Kovel, it is to the detriment of Marxism that it has not followed up Marx's notion of labor as that which is universal to human beings. Marxism, of course, is par excellence the theory that has described human work, the transformation of the world—what Althusser (1965f) calls "social practice." It is to psychoanalysis that we must turn for an understanding of the subjective aspect of labor, the transformation of and by the self (also to be understood as labor), remembering all the while that "the external world contains the internal world, as the internal world contains the external world" (Kovel 1988b: 391).

Allen Wheelis has postulated a helpful model of personality change that may throw light upon the processes of organized social change. Wheelis links together the following necessary elements of how people change:

CONFLICT—INSIGHT—WILL—ACTION—CHARACTER CHANGE

The ends of this chain are arbitrary in that conflict is not the original cause but the result of prior causes, and change becomes the cause of later events. Also, the elements isolated here are only the high points; for example, between "conflict" and "insight" the word "symptom" could have been written (Wheelis 1956: 290).

What Wheelis is adding to psychoanalytic theory is that he makes explicit elements that are only implicit in so much of the literature, viz. will and action. It is quite understandable why psychoanalysis has concentrated on conflict, insight, and change—it is here that the unconscious and analysis of the unconscious is emphasized, will and action being associated with naïve rationalist and voluntaristic approaches to psychology. However, we will see that for Wheelis a serious consideration of will and action is necessary, and that these must be understood within an understanding of unconscious determination.

Conflict

"Variation, opposition, and change inhere in the possibilities of code" (Bernstein 1981: 354). Absolutely central to psychoanalysis is a notion of conflict: internal psychic conflict and conflict between the internal and the external. And while such conflicts are in constant flux, they are in principle never fully resolvable. This is Freud's "pessimism" (Appel 1992b) which so many have found unbearable.

Almost always there will be, not one, but multiple conflicts of varying degrees
of urgency and consciousness, differing greatly in the extent of their relevance
to the events to follow, and each having some bearing on all the others. It is to
these hierarchies of opposing forces that one refers as *the* conflict. (Wheelis
1956: 290-91)

It is not necessary to spell out this theme, as it lies at the heart of every piece
of properly psychoanalytic literature. However, it is worth making a point here
about the relationship between the social and the personal. Wexler has argued
that CSOE has tended to see schooling as the "reproduction or replication of
integrated, rather than contradictory, social structures and processes" (1979:
253). In a study of a high school in Israel, he shows general social antagonisms
between an older pioneering and socialist ethos of the "society person," and a
newer individualized and careerist "salon" culture. Such conflicts are transmitted
into the school and on to the student, but, Wexler insists, not in a simple way;
they are transformed. So,

> an alternative model for the study of schooling would begin with structural
> contradictions and trace the process of their transmission and transformation from
> structural contradiction, through educational policy and school social organiz-
> ation, to individual conflict and ambivalence. (Wexler 1979: 254)

"Socialization," he says, "is a socialization into existing social contradictions.
Personal ambivalence and internal conflict are the result." This book is nothing
more than an attempt to flesh out what some of the processes of this socialization, the development of a "cultural super-ego" (Freud 1930: 141-44), might be.
Crucial to the study of education, though, is the fact that it is not only by
perpetuating dominant values or alienated social relations that the contradictory
social order is reproduced by schooling. Rather, it is maintained by "communi-
cating methods through which individuals can form stable identities in the face
of social contradiction" (Wexler 1979: 255). A little later we will see how the
recent work of Laclau and Mouffe and that of Žižek elaborates on this important
theoretical point.

Discursive self-formation, "becoming somebody" (Wexler 1992), is part of
collective redefinition, which is in turn a stage of collective action; and this
discursive self-formation is a "current active educational principle" (Wexler
1987: 176). External, external/internal, and internal conflicts are all to be
somehow settled within the mind of each person with the tools at his or her
disposal. The reader will recall the reference in Chapter 3 to Alain Badiou's
distinction between a "process of *transformation*" and a "process of *repetition*"
(quoted in Elliott 1987: 100). In order that "the temptations of conventionality"
(Kernberg 1989), habitual methods of adaptation, are not followed repeatedly
and ad nauseam, Wheelis insists that insight, will, and action are required.

Insight

Speaking simplistically, personal freedom exists where thoughts and behaviors are seen as internally elective, while necessity is when they are "determined by forces outside ourselves which we cannot alter" (Wheelis 1973: 24). But in every situation there are always areas of both freedom and restraint. "I receive an invitation to lecture, I automatically decline—this is a rule of mental operation. I think it is something I choose to *do* but it is something rather I have come to *be*. Though accompanied by a feeling of freedom it is deeply determined" (87).

Wheelis demonstrates the paradox at the heart of intended change: "the demonstration of necessity is simultaneously the proof of freedom" (1973: 84). He describes how *A*, his present way of life, has become, through his encounter with psychoanalysis, *B*, insight into the causal relation of *A* to his early experiences with his father. While *A* had appeared free, at *B* segment *A* is seen to have been determined by internalized childhood experiences. The demonstration by *B* that the apparent freedom of *A* was an illusion, that *A* was in fact determined, "has now the effect of creating a *real* freedom in *A*: the understanding of how something was necessarily brought about becomes the means to change it." "The ordinary assumption of scientific objectivity" would be satisfied with *B*, assuming that nothing had determined its emergence. But, as Wheelis says, "if I could be so mistaken about *A*, could I not be similarly mistaken about *B*?" (85). If *B* is now made an object of investigation, he says, it may well transpire that it too, now viewed from *C*, was determined (the insights from psychoanalysis are very different from other possible insights). And so the same movement can be reenacted at a further remove; segment *C*, demonstrating that *B* was really determined, makes it possible for *B* then to become freer. This is a crucial element of real intended change, although the moment of freedom quickly becomes the norm of determination. Crucially too, any particular condition *A* does not lead inexorably to specific insight *B*. To the question, "Why did I fail the exam?" one might answer, "Because the teacher asked that question" or "Because I did not study harder." "The way we understand the past is determined . . . by the future we desire" (115).

Of course, continuous movement in this "upward spiral" does not necessarily happen in anything like a rapid or regular cycle, indeed need not happen at all. Also, this book is not primarily concerned with the possibility of individual change, but instead the workings of the "sequence of collective states within a historical structure" (Wexler 1988: 314); the interlocking of the intrapsychic spiral with the interactive feedback of the interpersonal.

> Like any dialectic, psychoanalysis is a constant and fluid passage from one determination to another. At every stage of its spiral, conditions are transcended

and integrated anew. There is always a reciprocity between man and the world (the world of man being, before everything else, other men), rather than the linear, unilateral causality of metaphysics of mechanistic positivism. (Caruso 1965: 24)

In Wheelis's upward spiral, we can stand back from our lives to a certain degree and see what we are as having been determined; this creates a degree of freedom whereby one, through knowing about the determination, has the possibility to avoid that unfreedom. The relation between freedom and necessity, then,

> is one of complete alternativity: we are altogether free do as we choose, and we are altogether determined to do as we do. . . . The realm of experience is not, therefore, to be seen as divided like Ireland into the free and the ruled. The distinction is hierarchic. Any realm can, in principle, be demonstrated as determined, and in this process there will be created another realm, hierarchically removed, which is free and which may free the first realm which has just been proved to be determined. (Wheelis 1973: 89)

In order to change what one is, insight is not enough; effort and will are necessary. Insight illumines; it is a blueprint. But, while essential to building a house, a blueprint cannot build it; "a time comes when one must take up hammer and nails" (Wheelis 1973: 101).

Will

Crucially, says Wheelis, "will" should not be confused with "free will." "Will is a mental function, as fully determined as any other; and the sense of the necessity or freedom accompanying it is a mental state fully determined as any other" (Wheelis 1956: 290). And if will is not free will, we must also distinguish between will as intention to act (e.g., the intention to post a letter), and "will as it has a bearing on character change, that is to say a major act of will which issues out of needs in conflict and is directed toward a difficult and distant goal" (293). These two instances of will belong to a different order, the former being "conflict-free," while the latter is "the product of conflict and is drive motivated" (293). Obviously this book and CSOE are interested only in the latter type of will. Insight can lead to the formulation of a goal that attempts to reconcile conflicting needs, drawing energy from these needs. Goal formulation may in turn lead to "an intelligent consideration of means, and there is a downward shift of valence to the effect that means become cathected as intermediate ends" (294). Sometimes insight is the factor that enables change, at others it may be will, but "just as surely as will alone is ineffective, so insight alone is ineffective" (298). Wheelis's description of the processes of change is a useful one that the work of Laclau and Mouffe, and Žižek can be used to theorize more fully below.

It must be remembered that these compromise goals can never "promise full gratification of opposing needs; something of each must be renounced" (Wheelis 1956: 295).

> To proceed with awareness and imagination is to be affected by the memory of crossroads which one will never encounter again. Some persons sit at the cross roads, taking neither path because they cannot take both, cherish the illusion that if they sit there long enough the two ways will resolve themselves into one and hence both be possible. (295-96)

It is no easy matter to will change. The social is reproduced and maintained because people are "attached to their routines as elements of their self-constitution and identity" (Wexler 1981a: 258). We continue to address problems in habitual ways even when faced with rational counter-evidence: "unconscious commitments, as well as rational cognitions, connect the self to the social" (258). Collective change occurs when the social order is widely "*experienced* as hopelessly unsatisfying and unrewarding" with the result that people "withdraw the *emotional*, as well as their cognitive commitments" from their customary social relations. "Such a change is also painful, because it includes a self-denial, a renunciation of social identity to pursue untried and unfamiliar solutions" (258). The pain of renunciation is itself a form of inertia that blocks the possibility of change. Wheelis is loath to say, however, that the neurotic is powerless in the face of his or her unconscious conflicts. Giving the example of a neurotic who determinedly takes a number of steps in order to get into analytic treatment through which he eventually finds relief, Wheelis asks, "Could one say that his will had been ineffective?" (1956: 298).

It should not be overlooked, however, that an act of seemingly courageous will can in fact be a resistance to, and flight from, painful insight (Wheelis 1949). And conversely, insight may weaken the will necessary to produce change. Furthermore, will requires tremendous effort and is easily misguided or robbed of its purpose. One can only will with what one has at one's disposal: insight increasing the possibilities of will. Indeed, will is so intimately connected to unconscious motivation for the resolution of conflict that it must be considered to be a representation of libido. So, while an act of will is conscious, it emerges with a struggle from the unconscious, and it has as its aim the lessening of conflict. Will is an indispensable part of intended or desirable change. Will links insight to action; "insight without action is impotent; action without insight is chaotic" (Wheelis 1956: 301).

Action

In an early paper, Wheelis theorizes "The Place of Action in Personality Change" (1950). His question (and, changing "patients" for "groups," the question of critical theory and of Althusser) is, "Why—despite 'insight' and 'working through'—do some patients still cling to neurotic mechanisms and live in a twilight world of anger, frustration, and distorted, partial gratifications?" And conversely, of course, "Why do other patients get well?" (135). The short answer is, "Tension leads to action, and action to personality change" (137), and without (repeated) action, tension cannot produce change. While Wheelis uses outmoded mechanical terms, what he is saying is not far from Kovel's argument that desire leads to labor, and labor to transformation. To illustrate his point, Wheelis tells a story of a young man who, jilted by his lover (ostensibly) because of his lack of money, decides to remedy the situation by committing a robbery. Daydreaming is not enough, says Wheelis; only if the man goes through with his plan, and only if he as a consequence begins to lead a life of crime, will this previously honest man change psychically to become a criminal. One instance of positioning, then, will not produce a new subjective constellation. Personality changes are "new ways of feeling and reacting, new attitudes toward people, a new orientation to many aspects of living which are appropriate to that way of life." So, "a new mode of behavior and the emotional alterations which it produces comprise together a dynamic constituent of personality . . . thinking and feeling" (143).

As action is absolutely necessary to change, its characteristics should be amplified. Continuing with his metaphor of energy displacement, Wheelis asks, As thinking involves the discharge of energy, although in small quantities, is thinking therefore also action? He answers that, besides the quantitative difference, there is also a qualitative difference between action and thought: "Action usually has definite environmental or interpersonal consequences . . . [while] thought is largely confined within one's self, and—in and of itself—has no external consequences" (1950: 145). (Again we see the homology of "action" and "labor.") Action, however, is not limited to gross muscular behavior; an angry glance is a form of action, as are "any of the subtle and apparently slight manoeuvres of interpersonal exchange by which feeling or impulse is conveyed." So action is to be distinguished only from "intellectual, affectless contemplation" (145). While one can query whether any thought can be completely free of affect, Wheelis's point is plain: insight that is understood at a rational level but that does not penetrate more deeply—bodily—will not lead to personality change. On the other hand, deeply felt urges and notions, the kind that express themselves in the transference, may indeed lead to change and may also be regarded as action because, as we have seen in Ogden's work, transference, through projective identification, evokes countertransference—real change both

within the object and the subject. In analysis the following are typical examples
of action: "a friendly glance, a change in inflection, a smile, or crying with an
open acknowledgement of need. These things are more than the absence of
aggressiveness; *they are positive acts in their own right*" (Wheelis 1950: 147,
emphasis added).

Quite obviously, psychic determinism does not imply that people are the
pawns or dupes of larger forces. We are actively involved in our lives, albeit
that a major underbelly of that active involvement is unconscious. On the limited
power of insight and the necessity of action, Wheelis cites James Strachey's
classic declaration: "A mutative interpretation can only be applied to an id
impulse which is actually in a state of cathexis" (1950: 148). This is a statement
one would like to see stamped in large letters over every CSOE exhorta-
tion—what Richard Brosio (1990) calls its "motivational" emphasis—to change
through emancipatory pedagogy.

Change

"The suffering will not disappear without a change in the conflict, and a
change in the conflict amounts to a change in what one is and how one lives,
feels, reacts" (Wheelis 1973: 100). What Wheelis calls identity, or what this
book has called subjectivity, is "the integration of behavior" (11). Action that
defines one may at first have been "fumbling and uncertain," requiring
"attention, effort, will," but it eventually becomes "integrated within a larger
pattern which has an ongoing dynamism and cohesiveness, carries its own
authority" (11-12). Quite obviously, personality change, while it happens within
an individual person, is not a purely individual event. Each person is a social
product and actor, a member of a family, community, and society. Even the
most personal of psychic suffering, psychoanalysis shows, is a standard
repetition of earlier relations with other people, i.e., *social* relations. And the
labor of deep change seldom happens strictly within, and by the efforts of one
person. The analytic relationship, while only involving two people, is of course
also a social relationship. Transference/countertransference marks clinical
psychoanalysis as "a biographical process." "The analyst is at first its facilitator
and then, with the process set in motion, this re-enactment's *dramatis personae*"
(Frank 1991: 26). There is a complex interplay between one's own demons and
abilities and the frustrations and pleasures of the social world of which one is
part. It could be argued that all efforts at personality or identity change are
necessarily also social struggles, in that they impinge upon, are guided by, and
affect other people. Collective struggle would be the case of a more unified,
coherent movement, but it is important to recognize that the differences between
individual and collective attempts at self-construction lie only in the range of
people involved and their level of deliberate organization.

People resist change. We change only with great difficulty: spontaneously from within as a result of biological change; spontaneously from without as a result of changed external circumstance; or sometimes personality might be changed deliberately from within. This third case happens "never easily, never for sure, but slowly, uncertainly, and only with effort, insight, and a kind of tenacious creative cunning" (Wheelis 1973: 101). The upward spiral of change of which Wheelis speaks should not be taken to imply that some people ascend the spiral faster, thereby managing to approach ultimate Truth or Knowledge. For Wheelis, human beings are driven by a need to a "distant truth," which is, paradoxically, also the motivation that sends us searching (1980: 31). I have noted that Kovel (following Marx) states that what makes human beings different from animals is the ability to labor, and makes a convincing case that this is a universal human trait, whereby the self continually seeks to transform itself and the world. This impulse is driven by desire: "The longing of a subjectivity that has not been completed for an object it cannot name. . . . Desire is the wish as such, the experience of lack and impulsion, the want and not the need." Making itself known as passion, desire is "whatever is passionate in human experience" (Kovel 1988b: 387-88). As to why it is that we continually strive for the "object that cannot be named," one need go no further than Lacan, as we have seen in Chapter 6. The very entry into culture is marked by an incomplete, Symbolic relation to the Real, this relation being channeed according to the Imaginary. The lack that drives us is simultaneously the lack we seek to make whole. But it is a lack we can never approach except via the mediations of signification, each subsequent interpretation being only a movement along a chain of signification, not a movement closer to the Real. Or as Kovel puts it, "the referent of the word *nature* is obdurately real and denotes the universe outside of thought or subjectivity; and yet 'nature' can never be other than a human construction"—"All ideas of nature become variations on the theme of Otherness" (1988b: 374, 375).

Wheelis's work is in line with both that of Lacan and Kovel here. Wheelis makes a binary distinction: "the way things are" or the universal "unchanging backdrop," and "the schemes of things" or the historical "changing succession of stage sets." The way things are is "the raw nature of existence, unadorned, unmediated, overwhelming us with dread," while the schemes of things are the systems of meanings, seemingly fixed, that hide the way things are from view (Wheelis 1980: 28). For Žižek, as we shall see, social community only exists as long as people believe in it: "it is literally an effect of this belief in itself" (1990b: 53). Wheelis describes human life as a "search through a succession of schemes of things," always in the hope that each is not a scheme of things but reality, the way things are. But the human subject never finds the way things are. "As each scheme of things breaks down he falls into dread, that is, into unshielded contact with his own coming death. That dread is the goad that drives him to resume seeking, to find yet another scheme of things" (Wheelis 1980: 32). The scheme of things is our effort "to deal with the problem of growing up, aided by the illusion of an eternal future" (Roheim 1945: 249).

There is, then, misery that is not the result of mistreatment, but "that would remain, irredeemable, simply by virtue of . . . being a human being." "What portion of that mistreatment of man by man and of child by parent, all of which *appears* gratuitous, may prove to be the unavoidable outcome of conditions that define the human state?" (Wheelis 1980: 33, 34). The other side of the coin of fear of death is the urge to transcend death (135). "Work or wait—that's the problem" (136). We are impelled to live simultaneously in a mode of having to build monuments in order to gain redemption, and in a mode of having to live in the present; to be human and to live (178). And, it must be remembered, "we live by attachment, not by reason" (178). If there is not someone or something we care for, our lives are not worth preserving. Life has value because of care for others, care "*without (a) reason*! . . . The caring that justifies everything else is itself without justification. It is a leap" (179). Similarly, perhaps, for Wexler "the goal of social action is messianic—a collective return, and social redemption" (1987: 181).

We live within a scheme of things made from the way things are, "but we can never make the scheme of things identical with the way things are" (Wheelis 1980: 69). "A scheme of things can be as large as Christianity or as small as the Alameda County Bowling League" (72). The larger the scheme of things, the greater is its "promise of banishing dread" (72). What is the relationship between the historical and the ahistorical? In some ways the former "relieves the unbearable vision" of the latter (67). Schemes of things, Wheelis concludes, redeem the way things are by giving us strength to bear it, and it does this though interpretation as part of something grand.

> One's individual life is redeemed when it is in the service of the something grand.
> The beginning of the redemption of life is the beginning of culture. All culture is redemption. The history of culture, then, is the history of the changing forms by which a short and brutish life has been redeemed. (68)

And social change may be opposed precisely because the personal stress evoked weakens one's social defences to psychotic anxiety. Changes in social relationships require "restructuring of relationships at a phantasy level" (Jaques 1957: 498); change involves loss, and there must as such be mourning for the lost object in order that it not be repressed only to return as symptom (Freud 1917b).

Other than madness, there is no wholly individual scheme of things. "One's ambition may be secret, but the patterns of meanings that make possible the ambition and within which it may be realized is social" (Wheelis 1980: 71). That social form, the scheme of things, is a collective attempt at redemption in the face of the way things are. And, completing the circle, the nature of the ambition that drives the individual is the unfillable lack within the way things are.

This is the life cycle of a scheme of things. At first it is our view of the world, then it *becomes* our world. "We live within the space defined by its coordinates. It is self-evidently true" (Wheelis 1980: 69). Because of external changes the scheme of things sooner or later "loses authority, is less able to banish dread; its adherents fall away." With the passage of time it fades, becoming "quaint or primitive," a "myth." At this stage "one enters a state of dread. Life is then borne forward on waves of cynicism and dread" (73) until the establishment of a new way things are.

THEORIZING IDEOLOGICAL DISCOURSES

> Any given discourse is the potential sign of a movement within the sociohistor-
> ical filiations of identification, inasmuch as it constitutes, at the same time, a
> result of these filiations and the work (more or less conscious, deliberate, and
> constructed or not, but all the same traversed by unconscious determination) of
> displacement within their space: There is no completely "successful" identifica-
> tion. . . . This may even be one of the reasons why such things as society and
> history exist instead of merely a chaotic juxtaposition (or a perfect supra-organic
> integration) of human animals in interaction.
>
> —Michel Pêcheux
> "Discourse: Structure or Event?"

We have briefly considered Wheelis's model of the process of character change: what he later relabeled as suffering, insight, will, action, change (1973: 102). Although it cannot be elaborated in much detail here, an attempt will be made to show how Wheelis's highly evocative writings can be more fully theorized and integrated with my neo-Althusserian framework.

The reader who has worked through this book will be knee-deep in psychoanalysis. But we need to resist giving psychoanalysis the last word in cultural theory. When we say, as I believe we must, "social reality always exists for a subject," we recognize "a social *real*, whose sheer complexity, heterogeneity and contradictoriness generate dynamics which can only be apprehended symptomatically" (Donald 1991: 7). In this regard, Žižek has begun to theorize a political Lacanianism. Discussing Laclau and Mouffe's *Hegemony and Socialist Strategy* (1985), Žižek says its radical breakthrough is missed by most readers; its "basic proposition" is that "society doesn't exist." "The book's real achievement is to have theorized 'social antagonism'" whereby "the socio-symbolic field is conceived as structured around a certain traumatic impossibility, around a certain fissure which *cannot* be symbolized" (Žižek 1990a: 249).

We know from Althusser, says Žižek, that "the subject-position is a mode of how we recognize our position of an (interested) agent of the social process, of how we experience our commitment to a certain ideological cause" (251). Now we are able to realize that interpellation by definition overlooks "the radical dimension of the social antagonism, that is to say, the traumatic kernel the symbolization of which always fails" (251). Social antagonisms are neither logical contradictions nor objective oppositions, but rather the impossible relationship between two terms. Antagonisms happen outside, not inside, society; indeed, every antagonism "limits the societal effect": "each of them preventing the other from achieving its identity with itself, to become what it really is" (Laclau 1988: 255). The ideological illusion of the interpellations "proletarian," or "feminist," are illusions that the eventual destruction of the antagonistic Other will abolish the antagonism and that one will arrive at an identity with oneself (Žižek 1990a: 251). But this illusion is an inversion; it is not the external enemy that prevents self identity; "every identity is already itself blocked, marked by an impossibility, and the external enemy is simply the small piece, the rest of reality upon which we 'project' or 'externalize' this intrinsic, immanent impossibility." Indeed, it is at the moment of final victory over the enemy that we experience antagonism in its "most radical dimension, as a self-hindrance: far from enabling us finally to achieve full identity with ourselves, the moment of victory is the moment of greatest loss" (252).

This is why Žižek can agree that society doesn't exist. We must, he says, "distinguish between the experience of antagonism in its radical form, as a limit to the social, as the impossibility around which the social field is structured, from antagonism as the relation between antagonistic subject-positions: in Lacanian terms we must distinguish antagonism as *real* from the social *reality* of the antagonistic fight" (1990a: 253). In other words, he is talking about an antagonism around which every manifestation of the social is necessarily structured, not about particular social conflicts. What is at stake in subjectivization is the attempted avoidance of the traumatic experience of self-hindering, or self-blockage. This limit of the social is both that which subverts each subject position, and simltaneously that which sustains it: "the subject is a paradoxical entity which is so to speak its own negative, i.e., which persists only insofar as its full realization is blocked—the fully realized subject would be no longer subject but substance" (254). The subject (-in-general) is of a different order to actual instances of subjectivization; there is always "a certain left-over" of the given universe of meaning that cannot be integrated, "and the subject is precisely correlative to this object" (254).

What it is that holds a community together is not simply symbolic identification; "the bond linking its members always implies a shared relationship toward a Thing, toward Enjoyment [*jouissance*] incarnated" (Žižek 1990b: 51). Freud said as much when describing the libidinal ties of the group, "*a number of individuals who have put one and the same object in the place of their ego ideal*" (1921: 116). Communities never exist as isolated entities, they exist in relation to other communities—"Them": Freud's "narcissism of minor differences" (1930: 114). And what is always feared is the way They enjoy themselves, their enjoyment being experienced by us as theft by them of our own enjoyment. Our fantasies about "the Other's special, excessive enjoyment" are "precisely *so many ways, for us, to organize our own enjoyment*" (Žižek 1990b: 55). Enjoyment is always the enjoyment of the Other, or rather, of that imputed to the Other; and conversely, hatred of the Other's enjoyment is hatred of one's own desired excess of enjoyment. So, what drives this conflictual logic is "not immediate social reality—the reality of different ethnic communities living closely together—but the *inner antagonism to these communities*" (54).

The poststructural celebration of "difference," then, misses the point in this respect: not differences per se, but differences arising out of antagonisms. The possibility of a "politics of difference" (Lather 1991: 107-108) that is unifying and nonantagonistic does not make sense. "Which is it to be? Security and depression? Or freedom and panic? Claustrophobia or agoraphobia?" (de Mare 1975: 158). But there is much to be learned from poststructuralism with regard to theories and texts. Etienne Balibar, Althusser's old collaborator, has recently said that for Marxism the idea of a theory of ideology has usually functioned as filling a gap, "as an *ideal means of completing historical materialism.*" He says that, on the contrary, a program like Marxism can never be filled, "that the theory of ideology denotes no object other than that of the nontotalizable (or nonrepresentable within a given order) complexity of the historical process" (1988: 202, 2033).

Žižek has argued that what distinguishes ethnic subject positions is not just the different content of their symbolic identifications: "What categorically resists universalization is rather the particular structure of their relationship towards enjoyment." He goes on to quote Jacques-Alain Miller:

> The problem is apparently unsolvable as the Other is the Other in my interior. The root of racism is thus hatred of my own enjoyment. There is no other enjoyment but my own. If the Other is in me, occupying the place of extimacy, then the hatred is also my own. (In Žižek 1990b: 54)

What the myth of nationalism (and thus also racism) conceals from us is that the enjoyment that we allege the Other has stolen from us "*we never possessed.*" The root of these fantasies is clearly hatred of one's own enjoyment. Slovenes, for example, says Žižek, repress their own enjoyment by means of obsessional activity, and it is this very enjoyment which returns in the real, in the figure of the dirty and easy-going "Southerners" (55).

The subject "is the name of the void which cannot be filled out with subjectivation: the name of the subject is the point of failure of subjectivation." Perhaps we can then say that ideolo*gies* are phantasies, "imaginary scenario(s) the function of which is to provide a kind of positive support filling out the subject's constitutive void" (Žižek 1990a: 254). Any objectivity is, says Laclau, "crystallized myth." When a myth is thus realized, the subject (-in-general) is eclipsed and reabsorbed by the structure as particular subject position (Laclau 1990: 61). A myth or discourse or ideology, as we have seen, is not simply a set of ideas, it is a "mentality" (Vovelle 1990).

Flowing from Lacanian psychology, we then have two notions: the subject as an empty place or potential imbued in the antagonism; and social phantasy, the ideological mode of the realized antagonism. A myth, or an ideology, is a metaphor that is the product of the dialectic between "absence (dislocation of the structure) and presence (identification with an unachieved fullness)" (Laclau 1990: 63). This is the space of the subject (the lack within the structure). "The subject is the metaphor of an absent fullness," and "the concrete content of its forms of identification . . . function as the very representation of fullness, of all possible fullness" (Laclau 1990: 63). "Everyone," says the psychoanalyst Leonard Shengold, "wants everything" (quoted in Merkin 1991: 532). Myths or ideologies, because they are necessarily incomplete, operate as inverted representations of various instances of structural dislocation: the irony of an ideology is that its appearance of satisfying fullness is constituted by lack.

Along these lines, Laclau has provided some theoretical clarity to the kinds of problems that beset disciplines like CSOE. On the matter of the social agent/structure, he shows that the opposition of a structurally fully determined society and one that is the creation of social actors "is not an opposition between different conceptions of the social, but is inscribed in social reality itself"; "the subject exists because of dislocations in the structure" (254). Society is not a "sutured space," it is "an ultimate impossibility, an impossible object; it exists only as the attempt to constitute that impossible object or order." What is more, hegemonic relations and struggle, says Laclau, are inconceivable within a theory of fixed meanings or false consciousness. He gives the example of the signifier "woman," which out of its context has no meaning, but which can enter into "a relation of equivalence" with "family" and subordination to men or, alternatively, with oppressed people (1988: 255). Žižek (1989) has used the Lacanian notion of *point de capiton* to show how floating signifiers are discursively fixed and linked at a nodal point in an "ideological quilt." So, "dislocation is the source of freedom. *But this is not the freedom of a subject with a positive identity*—in which case it would just be a structural locus; rather it is merely the freedom of a structural fault which *can only construct an identity through acts of identification*" (Laclau 1990: 60, emphasis added). Althusser's theory of ideology-in-general has been developed in this book, and here we can begin to see how specific instances of projective identification produce subjectivities in antagonistically structured space.

Laclau also provides a way of thinking the power/subject relation that avoids externalizing power as something exercised on or by subjects. Any acts of identification or of decision are acts of power; and power is ambiguous, "to repress something entails the *capacity* to repress, which involves power; but it also entails the *need* to repress." Power is, then, "the trace of contingency," and objectivity "a power whose traces have been erased."

> On the one hand, then, we have decision—that is, identification as opposed to identity; and on the other, the discernable marks of contingency in the decision, that is, power. The ensemble of these marks cannot therefore be objective; it must be the location of an absence. This location is precisely that of the subject. Subject equals the pure form of the structure's dislocation, of its ineradicable distance from itself. (Laclau 1990: 60)

"There is politics because there is subversion and dislocation of the social." But while "*any* subject is, by definition, political" (61), to examine subject position- ing in contemporary societies is the same thing as inspecting the marks that historical circumstance has inscribed on what wrongly appears to be the objectivity of our societies. Dislocations and social demands are inscribed onto the surface, which is myth. Plainly, such an inscription must be incomplete, otherwise the inscription and the surface would be wholly symmetrical, "thus eliminating any distance between the act of expression and what is expressed by it." But, as the process is never complete, our attention may be directed away from what is inscribed to the process of inscription itself. Social myths, then, are "essentially incomplete: their content is constantly reconstituted and displaced" (63). Here Laclau shows the relationship between the in-general form of ideology, myths, and subject on the one hand, and particular ideologies, myths, and subject positions on the other.

Wheelis's schemes of things are ideologies or discourses. And, like Laclau, we are now in a position to answer the question, How are ideologies trans- formed? "The answer is: *through class struggle, which is carried out through the production of subjects and the articulation/dis-articulation of discourses*" (Laclau 1977: 109). But this formulation is a theoretical, analytical structure, not an instrument for political prediction. Politics has a "*necessary openness*"; "somebody else might have a more effective politics and organize the class around some other slogan; then the connections get forged in another way" (Hall 1988: 60).

A Word on Terminology

In this concluding chapter I have purposely introduced a range of terms as being more or less equivalent in meaning to the central concepts addressed in the body of the book, viz., ideology-in-general, ideologies, subjectivity, and interpellation. The following terms have cropped up: discourses, mentalities, myths, the ways things are, schemes of things, self, identity, and so on. The reason for allowing these terms is to demonstrate that this book is not by any manner of means the first attempt to address itself to issues of macro-micro linkages. Poststructuralism, especially the work of Foucault, is only the most fashionable of current theory that wishes to understand the social/self relation. Indeed, the mainstream sociologists Muench and Smelser put the matter very well:

> Both microscopic processes that constitute the web of interactions in society and the macroscopic frameworks that result from and condition these processes are essential levels for understanding and explaining social life. . . . It seems to us that to strive for better theoretical and empirical understanding of these processes constitutes a proper agenda for the coming years. (1987: 185)

There are many ways to take on these problems, and psychoanalysis via the Althusserian route is but one.

The basic terms of this theory of ideology-in-general carry baggage that seems impossible to shake off, that of ideology-as-false consciousness. The question then arises, As one cannot legislate how people use terms, is it not better to coin new terminology than redefine the old? To, say, restrict "ideology" to meaning mystification, and adopt "discourse" for the larger notion of system of significatory practices (Barrett 1991: 168). There are two problems that weaken this attempted solution. First, even the introduction of new terms does not guarantee the understanding of new concepts; there is no reason that a writer intellectually committed to an oppressor/oppressed understanding of history will accept what is assumed to be implied with the new term. Paul Willis and Philip Corrigan (1983), to give an example, use "discourse" and "cultural forms" as synonyms for "ruling class ideology" and "working class culture." Owen van den Berg (1986), to give another, uses the expressions "dominant discourse" and "useful rhetoric." The conceptual difficulty of some novel ideas, together with adherence to old notions, makes the adoption of new terms an unlikely strategy for overcoming terminological difficulties.

Second, it may be that one wants to build onto a concept despite the baggage borne by the term, even at the price of having to continually define one's own meaning. That has been the case in this book: while it is true that some theories of discourse say very nearly what a theory of ideology-in-general says, they do not have an adequate way of talking about subject production. (James Donald has shown the damaging absence of the unconscious in the neo-Foucauldian work of Ian Hunter and Nikolas Rose [1992: 89-97].) So, at the risk of talking in outdated language, Althusser's theories have been developed here. On top of his theory of subjectivity, his work represents a "point of no return within Marxism" (Barrett 1991: 109); it may be that by using his theoretical vessel of ideology-in-general the radical analysis of CSOE can begin dipping its fingers in the unconscious.

That having been said, there is no other sensible reason for hanging onto terms that demand excessive clarifications every time they are used. What is at stake is not the redemption of this or that *word*, but the development of a sophisticated and useful *concept*. This writer feels the need to transmit into CSOE ways of thinking about the rules for the rules that become "epistemo-logical enforcers" of what and how people think, live, and speak (Said 1988: 10). Althusser's theory of ideology-in-general can, I suggest, function as a *point de capiton* that quilts together Marxism, psychoanalysis, and poststructuralism. Whether this is called "ideology-in-general" or "discourse" is a minor matter of academic institutional strategy.

EDUCATION AND CHANGE

Now that we have the beginnings of a psychoanalytic theory of social stability and change compatible with Althusser's theory of ideology-in-general, the task becomes one of using this outline to explicate what happens in education.

Wexler has noted that, currently, "the relation between education and collective action is a contradictory one" (1983: 35). School is characterized by fragmentation, while collective action involves fairly unified action. This does not, of course, mean that group formation and struggle do not happen in schools, but rather that it is pointless simply to exhort people in educational institutions to optimism, resistance, and change; there are institutional and psychological reasons why intended, organized change is most difficult to effect. Writing, somewhat generously, of CSOE, Wexler notes that its adherents share "a commitment to social progress as well as to science, a hope for a more just and rational society." There is a danger, though, that the former commitment will come to dominate; he says it supplants "our scientific and craft criteria for knowledge and urges upon us the gauge of political efficacy" (1985c: 1). There is such a great felt need for "conscious collective action" that progressive educators "rush to market with packaged, dehistoricized plans for educational interventions into class formations, which we then call pedagogy" (Wexler 1983: 34). While it would be easy and comforting to promote a particular set of educational practices as liberating—as action research has done (Davidoff and van den Berg 1990)—the theory of ideology developed in this book does not lead inevitably to any particular pedagogical practice. Indeed, I have argued that theoretical work is never to be collapsed into policy work (Appel 1993).

Basil Bernstein says that in the end "it can be different: whether the 'it' refers to sociology or society, for in the end the two are the same." Taken as it stands, this is a statement that would be eagerly appropriated by critical pedagogues. But Bernstein proceeds to say that a sense of the possible should not come from socialization into a particular intellectual sect, but from "more dedication to a problem": the study of "the ambiguities and contradictions upon which our symbolic arrangements ultimately rest" (1975: 160). A critical pedagogy cannot be theorized in the academy and successfully implemented in schools with more than token effect (Wexler, Martusewicz, and Kern 1987: 228). Pedagogic activists, while they might benefit from understanding more of the depth and complexity of social and identity change, must develop their strategies in and out of their historical situations. We need to move "outward, and then back to the specific," to see education as part of a "wider social process" (Wexler 1986: 465). Just as no ahistoricized strategy can be regarded as appropriate in every historical instance, so no particular historical conjuncture is necessarily tied to any particular strategies. Or, to use the language of Laclau, "no collective imaginary appears essentially linked to a literal content." There is "no common measure between the dislocated structure and the discourse aiming to introduce a new order and a new articulation" (Laclau 1990: 65).

Enlightening and convincing descriptions of the postmodern condition abound, but I cannot agree with either those who lament this condition or those who applaud it. It seems to me that it is simply not true that the postmodern self is any more alienated that the self at any other time; identity, of whatever hue, is founded on fundamental structural splits: internal, external, internal/external. It may be that the multiplicity of subject positions is greater and more fleeting today than in the past, but there is no alteration in principle to subjectivity itself. With regard to "the *experience* of modernity—of what it is to be a modern 'subject'" (Frosh 1991: 8)—Laclau does suggest that no narrow discourse or myth will solve the ideological problems and demands of current postmodern dislocations: "the more the objective organization of that group has been dislocated, the more [the] 'basic principles' will have to be shattered, thereby widening the areas of social life that must be reorganized by a mythical space" (1990: 66). In other words, not only is wholeness as impossible as ever, today even the ideological *experience* of wholeness is increasingly difficult to achieve and sustain.

In relation to "closed mass culture," Wexler sees collective action to control the new means of semiotic production as the way in which the new subject becomes self-constituting. To develop this desire and capacity requires "a combination of defamiliarization and organization" of the "apparatus of meaning-production," which includes school knowledge (Wexler 1982a: 299). *"The relation between mass discourse and individual formation and motivation is the emergent educational relation"* (Wexler 1987: 175). Indeed, the common practices of the new social movements are what he means by education (1987: 183); "school is society" (Wexler 1990b). Schools are "places for making the CORE meaning of self or identity among young people" (3). Although expressed in different terms, perhaps what Wexler is saying is similar to what Laclau would have us believe about society as being "ultimately unrepresentable: any representation—and thus any space—is an attempt to constitute society, not to state what it is." "This final incompletion of the social is the main source of our political hope in the contemporary world: only it can assure the conditions for a radical democracy" (1990: 82). Wexler, too, is saying that society is not a finished thing but a making of meanings and identity, and education, broadly defined, is an important means by which this happens.

NEW DIRECTIONS

Once the can of worms that is psychoanalysis is opened, what to do next in the social analysis of education becomes a question with many possible answers. Following are two areas where it seems suitably psychoanalytic sociology can contribute to what we know about education: the level of the pedagogical relation and group psychology, and the level of discourse theory. To avoid the antinomies of CSOE, these should not be regarded as distinct areas, but rather as dialectically related levels of the same general object of study, education.

Group Dynamics in Educational Settings

The first level at which psychoanalysis can help to develop the social analysis of education is the classroom and school institutional level. Within any educational setting the defining relationship is that between teacher and student. Recollecting his own school days, Freud said that the emotional ties between student and teacher "was a perpetual undercurrent in all of us" and that the path to school knowledge leads through, or is blocked by, the teacher. It is "hard to decide whether what affected us more and was of greater importance to us was our concern with the sciences that we were taught or with the personalities of our teachers." (1914a: 242). Wexler's school ethnography throws light on the pedagogic relation between teacher and student as "the quintessential social relation where emotional commitment and caring are required for success" (1990b: 10). As Freud said, "only someone who can feel his way into the minds of children can be capable of educating them" (1913: 189). However, instead of finding the emotional dynamics of identification, attachment, and caring, in the three schools that he and his colleagues studied, Wexler found a "decline in the public sphere that is school": lack of care and withdrawal from interaction; desocialization and withdrawal from public life; and unintended assault of the self (1990b: 21). Future empirical studies of the pedagogic relation today would do well to start with Freud's *Group Psychology and the Analysis of the Ego* (1921) and Fritz Redl's (1942) excellent elaboration of the central person, the initiatory act, and the spatial repetition compulsion.

Group psychoanalysis should be able to throw light on both Cooley's groups: primary groups, where character development through affective interchange is basic; and secondary groups, which are "cold, impersonal, contractual and formal" (Bernard 1982). Indeed, schooling is an odd combination of these. Psychoanalytic tools can lead beyond the small group to society as "an intelligible field of study" through the study of groups: "society is present in the group; society and the group are present in the individual" (Khaleelee and Miller 1985: 382). Tom Main has suggested, for example, that an understanding of the workings of projection and projective identification may have particular value in the analysis of interpersonal behavior in large groups in institutions like the hospital (and, we might add, the school). Mutual projective processes alter not only the self but also the behavior of the world toward the self. R.D. Hinshel-wood (1987) has already gone some distance toward developing a model of how projective identification operates in the therapeutic group; it involves forms of dramatizations as well as verbalizations, barriers and alliances, roles, and scapegoating, and may produce demoralized and fragmented, or containing, groups. Psychosocial compromise formations reduce anxiety by projective identification with, as has been shown earlier, "the accompanying exchange between subject and object," thus strengthening group cohesion. "Seen in this light psychoanalysis is not merely representational psychology, a psychology of the subject, but also a psychology of the unconscious components of *real* interpersonal relationships" (Heigl-Evers and Heigl 1982: 234). Of course, for an understanding of any group to be sociological, it must be contextualized: "the group is always before the person. . . . It is the group which expresses the Self or the person" (Fiumara 1982: 179). Psychoanalysis can also help to show with some sophistication how a "kind of societal context creates a special type of personality structure" (Hopper and Weyman 1975: 187).

What is being suggested here is that considerable groundwork has been done for the analysis of group dynamics in educational institutions, whether schools or otherwise. But it remains unclear how to study, in a socially situated way, the drive-motivated dynamics of people in face-to-face interactions: "the individual in the communal, rather than to study a psychology of the community" (Hinshelwood 1987: 18). Similarly, we are a long way from knowing how to look at larger groups as the complex integration of a set of internal worlds. A group of twenty or more members is different from a group of eight, because in the larger group "a cultural texture comes into play which may be untenable in the smaller group" (de Mare and Piper 1982: 376). This book has raised some ways to conceptualize these problems—problems of CSOE too—like, how to affect change in small groups, and how to spread the change about a large institution (Menzies 1989: xi). It is here that a theory (based on a model of ideology-in-general—of the formation and nature of discourses) may be necessary. Yael Shalem (1992) has made an impressive foray with her study of identity production of white, English-speaking teachers in South Africa. In this study she puts empirical flesh onto the Laclau and Mouffe theory of social antagonisms, although there is a neglect in her study of unconscious desire.

(There is no need to "demand too much elegance in the lower-level theory if one wants to get on with one's research at the aggregate level" [Stinchcombe 1991: 386]. While lower-level theories must be pursued rigorously, it must be kept in mind that the task of the study of mechanisms is to improve higher-level theory, generally by making it more predictive.)

Discourse and Education

A second possible level at which psychoanalysis can enable social analysis of education is that of the study of particular ideologies or myths and their relation to education. Žižek uses the Lacanian notion of *jouissance* to understand the problem of the discourses of nationalism and racism. The scheme of things, or what Žižek calls with relation to nationalism "the Nation-Thing," is not reducible to a set of values of group identity. It is "our Thing," accessible only to us, but with noncomprehending others—"Them"—constituting a constant menace. Although our Thing appears to give fullness to our lives we cannot articulate it, resorting to empty tautologies like "the real thing," and "our way of life." "All we can do is enumerate disconnected fragments of the way our community organizes its feasts, its rituals of mating, its initiation ceremonies—in short, all the details by which is made visible the unique way a community *organizes its enjoyment*" (Žižek 1990b: 52). "Here we encounter the Real, that which 'always returns to its place' (Lacan), the kernel that persists unchanged in the midst of the radical change in society's symbolic identity" (56). It is not necessary here to do more than point toward the fact that *jouissance*, libido, energy, and love all bring into the foreground a notion of drive—"the cloven hoof of sex" (Riesman 1950: 187)—that is at the core of discourse, culture, ideology, social life. Plainly, then, discourse is not oppressive myth to be opposed by resistant cultural forms (Willis and Corrigan 1983). Or, to use Gramscian terminology, hegemony does not involve organizing elements whose class character never changes; rather, "hegemony is a process of rearticulation, of the internalization, through new articulations of something that was external" (Laclau 1988: 252).

"The pure discursive effect doesn't have enough 'substance' to exert the attraction proper to a Cause"; the "substance that must be added before a Thing can come into existence is 'the only 'substance' acknowledged by psychoanaly-sis"—*jouissance* (Žižek 1990b: 53). Or, in Winnicott's terms, the earliest transitional object, loved, attacked, and comforting, is the prototype of all future symbolizations. These are not dry ideas, but rather Imaginary, conflicted searches for a lost symbiosis. Once such a concept is accorded the necessary ambivalent affect by the educational investigator, it can provide a bridge between the early and the later, the inner and the outer, affect and cognition (Grolnick 1978). "A nation exists only as long as its specific enjoyment continues to be materialized in certain social practices, and transmitted in national myths that structure these practices" (Žižek 1990b). The suppressed classes can identify with their despised masters: they may see in them their ideals. Only relations of such a "fundamentally satisfying kind" can make comprehensible how so many societies "have survived so long in spite of the justifiable hostility of large human masses" (Freud 1927: 13). Deconstructionists who make the point that Nation is simply a "contingent discursive construction" are wrong here; they do not see "the role of a remainder of some real, non-discursive kernel of enjoyment which must be present" (Žižek 1990b: 53).

This focus upon the nondiscursive leads us to the work of Julia Kristeva. There is a contradiction at the heart of *signifiance*, as we saw in Chapter 6, which makes every instance of reproduction an instance of possible mutation. Indeed, Kristeva points to further instability within myths. All signification is premised upon the semiotic, and, because the semiotic is the product of the repression of elements undesirable to the Law of the Symbolic, signification is always in constant struggle with the semiotic. Michele Barrett (1988) is another who wants to rescue the aesthetic aspect of culture that Marxism's emphasis on meaning and meaning production simply rejects as reactionary mystification. It is not only poetic language, art, religion, and magic that bear the mark of the semiotic; indeed, all ideological practice must necessarily feel its disruptive influence. The catch-phrase "ideological struggle" thus gains a new complexity. Rather than bludgeoning people into insisting on its existence because it sounds undialectical not to do so, Kristeva, through Lacan and thus through Freud, provides us with an explanation of why ideology and the semiotic must and do exist in struggle.

It should be added that Kristeva's refinement does far more than this. She provides a theoretical road out of Eco's "world of unlimited semiosis." Kristeva proposes a cultural realm that is nondiscursive (if by discursive one means Symbolic). The theoretical ramifications of this are vast. Here we have a model that is somehow *post*-poststructuralist. While poststructuralism has argued that the "real" is a network of signifying discourses, Kristeva's focus on the preling-uistic and thus nonsignifying *semiotic chora* provides another way to develop an argument that there is more to social life than ever-absent Nature and its representations in discourse; this is the Imaginary and its unerasable traces of desire.

The unstable relation between Laclau's literal content of the mythical space and its representation of fullness denotes the potential of discursive disarticulation/rearticulation. If the form of fullness predominates, the myth becomes invisible and is experienced as hegemonic. This leads to more and more social demands being added to the literal content in order for their resolution into the greater fullness. It may be that the form of fullness cannot accommodate all the demands being made, and, gradually, or in a crisis of identity, the literal content of the mythical space begins to dominate with the decline in the ability to hegemonize. "The mythical space will lose its dimension of imaginary horizon. In practice, mythical spaces move on an unstable balance between these extremes: for longer or shorter periods they have a certain relative elasticity beyond which we witness their inexorable decline" (Laclau 1990: 67). When the moment of representation (as opposed to the inscription itself) comes to dominate, "myth is transformed into an imaginary"—a horizon or "absolute limit which structures a field of intelligibility and is thus the condition of possibility for the emergence of any object" (64). Social resistance—that great slogan of CSOE—then is to be explained as "the outcome of a dissonance which emerges in the agent herself between the different kinds of predicates which might be true of her" (Hinton 1988: 8).

Michael Ryan shows how difficult it has been for the academic Left to grasp what is at stake in some of the theories it appropriates: "social rupture and radical change . . . are not future events; they are permanent possibilities inscribed in the very structure of an inegalitarian society" (1988: 485). By now it should be clear that, given the theoretical premises driving his argument, there can be no such thing as an "egalitarian society," that society is by definition essentially antagonistic. This is not to say that life cannot be made better for people, but that the evaporation of inequalities of every kind is a wish being imposed on theory, to the detriment of theory. It sometimes seems that radical social theory cannot help essentializing the lower classes and their place in history: either they are the potentially revolutionary proletariat or the endlessly deluded masses of authoritarian society. But historical study, as long as it is reasonably free from such essentializations, reveals that in even the most extreme situations the conflictual symptoms of antagonisms have been present (Hall 1988: 72).

The theory of ideology-in-general can deal seriously with the emergence of apparently whole discourses and their dissolution. CSOE "fails to develop an alternative, liberating perspective, an alternative cultural basis for meaning and personal identity" (Wexler 1981a: 248), what Hall calls "a cultural politics capable of mobilizing alternative social identities" (1986). But this vision is not the same thing as an illumination of false consciousness, the demonstration to the oppressed that they are oppressed by class, gender, etc., forces, as much of critical pedagogy would have it. Žižek argues that

> the Bondsman frees himself from the Lord only when he experiences how the Lord was only embodying the auto-blockage of his own desire: what the Lord through his external repression was supposed to deprive him of, to prevent him from realizing, he—the Bondsman—never possessed. (1990a: 252)

How is a collective imaginary—"a point of coincidence" between egos (Freud 1921: 107)—constituted, and also undone? A social group "proposes" a mythical space of a social order made up of a series of measures to overcome its set of dislocations. As long as there is a direct link between the mythical space and a specific dislocation, the possibilities of expansion of the horizon are severely limited. But, we have seen, the mythical space is always more than and other than, the dislocation, and it therefore contains the potential for "radicalizing the metaphorical moment of the representation." What is needed for the myth to become autonomous from the "literality" of the original dislocation, and for the myth to become an imaginary horizon, is that other dislocations and demands be "added to the fullness that the mythical space must represent" (Laclau 1990: 64). Conversely, as a myth becomes able to integrate fewer dislocations and demands, the dissolution of the collective imaginary happens. Rob Nixon gives the example of South Africa where, since the political liberalizations of February 2 1990, the discursive antagonism of apartheid state/democratic movement has become blurred and "Everybody Claim Dem Democratic" (1992). "The space is, so to speak, re-literalized; its power of metaphorization is reduced, and its dimension of horizon is thus lost" (Hall 1988: 65).

The mythical space has two tasks, "expressing its concrete content and representing 'fullness' as such." But there is no necessary connection between the dislocation and the way it is to be represented. Therefore a myth which "presents itself as the embodiment of fullness" may be accepted by a group. Not just any discourse will be accepted, however; it must be credible and make no "clash with the basic principles informing the organization of the group" (Laclau 1990: 66).

For Žižek, Laclau has articulated "the contours of a political project based on an ethics of the real, of 'going through the fantasy (*la traversée du fantasme*),' an ethics of confrontation with an impossible, traumatic kernel not covered by any *ideal* (of the unbroken communication, of the invention of the self)" (1990a: 259). Such a confrontation entails not resignation, but "enthusiastic resignation": enthusiasm being used here in the Kantian sense of "experience of the object through the very failure of its adequate representation. Enthusiasm and resignation are not then two opposed moments: it is the 'resignation' itself, i.e. the experience of a certain impossibility, which incites enthusiasm" (259-60). (The potential overlap here with Buddhism needs to be explored. For a tantalizing start, see Epstein 1995.)

Much more work needs to be done on the details of a theory of ideology-in-general or discourse. Such work would be incalculably assisted by concrete studies of particular discourses, or "interpretive repertoires" (Potter et al. 1990) in educational settings. This suggests a productive reciprocity between the two levels of future research I have indicated: group psychology and discourse theory. For instance, empirical studies of groups in educational settings may help to develop, within a theory of social antagonism, a crucial area raised by Freud (1921), viz. that the libidinal bonds of groups are not only hatred of the pleasure of the Other, as Žižek has said, but also repressed envy of fellow group members as well as guilt over phantasized patricide. Another social antagonism, then, is that between the selfish demands of the individual and the altruistic demands of the group. It will be remembered that Lacan said that aggression is released "in any relation to the other, even in a relation involving the most Samaritan of aid" (1949: 6). The ambivalence of emotional ties must still be theoretically incorporated. Wexler's ethnography is a rare instance of a theoretically developed and developing study: he describes how internal tears and ambivalence define students' "work of becoming somebody," and he explains, in terms not dissimilar to those of Laclau and Mouffe and Žižek, that "'identity' is the denial of socially organized symbolic production" (Wexler 1988: 303).

Those who find the psychodynamic emphasis of this book convincing should beware—although psychoanalysis is regarded by many with scorn and abhorrence, it is all to easy, alternatively, to adopt some of its concepts without what is fundamental, namely drive. There are already several examples in the pedagogic literature that blithely advocate "breaking down student resistance" in order to "deprogram freshmen" and calling this "politics" (Davis 1987; Jay 1987; Ulmer 1987). Barbara Johnson (1982) advocates "teaching ignorance," "the pursuit of what is forever in the act of escaping, the inhabiting of that space where knowledge becomes the obstacle to knowing—*that* is the pedagogical imperative we can neither fulfil nor disobey" (1982: 182). Such deconstructionism is indeed impressive, showing as it does that *aporia*—Plato's "perplexity" and Freud's "everyday unhappiness"—should be a goal of pedagogy (Appel 1990). But it cannot begin to tell us "how children fail" in schools (Holt 1982). Pedagogy, like therapy, is not simply a matter of "changing people's minds, we are changing their interactions" (Schermer 1982: 204).

"The problem of education is a problem in the capacity of our cultural forms to engage the commitments and energies of the people who comprise society" (Wexler 1990b: 4-5). "Teaching is the everyday practice of creating culture," and educators stand "between the general culture and the individual. They link cultural drives, the expression of practical competence and personal identity with public issues" (8). "What is required is to rebuild the institutional core" (Wexler 1990b: 31). Of course Wexler does not sanction either the artificial, designer models of radical intellectuals or the romanticization of current practices of oppressed groups. Rebuilding the institutional core will happen in broad historical struggles and can only be addressed obliquely by isolated theoreticians.

I would agree that Wexler has pinpointed what is at stake in education if that core is understood as an incomplete and changing myth of fullness. The existence of a space for these relatively unifying new visions is theoretically elaborated by Laclau: "*The incomplete character of the mythical surfaces of inscription is the condition of possibility for the constitution of social imaginaries*" (1990: 63). Looking at the American curriculum scene, Johan Muller has extracted three general positions with regard to "the possibility and desirability of social and normative integration in late modern society" (1991: 14). The "thick" notion of the necessity of the unifying function of ideology and culture sees a community of values as constitutive of society as a nation. The "thin" view sees normative integration as neither possible nor desirable: "commonness can only be built on and out of difference" (15). In between these extremes is a Rortian "cheap" position of "thinness" plus western procedural justice and democracy. If, Muller says, there is any truth in the thin position, then "societies are heading for a world of difference" and a notion like, say, "the South African nation, at least in a strong sense, is a chimera" (16).

The social analysis of education needs to retain a certain realistic modesty in what it advocates. We will not, can not, find a stable "home" that does not depend on repressing differences (Bromley 1989); this is a "family romance" (Freud 1909) where the community is the longed-for, containing "mother" (Hinshelwood 1987). The theory of ideology-in-general elaborated in this book suggests that new interpellations cannot easily be imposed on people, and that at best we can achieve temporary fullness: but that this fullness is always achieved at a price. Unconscious acceptance of a myth always entails the development of an enemy, the Other of desire. There is the constant danger that the establishment of communities simultaneously and necessarily results in racism or other deep prejudice on which the community depends for its very existence. As mentioned in Chapter 3, Freud argued that all groups are loving internally and externally cruel (1921). And there are further prices to pay; drives inevitably come into conflict with the norms of civilization and are limited, denied, repressed. "Culture is repressive," writes Philip Rieff (1990: 369).

It might be asserted that the theory of ideology-in-general developed in this book is flawed in that it does not produce plans for action. Such a criticism would be both true and misguided. The theory developed above is not a program of action, nor does it aim to lead in any direct way to such a program. It is an attempt to construct a framework through which to answer (not in any final or scientistic way) some of the questions that sociology is "about," "the network of relationships we call society" (MacIver and Page 1950: v). But more than not setting out to come up with political strategy, this book suggests what political goals are; it leads us to the conclusion, for example, that desire for a Nation in a strong sense is, first, an infantile wish that cannot be achieved and, second, may of necessity lead to oppression. Also, calls for a "politics of difference" or a "pedagogy of the unknowable" (Ellsworth 1989: 318) have a very long way to go in order to become more than assertive posturing.

As for trying to theoretically justify programs for political unity (while claiming that this is different to all other totalitarianism), it might be worth reconsidering Freud's words: "Man's helplessness remains and along with it his longing for his father, and the gods" (1927: 17-18). Raymond Williams has called the argument for a "culture in common" dangerous and unreal. In a "common culture," on the other hand, "the only absolute will be the keeping of the channels and institutions of communication clear, so that all may contribute, and be helped to contribute" (1968: 38). In which case, the most we can and should hope to achieve as a communal alternative to "the dreadful loneliness of a society of comfortable, isolated monads connected to each other by the umbilical cord of the electronic society only," is education for democracy that "articulates with a *sense of possibility* which is necessary before struggles can sharpen their purpose and direction, can take specific curriculum issues as fightable and winnable" (Muller 1989b: 7). Michael Peters and James Marshall, two of the more sober CSOE writers to have embraced poststructuralist theories, suggest that "empowerment may depend upon a recognition of 'community-in-process'; that 'in-process' means an historical projection which, working through the differences of gender, race and class in collective self-reflection, can provisionally re-establish an unforced unity of community" (1991: 133). This provisionality is of a piece with the arguments outlined above, but it is some distance from proposing particular political/educational strategies. It suggests support for tolerance, but says nothing about socialism or any other political formations. Which is perhaps as it should be; an academic may sit and day-dream up a program of action that flows from activist wishes, but such a program is unlikely to be of any significant effect unless it happens to fulfill the wishes of other people's dreams and the murderous, incestuous, and selfish impulses that accompany these.

Another criticism of the theory of ideology-in-general might be that it replaces a hard economic determinism of Marxism with a hard psychoanalytic reductionism. While such a trend must be guarded against, it is not a necessary result: "What is constituted are the fragmentary subject positions that are then open to a range of subsequent interpellations" (Hall 1988: 68).

To end this long journey through Marxism and psychoanalysis, it is worth

considering the richness of Kovel's words about human nature; such a notion
may yet enliven and move forward the social analysis of education.

> The world is intensely differentiated according to the values projected upon it by
> desire and praxis. Inasmuch as the self is forever incomplete, it is forever seeking
> itself in the world. And inasmuch as desire is for the original others, while praxis
> recognizes the mutual interdependence of producers, the world as it matters to
> us is the world populated with other humans: society. Thus to say that the self
> seeks its creation and expression through the transformation of the world is to
> claim nothing more or less than that the cardinal dispossession of human nature
> is to make history. For history is the transformation of society through the
> transformation of nature. And so our human nature is to be historical, i.e., to
> transform itself. We are the creature that expresses its nature through the refusal
> of nature, that projects its being into the world and thereby makes itself. (Kovel
> 1988b: 391)

BIBLIOGRAPHY

Note: A standard abbreviation used in this bibliography is *SE*, which stands for *The Standard Edition of the Complete Psychological Works of Sigmund Freud*, James Strachey (ed.) (London: Hogarth, 1953).

Adamson, Walter (1980). *Hegemony and Revolution: A Study of Antonio Gramsci's Political and Cultural Theory* (Berkeley: University of California Press).

Adler, Gerald (1989). Transitional phenomena, projective identification, and the essential ambiguity of the psychoanalytic situation, *Psychoanalytic Quarterly*, 58, 81-104.

Allport, Gordon W. (1968). The historical background of modern psychology, in Gardner Lindzey and Eliot Aronson (eds.), *The Handbook of Social Psychology*, 2nd ed. (Reading, Mass.: Addison-Wesley), 1-80.

Althusser, Louis (1964). Freud and Lacan, in *Lenin and Philosophy and Other Essays*, 189-219.

———. (1965a). Contradiction and overdetermination, in Althusser, *For Marx*, 87-128.

———. (1965b). *For Marx* (London: Allen Lane, 1969).

———. (1965c). Theory, theoretical practice and theoretical formation: Ideology and ideological struggle, in Althusser, *Philosophy and the Spontaneous Philosophy of the Scientist, and Other Essays* (London: Verso, 1990), 1-40.

———. (1965d). From *Capital* to Marx's philosophy, in Althusser with Balibar, *Reading Capital*, 11-69.

———. (1965e). The object of *Capital*, in Althusser with Balibar, *Reading Capital*, 73-198.

———. (1965f). On the materialist dialectic, in Althusser, *For Marx*, 161-217.

———. (1965g). Marxism and humanism, in Althusser, *For Marx*, 219-247.

———. (1967). To my English readers, in Althusser, *For Marx*, 9-15.

———. (1970). Ideology and ideological state apparatuses (Notes towards an investigation), in Althusser, *Lenin and Philosophy and Other Essays*, 121-173.

———. (1971a). *Lenin and Philosophy and Other Essays* (London: New Left Books).

———. (1971b). Freud and Lacan, in Althusser, *Lenin and Philosophy and Other*

Essays, 195-219.

―――. (1972). *Politics and History: Montesquieu, Hegel and Marx* (London: New Left Books).

―――. (1974). Elements of self-criticism, in Althusser, *Essays in Self-Criticism*, 101-161.

―――. (1976). *Essays in Self-Criticism* (London: New Left Books).

―――. (1993). *The Future Lasts a Long Time, and The Facts* (London: Chatto & Windus).

Althusser, Louis with Balibar, Etienne (1965). *Reading Capital* (London: New Left Books, 1970).

Anderson, Perry (1977). The antinomies of Antonio Gramsci, *New Left Review*, 100, 5-78.

―――. (1980). *Arguments Within English Marxism* (London: New Left Books).

―――. (1983). *In the Tracks of Historical Materialism* (London: Verso).

Angel, Klaus (1972). The role of the internal object and external object in object relationships, separation anxiety, object constancy and symbiosis, *International Journal of Psycho-Analysis*, 53, 541-547.

Appel, Stephen (1990). Wrong opinions, repressions and pedagogy: Toward "perplexity" and "everyday unhappiness," *Educational Philosophy and Theory*, 22 (2), 1-7.

―――. (1992a). Problems of transferring concepts across paradigms: The case of the Matthew effect, *Acta Academica*, 24 (2), 1-15.

―――. (1992b). Freud's "pessimism": Drives and civilization, *South African Journal of Philosophy*, 11 (2), 41-43.

―――. (1993). Like chalk and cheese, *Perspectives in Education*, 14 (2), 229-238.

Appignanesi, Lisa (ed.) (1987). *Identity* (London: Institute of Contemporary Arts).

Apple, Michael W. (1971). The hidden curriculum and the nature of conflict, *Interchange*, 2 (4), 27-40.

Arnold, Roslyn (1994). The theory and principles of psychodynamic pedagogy, *Forum of Education*, 49 (2), 21-33.

Arnot, Madeleine, and Weiner, Gaby (eds.) (1987). *Gender and the Politics of Schooling* (London: Hutchinson).

Aronowitz, Stanley (1981). *The Crisis in Historical Materialism* (New York: Praeger).

―――. (1988). The production of scientific knowledge: Science, ideology, and Marxism, in Nelson and Grossberg (eds.), *Marxism and the Interpretation of Culture*, 519-541.

―――. (1991). Postmodernism and the discourse of educational criticism, in Aronowitz and Giroux, *Postmodern Education: Politics, Culture, and Social Criticism*.

Aronowitz, Stanley, and Giroux, Henry (1985) *Education Under Seige: The Conservative, Liberal and Radical Debate Over School* (South Hadley, Mass.: Bergin & Garvey).

―――. (1991). *Postmodern Education: Politics, Culture, and Social Criticism* (Minneapolis and Oxford: University of Minnesota Press).

Auerbach, Paul (1992). On socialist optimism, *New Left Review*, 192, 5-35.

Bak, Robert C. (1973). Being in love and object loss, *International Journal of Psycho-Analysis*, 54, 1-8.

Balibar, Etienne (1988). The vacillation of ideology, in Nelson and Grossberg (eds.),

Marxism and the Interpretation of Culture, 159-210.

———. (1991). For Louis Althusser, *Rethinking Marxism*, 4 (1), 9-12.

Ball, Stephen J. (1986). The sociology of the school: Streaming and mixed ability and social class, in Rick Rogers (ed.), *Education and Social Class* (Sussex, UK: Falmer Press), 83-100.

———. (1992). Review of Stanley Aronowitz and Henry Giroux *Postmodern Education: Politics, Culture, and Social Criticism*, *Sociological Review*, 40, 184-187.

———. (1994). *Education Reform: A Critical and Post-structural Approach* (Buckingham and Philadelphia: Open University Press).

Barrett, Michèle (1988). The place of aesthetics in Marxist criticism, in Nelson and Grossberg (eds.), *Marxism and the Interpretation of Culture*, 697-714.

———. (1991). *The Politics of Truth: From Marx to Foucault* (Cambridge, UK: Polity).

———. (1993). Althusser's Marx, Althusser's Lacan, in E. Ann Kaplan and Michael Sprinker (eds.), *The Althusserian Legacy* (London and New York: Verso), 169-182.

Barrows, Susanna (1981). *Distorting Mirrors: Visions of the Crowd in Late Nineteenth-Century France* (New Haven and London: Yale University Press).

Barton, Len, Meighan, Roland, and Walker, Stephen (eds.) (1980). Introduction, in *Schooling, Ideology and the Curriculum* (Sussex, UK: Falmer Press), 1-10.

Barton, Len and Walker, Stephen (eds.) (1985). Introduction, in *Education and Social Change* (London: Croom Helm), i-ix.

Bennett, Tony (1980). The not-so-good, the bad and the ugly, *Screen Education*, 36, 119-130.

Bennett, Tony, Martin, Graham, Mercer, Colin, and Woolacott, Janet (1981a). Antonio Gramsci, in *Culture, Ideology and Social Process*, 191-218.

———. (eds.) (1981b). *Culture, Ideology and Social Process: A Reader* (London: Batsford Academic).

Bensusan, David, and Shalem, Yael (1993). The crooked path of pedagogy, presented at Kenton Education Conference, Olwandle, South Africa.

Benton, Ted (1984). *The Rise and Fall of Structural Marxism: Althusser and His Influence* (Basingstoke and London: Macmillan).

Benvenuto, Bice, and Kennedy, Roger (1986). *The Works of Jacques Lacan: An Introduction* (London: Free Association).

Bernard, Marcos (1982). The structure of roles and the status of the unconscious, in Malcolm Pines and Lisa Rafaelsen (eds.), *The Individual and the Group: Boundaries and Interrelations*, vol. 2. *Practice* (London, and New York: Plenum), 31-37.

Bernstein, Basil (1967). Open schools, open society? *New Society*, 14 September, 351-353.

———. (1975). The sociology of education: A brief account, in Bernstein, *Class, Codes and Control*, vol. 3. *Towards a Theory of Educational Transmissions* (London, and Boston: Routledge & Kegan Paul), 146-162.

———. (1981). Codes, modalities, and the process of cultural reproduction: A model, *Language in Society*, 10 (3), 327-363.

———. (1990). *The Structuring of Pedagogic Discourse. Class, Codes and Control*, vol. 4 (London and New York: Routledge).

Beyer, L., and Liston, Daniel (1992). Discourse or moral action? A critique of postmodernism, *Educational Theory*, 42, 371-393.

Bion, Wilfred R. (1957). Group dynamics: A review, in Klein, Heimann, and Money-Kyrle (eds.), *New Directions in Psycho-Analysis*, 440-477.

————. (1959a). *Experiences in Groups, and Other Papers* (New York: Basic Books).

————. (1959b). Attacks on linking, *International Journal of Psycho-Analysis*, 40, 308-315.

————. (1962). *Learning from Experiece* (London: Heinemann).

————. (1963). *Elements of Psycho-Analysis* (London: Heinemann).

Bollas, Christopher (1979). The transformational object, *International Journal of Psycho-Analysis*, 60, 97-107.

————. (1982). On the relation to the self as an object, *International Journal of Psycho-Analysis*, 63, 347-359.

————. (1987). *The Shadow of the Object: Psychoanalysis of the Unthought Known* (London: Free Association).

Boris, Harold N. (1990). Identification with a vengence, *International Journal of Psycho-Analysis*, 71, 127-140.

Bourdieu, Pierre, and Passeron, Jean-Claude (1977). *Reproduction: In Education, Society, Culture* (London: Sage).

Bowers, C. (1991). Some questions about the anachronistic elements in the Giroux-McLaren theory of critical pedagogy, *Curriculum Inquiry*, 21, 239-252.

Bowie, Malcolm (1979). Jacques Lacan, in John Sturrock (ed.), *Structuralism and Since* (Oxford: Oxford University Press), 116-153.

————. (1991). *Lacan* (London: Fontana).

Bowles, Samuel, and Gintis, Herbert (1976). *Schooling in Capitalist America: Educational Reform and the Contradictions of Economic Life* (New York: Basic Books).

Brandes, Charles E. (1986). The meaning of work as transitional phenomena for men at mid-life, Ph.D. dissertation, The Wright Institute, Berkeley, California.

Breen, C. (1991/1992). Teacher education and mathematics: Conflicting preconceptions, *Perspectives in Education*, 13, 33-44.

Breuer, Josef, and Freud, Sigmund (1895). *Studies on Hysteria*, *SE*, 2.

Britzman, Deborah (1986). Cultural myths in the making of a teacher: Biography and social structure, *Harvard Educational Review*, 56 (4), 442-456.

Bromley, Hank (1989). Identity politics and critical pedagogy, *Educational Theory*, 39 (3), 207-223.

Brosio, Richard A. (1990). Teaching and learning for democratic empowerment: A critical evaluation, *Educational Theory*, 40 (1), 69-81.

Buci-Glucksman, Christine (1980). *Gramsci and the State* (London: Lawrence & Wishart).

Burbules, Nicholas C. (1986). *Tootle*: A parable of schooling and destiny, *Harvard Educational Review*, 56 (3), 239-256.

Burbules, Nicholas C., and Rice Suzanne (1991). Dialogue across differences: Continuing the conversation, *Harvard Educational Review*, 61, 393-416.

Busch, Fred, with McKnight, Judith (1977). Theme and variation in the development of the first transitional object, *International Journal of Psycho-Analysis*, 58, 479-

495.

Calogeras, Roy C. and Alston, Toni M. (1985). Family pathology and the infantile neurosis, *International Journal of Psycho-Analysis*, 66, 359-373.

Campbell, Helen (1995). Projective identification and countertransference, *NZAP Forum*, 1, 51-59.

Carr, Wilfred and Kemmis, Stephen (1986). *Becoming Critical: Education, Knowledge, and Action Research*, rev. ed. (London and Philadelphia: Falmer).

Caruso, Igor (1965). Psychoanalysis and society, *New Left Review*, 32, 24-31.

Castoriadis, Cornelius (1987). The imaginary: Creation in the social-historical domain, in Appignanesi (ed.), *Identity*, 39-43.

———. (1994). Psychoanalysis and politics, in Sam Shamdasani and Michael Münchow (eds.), *Speculations After Freud: Psychoanalysis, Philosophy and Culture* (London, and New York: Routledge), 2-12.

Cathcart, Heather, and Esland, Geoff (1985). The compliant-creative worker: The ideological reconstruction of the school learner, in Barton and Walker (eds.), *Education and School Change*, 173-192.

Chediak, Charles (1979). Counter-reactions and countertransference, *International Journal of Psycho-Analysis*, 60, 117-129.

Cherryholmes, Cleo H. (1988). *Power and Criticism: Poststructural Investigations in Education* (New York and London: Teachers College Press).

Chicago Psychoanalytic Literature Index, (1985-1988). (Chicago: Institute for Psychoanalysis).

Chisholm, Linda and Sole, Kelwyn (1981). Education and class struggle, *Perspectives in Education*, 5 (2), 110-117.

Clarke, Simon (1980). Althusserian Marxism, in Clarke et al., *One-Dimensional Marxism*, 7-102.

Clarke, Simon, Seider, Victor, McDonnell, Kevin, Robins, Kevin, and Lovell, Terry (1980). *One-Dimensional Marxism: Althusser and the Politics of Culture* (New York and London: Allison & Busby).

Colletti, Lucio (1972). Marxism: Science or revolution?, in Robin Blackburn (ed.), *Ideology in Social Science: Readings in Critical Social Theory* (New York: Pantheon), 369-377.

Cook, J.A. (1973). Language and socialization, in Bernstein (ed.), *Class, Codes and Control*, 293-341.

Critchlow, Warren (1992). A social analysis of black youth commitment and disaffection in an urban high school, Ed.D. dissertation, University of Rochester, Rochester, N.Y.

Crook, Stephen (1991). *Modernist Radicalism and Its Aftermath* (London and New York: Routledge).

Dale, Roger (1992). Recovering from a Pyrrhic victory? Quality, relevance and impact in the sociology of education, in Madeleine Arnot and Len Barton (eds.), *Voicing Concerns: Sociological Perspectives on Contemporary Education Reforms* (Wallington, UK: Triangle), 201-217.

Davidoff, Sue, and van den Berg, Owen (1990). *Changing Your Teaching: The Challenge of the Classroom* (Pietermaritzburg, South Africa: Centaur).

Davies, Bronwyn (1990). The problem of desire, *Social Problems*, 37, 501-516.

————. (1992). A feminist poststructuralist analysis of discursive practices in the classroom and playground, *Discourse*, 13 (1), 49-66.

Davies, Bronwyn, and Banks, Chas (1992). The gender trap: A feminist post-structuralist analysis of primary school children's talk about gender, *Journal of Curriculum Studies*, 24, 1-25.

Davies, Bronwyn, and Harré, Rom (1990). Positioning: The discursive production of selves, *Journal for the Theory of Social Behaviour*, 20, 43-63.

Davis, Robert Con (1987). Pedagogy, Lacan, and the Freudian subject, *College English*, 49 (7), 749-755.

De Bea, Eulalia Torras (1989). Projective identification and differentiation, *International Journal of Psycho-Analysis*, 70, 265-274.

De Folch, Tertu Eskelinen (1983). We versus I and you, *International Journal of Psycho-Analysis*, 64, 309-320.

de Jonghe, F., Rijnierse, P., and Janssen, R. (1991). Aspects of the analytic relationship, *International Journal of Psycho-Analysis*, 72, 693-707.

Demaine, Jack (1989). Race, categorization and educational achievement, *British Journal of Sociology of Education*, 10 (2), 195-214.

De Man, Paul (1979). *Allegories of Reading: Figural Language in Rousseau, Nietzsche, Rilke and Proust* (New Haven: Yale University Press).

de Mare, Patrick (1975). The politics of large groups, in Kreeger (ed.), *The Large Group*, 145-158.

de Mare, Patrick, and Piper, Robin (1982). Large group perspectives, in Pines and Rafaelsen (eds.), *The Individual and the Group*, 365-377.

Derrida, Jacques (1976). *Of Grammatology*, Gayatri Spivak (trans.) (Baltimore: Johns Hopkins University Press).

————. (1990). Let us not forget—Psychoanalysis, *Oxford Literary Review*, 12, 3-7.

————. (1993). Politics and friendship: An interview with Jacques Derrida, in E. Ann Kaplan and Michael Sprinker (eds.), *The Althusserian Legacy* (London, and New York: Verso), 183-231.

Descombes, V. (1991). Apropos of the critique of "the subject" and the critique of the critique, in E. Cadava, P. Connor, and J.L. Nancy (eds.), *Who Comes After the Subject?* (New York and London: Routledge).

Dippo, D., Gelb, S., Turner, I. and Turner, T. (1991). Making the political personal: Problems of privilege and power in post-secondary teaching, *Journal of Education*, 173, 81-95.

Donald, James (1991). On the threshold: Psychoanalysis and cultural studies, in Donald (ed.), *Psychoanalysis and Cultural Studies* (Basingstoke and London: Macmillan).

————. (1992a). Dewey-eyed optimism: The possibility of democratic education, *New Left Review*, 192, 133-144.

————. (1992b). *Sentimental Education: Schooling, Popular Culture, and the Regulation of Liberty* (New York and London: Verso).

Dostoyevsky, Fyodor (1866). *Crime and Punishment* (Harmondsworth, UK: Penguin, 1951).

du Preez, J.M. (1983). *Africana Afrikaner—Master Symbols in South African School Textbooks* (Alberton, South Africa: Librarius).

Eagleton, Terry (1986). *Against the Grain: Essays, 1975-1985* (London: Verso).
———. (1990). *Ideology of the Aesthetic* (Cambridge, Mass.: Blackwell).
Eco, Umberto (1973). Social life as a sign system, in David Robey (ed.), *Structuralism: An Introduction* (Oxford: Clarendon), 57-72.
Elliott, Gregory (1987). *Althusser: The Detour of Theory* (New York and London: Verso).
Ellsworth Elizabeth (1989). Why doesn't this feel empowering? Working through the repressive myths of critical pedagogy, *Harvard Educational Review*, 59 (3), 297-324.
Elmhirst, Susanna Isaacs (1980). Transitional objects in transition, *International Journal of Psycho-Analysis*, 61, 367-373.
Epstein, Mark (1995). *Thoughts Without a Thinker: Psychotherapy from a Buddhist Perspective* (New York: basic Books).
Erben, Michael, and Gleeson, Denis (1977). Education as reproduction: A critical examination of some aspects of the work of Louis Althusser, in Whitty and Young (eds.), *Society, State and Schooling*, 73-92.
Etchegoyen, R. Horacio (1985). Identification and its vicissitudes, *International Journal of Psycho-Analysis*, 66, 3-18.
Evans, John, Davies, Brian, and Penny, Dawn (1994). Whatever happened to the subject and the state in policy research in education? *Discourse*, 14 (2), 57-64.
Everhart, Robert B. (1983). *Reading, Writing and Resistance: Adolescence and Labor in a Junior High School* (Boston: Routledge & Kegan Paul).
Felman, Shoshana (1986). Psychoanalysis and education: Teaching terminable and interminable, *Yale French Studies*, 63, 21-44.
———. (1987). *Jacques Lacan and the Adventure of Insight: Psychoanalysis in Contemporary Culture* (Cambridge, Mass., and London: Harvard University Press).
Felman, Shoshana, and Laub, Dori (1992). *Testimony: Crises of Witnessing in Literature, Psychoanalysis, and History* (New York: Routledge).
Femia, Joseph (1981). *Gramsci's Political Thought* (London: Clarendon).
Fenichel, Otto (1925). Introjection and the castration complex, in *The Collected Papers of Otto Fenichel*, first series (New York: Norton), 39-70.
Ferenczi, Sandor (1909). Introjection and transference, in Ferenczi, *Contributions to Psycho-Analysis* (Boston: Richard G. Badger, 1916).
———. (1912). On the definition of introjection, in Ferenczi, *Final Contributions to Psycho-Analysis* (London: Hogarth, 1955).
Feyerabend, Paul (1975). *Against Method: Outline of an Anarchistic Theory of Knowledge* (London: New Left Books).
Fine, Michelle (1988). Sexuality, schooling, and adolescent females: The missing discourse of desire, *Harvard Educational Review*, 58 (1), 29-53.
Fiumara, Romano (1982). The person as expression of the group, in Pines and Rafaelsen (eds.), *The Individual and the Group*, 169-179.
Fitzclarence, Lindsay (1992). *Shame/emotions/violence—Issues for educational research*, working paper, Deakin Centre for Education and Change, Geelong, Australia.
Forrester, John (1987). A brief history of the subject, in Appignanesi (ed.), *Identity*, 13-16.

Foucault, Michel (1977a). *Discipline and Punish: The Birth of the Prison* (New York: Peregrine, 1982).
————. (1977b). *The Archeology of Knowledge* (Tavistock: London).
Frank, Alvin (1991). Psychic change and the analyst as biographer: Transference and reconstruction, *International Journal of Psycho-analysis*, 70 (1), 22-26.
Frazer, Elizabeth (1989). Problems with the theory of ideology, *Cogito*, 3 (2), 117-122.
Freire, Paulo (1970). *The Pedagogy of the Oppressed* (New York: Seabury Press).
Freud, Anna (1936). *The Ego and the Mechanisms of Defence* (New York: International Universities Press).
————. (1965). *Normality and Pathology in Childhood* (New York: International Universities Press).
Freud, Sigmund (1895). Draft H. Paranoia, in Masson (trans. and ed.), *The Complete Letters of Sigmund Freud to Wilhelm Fliess*, 107-112.
————. (1900). *The Interpretation of Dreams, SE*, 4.
————. (1901). *The Psychopathology of Everyday Life, SE*, 6.
————. (1905a). Fragment of an analysis of a case of hysteria, *SE*, 7, 1-122.
————. (1905b). *Three Essays on the Theory of Sexuality, SE*, 7, 125-243.
————. (1905c). *Jokes and their Relation to the Unconscious, SE*, 8.
————. (1907a). Obsessive acts and religious practices, *SE*, 9, 115-127.
————. (1907b). Creative writers and day-dreaming, *SE*, 9, 141-153.
————. (1908). "Civilized" sexual morality and modern nervousness, *SE*, 9, 177-204.
————. (1909). Family romances, *SE*, 9, 235-244.
————. (1910a). Five lectures on psycho-analysis, *SE*, 11, 3-55.
————. (1910b). *Leonardo da Vinci and a Memory of his Childhood, SE*, 11, 59-127.
————. (1911a). Psycho-analytic notes upon an autobiographical account of a case of paranoia (dementia paranoides), *SE*, 12, 9-79.
————. (1911b). Formulations on the two principles of mental functioning, *SE*, 12, 215-226.
————. (1912). A note on the unconscious in psycho-analysis, *SE*, 12, 255-266.
————. (1912-1913). *Totem and Taboo: Some Points of Agreement between the Mental Lives of Savages and Neurotics, SE*, 13, xiii-162.
————. (1913). The claims of psycho-analysis to scientific interest, *SE*, 13, 165-190.
————. (1914a). Some reflections on schoolboy psychology, *SE*, 13, 241-244.
————. (1914b). On narcissism: An introduction, *SE*, 14, 69-102.
————. (1915a). Insticts and their vicissitudes, *SE*, 14, 105-140.
————. (1915b). Thoughts for the time on war and death, *SE*, 14, 273-302.
————. (1915c). The unconscious, *SE*, 14, 159-215.
————. (1915d). Repression, *SE*, 14, 141-158.
————. (1916-1917). *Introductory Lectures on Psycho-Analysis, SE*, 15.
————. (1917a). A metapsychological supplement to the theory of dreams, *SE*, 14, 222-235.
————. (1917b). Mourning and melancholia, *SE*, 14, 237-258.
————. (1919). Preface to Reik's *Ritual: Psychoanalytic Studies, SE*, 17, 257-263.
————. (1920). *Beyond the Pleasure Principle, SE*, 18, 3-64.
————. (1921). *Group Psychology and the Analysis of the Ego, SE*, 18, 65-143.

———. (1922). Some neurotic mechanisms in jealousy, paranoia and homosexuality, *SE*, 18, 221-232.

———. (1923). *The Ego and the Id, SE*, 19, 3-66.

———. (1924). The economic problem of masochism, *SE*, 19, 159-170.

———. (1925). *An Autobiographical Study, SE*, 20, 3-74.

———. (1926). *Inhibitions, Symptoms and Anxiety, SE*, 20, 87-174.

———. (1927). *The Future of an Illusion, SE*, 21, 3-56.

———. (1930). *Civilization and Its Discontents, SE*, 21, 59-145.

———. (1933). *New Introductory Lectures on Psycho-Analysis, SE*, 22, 3-182.

———. (1935). Postscript *An Autobiographical Study, SE*, 20, 71-74

———. (1937). Analysis terminable and interminable, *SE*, 23.

———. (1939). *Moses and Monotheism: Three Essays, SE*, 23, 3-137.

———. (1941). Findings, ideas, problems, *SE*, 22, 5-182.

Frosh, Stephen (1987). *The Politics of Psychoanalysis* (Basingstoke, UK: Macmillan).

———. (1991). *Identity Crisis: Modernity, Psychoanalysis and the Self* (New York: Routledge).

Furlong, V.J. (1991). Disaffected pupils: Reconstructing the sociological perspective, *British Journal of Sociology of Education*, 12, 292-307.

Gallop, Jane (1992). Knot a love story, *Yale Journal of Criticism*, 5, 209-218.

———. (1995). The teacher's breasts, in Gallop (ed.), *Pedagogy: The Question of Impersonation* (Bloomington and Indianapolis: Indiana University Press), 79-89.

Gay, Peter (1985). *Freud for Historians* (New York and Oxford: Oxford University Press).

Gedo, John (1989). An epistemology of transference, *The Annual of Psychoanalysis*, 17, 3-15.

Geras, Norman (1972). Althusser's Marxism: An account and assessment, in Geras, *Literature of Revolution: Essays on Marxism* (London: Verso, 1986), 91-131.

———. (1983). *Marx and Human Nature: Refutation of a Legend* (London: Verso).

Gerth, Hans, and Mills, C. Wright (1954). *Character and Social Structure: The Psychology of Social Institutions* (London: Routledge & Kegan Paul).

Gill, Harwant S. (1991). Internalization of the absent father, *International Journal of Psycho-Analysis*, 72, 243-252.

Giroux, Henry A. (1983a). *Theory and Resistance: A Pedagogy for the Opposition* (South Hadley, Mass.: Bergin & Garvey).

———. (1983b). Theories of reproduction and resistance in the new sociology of education: A critical analysis, *Harvard Educational Review*, 53 (3), 257-293.

Giroux, Henry, and McLaren, Peter (1992). Writing from the margins: Geographies of identity, pedagogy, and power, *Journal of Education*, 174, 7-30.

Gramm, Tomas (1988). Education for humanization: Applying Paulo Freire's pedagogy to learning a second language, *Harvard Educational Review*, 58 (4), 433-448.

Gramsci, Antonio (1971). *Selections from the Prison Notebooks of Antonio Gramsci*, Quintin Hoare and Geoffrey Newell Smith (eds.), (New York: International Universities Press).

Green, André (1975). The analyst, symbolization and absence in the analytic setting (Or changes in analytic pratice and analytic experience), *International Journal of Psycho-Analysis*, 56, 1-22.

Greenberg, Jay R., and Mitchell, Stephen A. (1983). *Object Relations in Psychoanalytic Theory* (Cambridge, Mass., and London: Harvard University Press).

Greenson, R.R., and Wexler, M. (1969). The non-transference relationship in the psychoanalytic situation, *International Journal of Psycho-Analysis*, 50, 27-39.

Grolnick, Simon A. (1978). Epilogue, in Simon A. Grolnick and Leonard Barkin with Werner Muensterberber (eds.), *Between Reality and Fantasy: Transitional Objects and Phenomena* (New York and London: Jason Aronson), 537-538.

Grossberg, Lawrence (1993). Articulation and agency, in Grossberg (ed.), *We Gotta Get Out of This Place: Popular Conservatism and Postmodern Culture* (New York and London: Routledge), 113-27.

Grundy, Shirley (1994). Being and becoming an Australian: Classroom discourse and the construction of identity, *Discourse*, 15 (1), 16-31.

Guess, Dieter (1981). *The Idea of Critical Thinking* (Cambridge: Cambridge University Press).

Gurko, J. (1982). Sexual energy in the classroom, in Margaret Cruikshank (ed.), *Lesbian Studies Present and Future* (New York: Feminist Studies).

Hall, Stuart (1980). Recent developments in theories of language and ideology: A critical note, in Stuart Hall, et al. (eds.), *Culture, Media, Language*, 157-162.

———. (1981). Notes on deconstructing "the popular," in Raphael Samuel (ed.), *People's History and Socialist Theory* (London: Routledge & Kegan Paul), 232-239.

———. (1985). Signification, representation, ideology: Althusser and the post-structuralist debates, *Critical Studies in Mass Communication*, 2 (2), 91-114.

———. (1986). No light at the end of the tunnel, *Marxism Today*, December, 12-16.

———. (1987). Minimal selves, in Appignanesi (ed.), *Identity*, 44-46.

———. (1988). The toad in the garden: Thatcherism among the theorists, in Nelson and Grossberg, *Marxism and the Interpretation of Culture*, 35-73.

Hall, Stuart, Hobson, D., Lowe, A., and Willis, P. (eds.), (1980). *Culture, Media, Language: Working Papers in Cultural Studies, 1972—1979* (London: Hutchinson).

Hamilton, N. Gregory (1986). Positive projective identification, *International Journal of Psycho-Analysis*, 67, 489-496.

———. (1990). The containing function and the analyst's projective identification, *International Journal of Psycho-Analysis*, 71, 445-453.

Hartmann, Heinz (1939). *Ego Psychology and the Problem of Adaptation* (New York: International Universities Press).

Hayes, Grahame (1989). Psychology and ideology: The case of Althusser, *South African Journal of Psychology*, 19 (2), 84-90.

———. (1990). Psychoanalysis, Lacan, and social theory, *Psychology in Society*, 14, 28-46.

Hayman, Anne (1989). What do we mean by "phantasy"?, *International Journal of Psycho-Analysis*, 70, 105-114.

Heigl-Evers, A., and Heigl, F. (1982). Psychological compromise formation as the changeover point between intrapsychic and interpersonal relationships, in Pines and Rafaelsen (eds.), *The Individual and the Group*, 225-235.

Heimann, Paula (1950). On counter-transference, *International Journal of Psycho-Analysis*, 31, 81-84.

Heller, Agnes (1990). The death of the subject, *Thesis Eleven*, 25, 22-38.

Hernandez, Max (1988). Group formation and ideology: Text and context, *International Journal of Psycho-Analysis*, 69 (2), 163-170.

Hindess, Barry, and Hirst, Paul (1975). *Pre-Capitalist Modes of Production* (London, and Boston: Routledge & Kegan Paul).

———. (1977). *Mode of Production and Social Formation: An Auto-Critique of Pre-Capitalist Modes of Production* (London: Macmillan).

Hinshelwood, R.D. (1987). *What Happens in Groups: Psychoanalysis, the Individual and the Community* (London: Free Association).

Hinton, Tim (1988). Some problems in the sociology of education, seminar, University of the Witwatersrand, Johannesburg, South Africa.

Hirst, Paul (1985). *Marxism and Historical Writing* (London: Routledge & Kegan Paul).

Holland, Norman N. (1985). *The I* (New Haven and London: Yale University Press).

Holt, John (1982). *How Children Fail*, 2nd ed. (Harmondsworth, UK: Penguin).

hooks, bell (1994). Eros, eroticism, and the pedagogical process, in hooks, *Teaching to Transgress: Education as the Practice of Freedom* (New York and London: Routledge), 191-199.

Hopper, Earl, and Weyman, Anne (1975). A sociological view of large groups, in Kreeger (ed). *The Large Group*, 159-189.

Hunter, Virginia (ed.) (1984). *Psychoanalysts Talk* (New York and London: Guilford).

Isaacs, Susan (1952). The nature and function of phantasy, in Klein and Riviere, *Developments in Psycho-Analysis*.

Jaffe, D.S. (1968). The mechanism of projection: Its dual role in object relations, *International Journal of Psycho-Analysis*, 49, 662-677.

Jakobson, Roman (1956). Two aspects of language and two types of aphasic disturbances, in Roman Jakobson and Morris Halle, *Fundamentals of Language* (The Hague: Mouton), 55-82.

Jameson, Fredric (1977). Imaginary and symbolic in Lacan: Marxism, psychoanalytic criticism and the problem of the subject, *Yale French Studies*, 55/56, 338-395.

———. (1981). *The Political Unconscious: Narrative as Socially Symbolic Act* (Ithaca, N.Y.: Cornell University Press).

Jaques, Elliott (1957). Social systems as defence against persecutory and depressive anxiety, in Klein, Heimann, and Money-Kyrle, *New Directions in Psycho-Analysis*, 478-498.

Jay, Gregory S. (1987). The subject of pedagogy: Lessons in psychoanalysis and politics, *College English*, 49 (7), 785-800.

Johnson, Barbara (1982). Teaching ignorance: *L'Ecole des Femmes*, *Yale French Studies*, 63, 165-182.

Johnson, J. Alleyne (1995). Life after death: Critical pedagogy in an urban classroom, *Harvard Educational Review*, 65 (2), 213-230.

Jones, Alison (1993). Becoming a "girl": Post-structuralist suggestions for educational research, *Gender and Education*, 5, 157-166.

Jones, Ernest (1957). *The Life and Work of Sigmund Freud*, vol. 3 (New York: Basic Books).

Joseph, Betty (1985). Transference: The total situation, *International Journal of Psycho-Analysis*, 66, 447-454.

———. (1987). Projective identification: Clinical aspects, in Sandler (ed.), *Projection, Identification, Projective Identification*, 65-76.

Kalmar, David A., and Sternberg, Robert J. (1988). Theory knitting: An integrative approach to theory development, *Philosophical Psychology*, 1 (2), 153-170.

Kanpol, Barry (1992a). Postmodernism in education revisited: Similarities within differences and the democratic imaginary, *Educational Theory*, 42, 217-229.

———. (1992b). *Towards a Theory and Practice of Teacher Cultural Politics: Continuing the Postmodern Debate* (Norwood, N.J.: Ablex).

Karol, K.S. (1980). The tragedy of the Althussers, *New Left Review*, 124, 93-95.

Kenway, Jane (1995). Masculinities in schools: Under siege, on the defensive and under reconstruction?, *Discourse*, 16 (1), 59-79.

Kernberg, Otto (1965). Notes on countertransference, *Journal of the American Psychoanalytic Association*, 13, 38-56.

———. (1987). .Projection and projective identification: Developmental and clinical aspects, in Sandler (ed.), *Projection, Identification, Projective Identification*, 93-115.

———. (1989). The temptations of conventionality, *International Review of Psycho-Analysis*, 16 (1). 191-205.

Khaleelee, Olya, and Miller, Eric (1985). Beyond the small group: Society as an intelligible field of study, in Malcolm Pines (ed.), *Bion and Group Psychotherapy* (London: Routledge & Kegan Paul), 354-385.

Klein, Melanie (1926). The psychological principles of infant analysis, in J. Mitchell (ed.), *The Selected Melanie Klein*, 57-68.

———. (1929). Personification in the play of children, in Klein, *Love, Guilt and Reparation*, 248-257.

———. (1930). The importance of symbol formation in the development of the ego, in Klein, *Love, Guilt and Reparation*, 219-232.

———. (1931). A contribution to the theory of intellectual inhibition, in Klein, *Love, Guilt and Reparation*, 236-247.

———. (1932). *The Psycho-Analysis of Children* (London: Hogarth).

———. (1935). A contribution to the psychoanalysis of manic-depressive states, in Klein, *Love, Guilt and Reparation*, 262-289.

———. (1940). Mourning and its relation to manic depressive states, *International Journal of Psycho-Analysis*, 20.

———. (1946). Notes on some schizoid mechanisms, in *Envy and Gratitude and Other Works*, 1-24.

———. (1955). On identification, in Klein et al., *New Directions in Psycho-Analysis*, 309-345.

———. (1957). Envy and gratitude, in Klein, *Envy and Gratitude*.

———. (1959). Our adult and its roots in infancy, *Human Relations*, 12 (4), 291-303.

———. (1963). On the sense of loneliness, in Klein, *Envy, and Gratitude and Other Works*, 300-313.

———. (1975a). *Love, Guilt and Reparation and Other Works, 1921-1945* (London: Hogarth).

————. (1975b). *Envy and Gratitude and Other Works, 1946-1963* (London: Hogarth).

Klein, Melanie, Heimann, Paula, and Money-Kyrle, R.E. (eds.), (1957). *New Directions in Psycho-Analysis: The Significance of Infant Conflict in the Pattern of Adult Behaviour* (New York: Basic Books).

Klein, Melanie, and Riviere Joan (eds.), (1952). *Developments in Psycho-Analysis* (London: Hogarth).

Knapp, Harriet D. (1989). Projective identification: Whose projection-whose identity?, *Psychoanalytic Psychology*, 6, 47-58.

Kovel, Joel (1988a). The Marxist view of man and psychoanalysis, in Kovel, *The Radical Spirit*, 167-188.

————. (1988b). On the notion of human nature: A contribution toward a philosophical anthropology, in Stanley B. Messer, Louis A. Sass, and Robert L. Woolfolk (eds.), *Hermeneutics and Psychologocal Theory: Interpretive Perspectives on Personality, Psychotherapy, and Psychopathology* (New Brunswick, N.J.: Rutgers University Press), 370-399.

————. (1988c). *The Radical Spirit: Essays on Psychoanalysis and Society* (London: Free Association Books).

Kreeger, Lionel (ed.), (1975). *The Large Group: Dynamics and Therapy* (London: Constable).

Kringas, Paul, and Steward, Ian (1992). Class, race and education: An Australian case study, *Discourse*, 13 (1), 20-35.

Kristeva, Julia (1980). *Desire in Language: A Semiotic Approach to Literature and Art* (Oxford: Basil Blackwell).

————. (1986). *The Kristeva Reader* (Oxford: Basil Blackwell).

————. (1993). The speaking subject is not innocent, in Barbara Johnson (ed.), *Freedom and Interpretation: The Oxford Amnesty Lectures* 1992 (New York: Basic Books), 147-174.

Kulevski, B. (1984). The educative eros: Teacher pupil intimacy and aspects of pedagogic domination in Plato's Academy, *History of Education Review*, 13 (1), 14-28.

Lacan, Jacques (1948). Aggressivity in psychoanalysis, in Lacan, *Ecrits*, 8-29.

————. (1949). The mirror stage as formative of the function of the I, in Lacan, *Ecrits*, 1-7.

————. (1953). The function and field of speech and language in psychoanalysis, in Lacan, *Ecrits*, 30-113.

————. (1956). The seminar on Poe's "Purloined letter," *Yale French Studies*, 1972, 48, 38-72.

————. (1957). The agency of the letter in the unconscious or reason since Freud, in Lacan, *Ecrits*, 146-178.

————. (1960). The subversion of the subject and the dialectic of desire in the Freudian unconscious, in Lacan, *Ecrits*, 292-325.

————. (1964). *The Four Fundamentals of Psychoanalysis*, (Harmondsworth, UK: Penguin, 1977).

————. (1968). The mirror stage, *New Left Review*, 51, 71-77.

————. (1977). *Ecrits: A Selection*, A. Sheridan (ed.), (New York and London: Norton).

Laclau, Ernesto (1977). *Politics and Ideology in Marxist Theory* (London: New Left

Books).

———. (1988). Metaphor and social antagonisms, in Nelson and Grossberg, *Marxism and the Interpretation of Culture*, 249-267.

———. (1990). *New Reflections on the Revolution of our Time* (London: Verso).

———. (1993). Political frontiers, identification and political identities, conference on Ethnicity, Identity and Nationalism in South Africa: Comparative Perspectives, Grahamstown, South Africa.

Laclau, Ernesto, and Mouffe, Chantal (1985). *Hegemony and Socialist Strategy: Towards a Radical Democratic Politics* (London: Verso).

Langs, Robert (1975). Therapeutic misalliances, *International Journal of Psychoanalytic Psychotherapy*, 4, 77-105.

———. (1976). *The Therapeutic Interaction* (New York: Jacob Aronson).

Lather, Patti (1991). *Getting Smart: Feminist Research and Pedagogy With/in the Postmodern* (New York and London: Routledge).

Le Bon, Gustave (1895). *La Psychologie des foules* (Paris: Alcan).

———. (1913). *Aphorismes du Temps Present*, in Widener (ed.), *Gustave Le Bon*, 267-305.

Leavy, Stanley A. (1990). Lacan's words, *Psychoanalytic Quarterly*, 59, 437-443.

Lee, Anne (1989). "Together we learn to read and write": Sexism and literacy, in Dale Spender and Elizabeth Sarah (eds.), *Learning to Lose: Sexism and Education*, rev. ed. (London: Women's Press), 121-127.

Lee, Elaine (1983). Ideology and the individual, *Perspectives in Education*, 7 (1), 25-39.

Lehman, David (1991). *Signs of the Times: Deconstruction and the Fall of Paul de Man* (London: Andre Deutch).

Lemaire, Anika (1970). *Jacques Lacan*, David Macey (trans.) (London: Routledge & Kegan Paul).

Levine, Ellen Greengross (1982). Psychoanalysis and symbolism: The space between self and world, Ph.D. dissertation, York University, Toronto, Canada.

Lindroos, Maarit (1995). The production of "girl" in an educational setting, *Gender and Education*, 7 (2), 143-155.

Livingstone, David (1995). Searching for missing links: Neo-Marxist theories of education, *British Journal of Sociology of Education*, 16 (1), 53-73.

Loewald, Hans (1962). Internalization, separation, mourning, and the superego, in Loewald, *Papers on Psychoanalysis* (New Haven: Yale University Press, 1980).

Loptson, Peter (1991). Compatibilism, *Cogito*, 5 (1), 24-30.

Lukács, Georg (1923). *History and Class Consciousness: Studies in Marxist Dialectics* (Cambridge: MIT Press, 1971).

Luke, Carmen (1994). Women in the academy: The politics of speech and silence, *British Journal of Sociology of Education*, 15 (2), 211-230.

Lussier, André (1988). The limitations of the object relations model, *Psychoanalytic Quarterly*, 57, 528-546.

MacDonell, Diane (1986). *Theories of Discourse: An Introduction* (Oxford and New York: Basil Blackwell).

Macherey, Pierre (1966). *A Theory of Literary Production* (London: Routledge & Kegan Paul, 1978).

MacIver, R.M., and Page, Charles H. (1950). *Society: An Introductory Analysis* (London:

Macmillan).

Malin, A., and Grotstein, J.S. (1966). Projective identification in the therapeutic process, *International Journal of Psycho-Analysis*, 47, 26-31.

Mao Tse-tung (1953). *On Contradiction* (New York: International Publishers).

Martin, Jay (1988). *Who Am I This Time? Uncovering the Fictive Personality* (New York and London: Norton).

Marx, Karl (1857-1859). *Grundrisse* (Harmondsworth, UK: Penguin, 1973).

Marx, Karl, and Engels, Friedrich (1846). *The German Ideology* (London: Lawrence & Wishart, 1965).

————. (1975). *Karl Marx and Friedrich Engels: Selected Correspondence* (Moscow: Progress Publishers).

Masson, Jeffrey M. (trans. and ed.), (1985). *The Complete Letters of Sigmund Freud to Wilhelm Fliess, 1887-1904* (Cambridge, Mass., and London: Belknap).

Mateu, Pere Folch (1986). Identification and its vicissitudes, as observed in the neuroses, *International Journal of Psycho-Analysis*, 67, 209-218.

Mathews, Julie (1994). . . . if radical education is to be anything more than radical pedagogy, *Discourse*, 15 (2), 60-72.

McCarthy, Cameron R. (1988). Rethinking liberal and radical perspectives on racial inequality in schooling: Making a case for nonsynchrony, *Harvard Educational Review*, 58 (3), 265-279.

McDougall, W. (1920). *The Group Mind* (New York: Putnam).

McLaren, Peter (1988). Culture or canon? Critical pedagogy and the politics of literacy, *Harvard Educational Review*, 58 (2) 213-234.

————. (1991). Critical pedagogy: Constructing an arch of social dreaming and a doorway to hope, *Journal of Education*, 173, 9-34.

McLennan, Gregor, Molina, Victor, and Peters, Roy (1977). Althusser's theory of ideology, in Centre for Contemporary Cultural Studies, *On Ideology* (London: Hutchinson), 77-105.

Meissner, W.W. (1970). Notes on identification: I. Origins in Freud, *Psychoanalytic Quarterly*, 39, 563-589.

————. (1971). Notes on identification: II. Clarification of related concepts, *Psychoanalytic Quarterly*, 40, 277-302.

————. (1972). Notes on identification: III. The concept of identification, *Psychoanalytic Quarterly*, 41, 224-260.

————. (1980). A note on projective identification, *Journal of the American Psychoanalytic Association*, 28, 43-67.

————. (1981). *Internalization in Psychoanalysis* (New York: International Universities Press).

————. (1987). Projection and projective identification, in Sandler (ed.), *Projection, Identification, Projective Identification*, 27-50.

Meltzer, Donald (1986). On first impressions, *Contemporary Psychoanalysis*, 22, 467-470.

Menninger, Karl A. (1938). *Man Against Himself* (New York: Harcourt Brace).

Menzies, Isabel Lyth (1989). *The Dynamics of the Social* (London: Free Association).

Merkin, Daphne (1991). The talking cure blues, *Partisan Review*, 58 (3), 526-532.

Mitchell, Juliet (ed.), (1986). *The Selected Melanie Klein* (Harmondsworth, UK:

Penguin).

————. (1988). An interview, by Angela McRobbie, *New Left Review*, 170, 80-91.

Mitchell, Stephen A. (1988). *Relational Concepts in Psychoanalysis: An Integration* (Cambridge: Harvard University Press).

Modell, Arnold H. (1975). *The Ego and the Id: Fifty years later*, *International Journal of Psycho-Analysis*, 56, 57-68.

Molteno, Frank (1987). Students take control: The 1980 boycott of coloured education in the Cape Peninsula, *British Journal of Sociology of Education*, 8 (1), 3-22.

Moore, R. (1991). New departures? Arrivals pending: Curriculum, theory and practice, *British Journal of Sociology of Education*, 12 (1), 115-123.

Morley, Dave (1980). Texts, readers, subjects, in Hall et al. (eds.), *Culture, Media, Language*, 163-173.

Moscovici, Serge (1993a). The return of the unconscious, *Social Research*, 60, 39-93.

————. (1993b). *The Invention of Society: Psychological Explanations of Social Phenomena* (Cambridge: Polity).

Mouffe, Chantal (1979). *Gramsci and Marxist Theory* (London: Routledge & Kegan Paul).

————. (1981a). Hegemony and ideology in Gramsci, in Bennett et al., *Culture, Ideology and Social Practice*, 219-234.

————. (1981b). Hegemony and the integral state in Gramsci: Towards a new concept of politics, in George Bridges and Rosiland Brunt (eds.), *Silver Linings: Some Strategies for the Eighties* (London: Lawrence & Wishart), 167-187.

Mouzelis, Nicos (1978). Ideology and class politics: a critique of Ernesto Laclau, *New Left Review*, 112, 45-61.

Muench, Richard, and Smelser, Neil J. (1987). Relating the micro and macro, in Jeffrey C. Alexander, Bernhard Giesen, Richard Muench, and Neil J. Smelser (eds.), *The Micro-Macro Link* (Berkeley: University of California Press), 356-387.

Muller, Johan (1985). The end of psychology: Review of Henriques et al., *Changing the Subject*, Psychology in Society, 3, 33-42.

————.(1989a). Review of Philip Wexler, *Social Analysis of Educaton: After the New Sociology*, Perspectices in Education, 11 (1), 73-79.

————. (1989b). The question of the curriculum, seminar, University of Cape Town.

————. (1991). Difference, identity and community: American perspectives on the curriculum, Kenton-at-Katberg Education Conference, South Africa.

Muller, Johan and Crewe, Mary (1981). Subjects and subjection: A comment, *Perspectives in Education*, 5 (2), 118-123.

————. (1983). Shadow boxing, *Perspectives in Education*, 7 (1), 3-7.

Nash, James L., and McGehee, James B. (1986). Acting out the countertransference, *Bulletin of the Menninger Clinic*, 50, 379-384.

Nelson, Cary and Grossberg, Lawrence (eds.) (1988). *Marxism and the Interpretation of Culture* (Urbana and Chicago: University of Illinois Press).

Nespor, J., and Barber, L. (1991). The rhetorical construction of "the teacher," *Harvard Educational Review*, 61, 417-433.

Nilan, Pam (1995). Making up men, *Gender and Education*, 7 (2), 175-187.

Nixon, Rob (1992). "An everybody claim dem democratic": Notes on the "new" South Africa, *Transition*, 54, 20-35.

Noguera, Pedro A. (1995). Preventing and producing violence: A critical analysis of responses to school violence, *Harvard Educational Review*, 65 (2), 189-212.

Nunberg, Herman, and Federn, Ernst (eds.) (1962-1975). *Minutes of the Vienna Psychoanalytic Society*, vol. 2.

Nye, Robert A. (1973). Two paths to a psychology of social action: Gustave Le Bon and Georges Sorel, *Journal of Modern History*, 45 (3), 411-438.

———. (1975). *The Origins of Crowd Psychology: Gustave Le Bon and the Crisis of Mass Democracy in the Third Republic* (London, and Beverly Hills: Sage).

Ogden, Thomas H. (1979). On projective identification, *International Journal of Psycho-Analysis*, 60, 357-373.

———. (1982). *Projective Identification and Psychotherapeutic Technique* (New York and London: Jason Aronson).

———. (1983). The concept of internal object relations, *International Journal of Psycho-Analysis*, 64, 227-241.

———. (1985). On potential space, *International Journal of Psycho-Analysis*, 66, 129-141.

———. (1988). On the dialectical structure of experience, *Contemporary Psychoanalysis*, 24, 17-45.

———. (1989). *The Primitive Edge of Experience* (Northvale, N.J., and London: Jason Aronson).

———. (1991). Analyzing the matrix of transference, *International Journal of Psycho-Analysis*, 72, 593-605.

O'Neill, John (1982). *For Marx Against Althusser and Other Essays* (Washington, D.C.: Center for Advanced Research in Phenomenology & University Press of America).

Ornston, Darius (1978). On projection: A study of Freud's usage, *Psychoanalytic Study of the Child*, 33, 117-166.

O'Shaughnessy, Edna (1986). A 3 1/2-year-old boy's melancholic identification with an original object, *International Journal of Psycho-Analysis*, 67, 173-179.

Pêcheux, Michel (1983). *Language, Semiotics and Ideology: Stating the Obvious* (London: Macmillan).

———. (1988). Discourse: Structure or event?, in Nelson and Grossberg (eds.), *Marxism and the Interpretation of Culture*, 633-650.

Peters, Bernhard (1994). Why is it so hard to change the world?, *International Sociology*, 9 (3), 275-293.

Peters, Michael (1993). Against Finkielkraut's *La Défaite de la Pénsee*: Culture, postmodernism and education, *French Cultual Studies*, 4, 91-106.

Peters, Michael, and Marshall, James (1991). Education and empowerment: Postmodernism and the critique of humanism, *Education and Society*, 9 (2), 123-134.

Pines, Malcolm, and Rafaelsen, Lisa (eds.) (1982). *The Individual and the Group: Boundaries and Interrelations*, vol. 1, *Theory* (New York and London: Plenum).

Poe, Edgar Allen (1839). William Wilson, in *Tales of Mystery and Imagination* (London: Dent, 1968).

Porder, Michael S. (1987). Projective identification: An alternative hypothesis, *Psycho-

analytic Quarterly, 56, 431-451.

Potter, Jonathon, Wetherell, Margaret, Gill, Ros, and Edwards, Derek (1990). Discourse: Noun, verb or social practice? *Philosophical Psychology*, 3 (2), 205-217.

Racker, H. (1968). *Transference and Countertransference* (New York: International Universities Press).

Rapaport, David (1967). A theoretical analysis of the super-ego concept, in *The Collected Papers of David Rapaport* (New Haven: Yale University Press).

Redl, Fritz (1942). Group emotion and leadership, in Saul Scheidlinger (ed.), *Psychoanalytic Group Dynamics* (New York: International Universities Press, 1980), 15-71.

Ricoeur, Paul (1986). *Lectures on Ideology and Utopia*, (New York: Columbia University Press).

Rieff, Philip (1990). Sentences, in Rieff, *The Feeling Intellect: Selected Writings* (Chicago: University of Chicago Press), 367-385.

Riesman, David (1950). Authority and liberty in the structure of Freud's thought, *Psychiatry*, 13, 167-187.

Roheim, Geza (1945). *The Eternal Ones of the Dream: A Psychoanalytic Interpretation of Australian Myth and Ritual* (New York: International Universities Press).

Rose, Gilbert J. (1978). The creativity of everyday life, in Simon A. Grolnick and Leonard Barkin with Werner Muensterberger (eds.), *Between Reality and Fantasy: Transitional Objects and Phenomena* (New York and London: Jason Aronson), 347-362.

Rosenfeld, Herbert (1983). Primitive object relations and mechanisms, *International Journal of Psycho-Analysis*, 64, 261-267.

Roudinesco, Elizabeth (1990). *Jacques Lacan and Co.: A History of Psychoanalysis in France* (Chicago: University of Chicago Press).

Ryan, Michael (1988). The politics of film: Discourse, psychoanalysis, ideology, in Nelson and Grossberg (eds.), *Marxism and the Interpretation of Culture*, 477-488.

Said, Edward (1988). Michel Foucault, 1926-1984, in Jonathon Arac (ed.), *After Foucault* (New Brunswick, N.J.: Rutgers University Press).

Sandler, Joseph (1961). Identification in children, parents and doctors, in R. MacKeith and J. Sandler (eds.), *Psychosomatic Aspects of Paediatrics* (London: Pergamon), 16-26.

———. (1976). Countertransference and role-responsiveness, *International Journal of Psycho-Analysis*, 3, 43-47.

———. (1987a). The concept of projective identification, in Sandler (ed.), *Projection, Identification, Projective Identification*, 13-26.

———. (ed.) (1987b). *Projection, Identification, Projective Identification* (Madison, Conn.: International Universities Press).

Sandler, Joseph, and Dare, C. (1970). The psychoanalytic concept of orality, *Journal of Psychosomatic Research*, 14, 211-222.

Sandler, Joseph, and Joffe, W.G. (1967). The tendency to persistence in psychological function and development, with special reference to fixation and regression, *Bulletin of the Menninger Clinic*, 31, 257-271.

Sandler, Joseph, and Perlow, Meir (1987). Internalization and externalization, in Sandler (ed.), *Projection, Identification, Projective Identification*, 1-11.

Sandler, Joseph, and Rosenblatt, B. (1962). The concept of the representational world, *Psychoanalytic Study of the Child*, 17, 128-162.

Sandler, Joseph, and Sandler, Anna-Marie (1978). On the development of object relationships and affects, *International Journal of Psycho-Analysis*, 59, 285-296.

Sassoon, Anne Showstack (1980). *Gramsci's Politics* (London: Croom Helm).

Saussure, Ferdinand de (1915). *Course in General Linguistics*, (New York: McGraw-Hill, 1959).

Schafer, Roy (1968). *Aspects of Internalization* (New York: International Universities Press).

Scharff, David E. (1988). Epilogue: Transference as the interface between the intrapsychic and the interpersonal, *Psychoanalytic Inquiry*, 8, 598-602.

Schermer, Victor L. (1982). Interactive concepts in psychoanalytic developmental psychology: Their relevance to the individual/group linkage, in Pines and Rafaelsen (eds.), *The Individual and the Group*, 193-207.

Schneider, Michael (1973). *Neurosis and Civilization: A Marxist/Freudian Synthesis*, Michael Roloff (trans.) (New York: Seabury, 1975).

Schneiderman, Stuart (1983). *Jacques Lacan: The Death of an Intellectual Hero* (Cambridge: Harvard University Press).

Schrag, Francis (1992). Review of Stanley Aronowitz and Henry Giroux, *Postmodern Education: Politics, Education, and Social Criticism, Educational Studies*, 23, 200-208.

Segal, Hannah (1974). *Introduction to the Work of Melanie Klein* (New York: Basic Books).

⸻. (1952). A psychoanalytic contribution to aesthetics, in Rita V. Frankiel (ed.), *Essential Papers on Object Loss* (New York: New York University, 1994).

Shakespeare, William (1984). *Julius Caesar* (Oxford: Clarendon).

Shalem, Yael (1992). Teachers' struggle: The case of white English-speaking teachers in Soouth Africa, *British Journal of Sociology of Education*, 13 (3), 307-328.

Shapiro, T. (1981). On the quest for the origins of conflict, *Psychoanalytic Quarterly*, 50, 1-21.

Shapiro, Svi (1987). If you won't work Sunday, don't come in on Monday, in Stevens and Wood (eds.), *Justice, Ideology, and Education*, 141-145.

Sharp, Rachel (1982). Response to Wexler, *Interchange*, 13 (3), 68-75.

Sheridan, Alan (1977). Translator's note, in Lacan, *Ecrits*, vii-xii.

Shilling, Chris (1991). Educating the body: Physical capital and the production of social inequalities, *Sociology*, 25 (4), 653-672.

⸻. (1992a). Schooling and the production of physical capital, *Discourse*, 13 (1), 1-19.

⸻. (1992b). Reconceptualising structure and agency in the sociology of education: Structuration theory and schooling, *British Journal of Sociology of Education*, 13 (1), 69-87.

⸻. (1993). The demise of sociology of education in Britain?, *British Journal of Sociology of Education*, 14, 105-112.

Simenauer, Erich (1985). Identification in the theory and technique of psychoanalysis:

Some thoughts on its farther reaches and functions, *International Journal of Psycho-Analysis*, 66, 171-184.

Simon, Roger (1982). Gramsci's Political Thought (London: Lawrence & Wishart).

Skeggs, B. (1991). Postmodernism: What is all the fuss about? *British Journal of Sociology of Education*, 12, 255-267.

Smith, Steven (1984). *Reading Althusser: An Essay on Structural Marxism* (Ithaca, N.Y., and London: Cornell University Press).

Smith, Sydney (1977). The golden fantasy: A regressive reaction to seperation anxiety, *International Journal of Psycho-Analysis*, 58, 311-324.

Spillius, Elizabeth Bott (1983). Some developments from the work of Melanie Klein, *International Journal of Psycho-Analysis*, 64, 321-332.

Spruiell, Vann (1988). Crowd psychology and ideology: A psychoanalytic view of the reciprocal effects of folk philosophies and personal actions, *International Journal of Psycho-Analysis*, 69 (2), 171-178.

Stalin, Joseph (1938). Dialectical and Historical Materialism (Moscow: Foreign Languages Publishing House, 1939).

Stanton, Martin (1983). *Outside the Dream: Lacan and French Style Psychoanalysis* (London: Routledge & Kegan Paul).

Stevens, Edward, and Wood, George (eds.) (1987). *Justice, Ideology, and Education: An Introduction to the Social Foundations of Education* (New York: Random House).

Stinchcombe, Arthur L. (1991). The conditions of fruitfulness of theorizing about mechanisms in social science, *Philosophy of the Social Sciences*, 21 (3), 367-387.

Symington, Neville (1985). Phantasy effects that which it represents, *International Journal of Psycho-Analysis*, 66, 349-357.

Talbot, Margaret (1994). A most dangerous method, *Lingua Franca*, January/February, 24-40.

Therborn, Goran (1980). *The Ideology of Power and the Power of Ideology* (London: New Left Books).

Thompson, E.P. (1963). *The Making of the English Working Class* (New York: Vintage Books).

———. (1978). The poverty of theory: Or, An orrery of errors, in Thompson, *The Poverty of Theory and Other Essays* (London: Merlin), 1-210.

———. (1981). The politics of theory, in Raphael Samuel (ed.), *People's History and Socialist Theory* (London: Routledge & Kegan Paul), 396-408.

Trotter, W. (1916). *Instincts of the Herd in Peace and War* (London: T.F. Unwin).

Turkle, Sherry (1979). *Psychoanalytic Politics: Freud's French Revolution* (London: Burnett).

Ulman, Richard B. and Stolorow, Robert D. (1985). The "transference—countertransference neurosis" in psychoanalysis: An intersubjective view, *Bulletin of the Menninger Clinic*, 49, 37-51.

Ulmer, Gregory L. (1987). Textshop for psychoanalysis: On deprogramming freshman Platonists, *College English*, 49 (7) 756-769.

Unger, S. (1986). The professor of desire, *Yale French Studies*, 63, 81-97.

van den Berg, Owen (1986). Power, discourse and the teacher, *Perspectives in*

Education, 9 (1), 4-16.

van Ginneken, Jaap (1992). *Crowds, Psychology, and Politics, 1871-1899* (Cambridge: Cambridge University Press).

Vovelle, Michel (1990). *Ideologies & Mentalities* (Cambridge: Polity).

Walcott, Rinaldo (1994). Pedagogical desire and the crisis of knowledge, *Discourse*, 15 (1), 64-74.

Walker, J.C. (1988). *Louts and Legends: Male Youth Culture in an Inner-City School* (Sydney: Allen & Unwin).

Walkerdine, Valerie (1986). Progressive pedagogy and political struggle, *Screen and Screen Education*, 27, 54-60.

————. (1990). *Schoolgirl Fictions* (London, and New York: Verso).

Ward, Janie V. (1995). Cultivating a morality of care in African American adolescents, *Harvard Educational Review*, 65 (2), 175-188.

Weiler, K. (1991). Freire and a feminist pedagogy of difference, *Harvard Educational Review*, 61, 449-474.

Wertheimer, Michael (1988). Obstacles to the integration of competing theories in psychology, *Philosophical Psychology*, 1 (1), 131-137.

West, L.J. (1968). The "Othello syndrome," *Contemporary Psychoanalysis*, 4, 103-110.

Wexler, Philip (1976). *The Sociology of Education: Beyond Equality* (Indianapolis: Bobbs-Merrill).

————. (1979). Educational change and social contradiction, *Comparative Review of Education*, 23 (2), 240-255.

————. (1981a). Body and soul: Sources of social change and strategies of education, *British Journal of Sociology of Education*, 2 (3), 247-263.

————. (1981b). Review of Paul Willis *Learning to Labour: How Working Class Kids Get Working Class Jobs*, *Contemporary Sociology*, 10 (1), 158-159.

————. (1982a). Structure, text and subject: A critical sociology of school knowledge, in Michael W. Apple (ed.), *Cultural and Economic Reproduction in Education* (London, and Boston: Routledge & Kegan Paul), 275-303.

————. (1982b). Ideology and education: From critique to class action, *Interchange*, 13 (3), 53-68.

————. (1983). Movement, class and education, in Len Barton and Stephen Walker (eds.), *Race, Class and Education* (London, and Canberra: Croom Helm), 17-39.

————. (1985a). Organizing the unconscious: Towards a social psychology of education, in Barton and Walker (eds.), *Education and Social Change*, 218-228.

————. (1985b). Social change and the practice of education, *Social Education*, 49 (5), 390-394.

————. (1985c). Editor's foreword, *Sociology of Education*, 58 (1), 1-2.

————. (1986). Radical antinomies, *British Journal of Sociology of Education*, 7 (4), 461-465.

————. (1987). *Social Analysis of Education: Beyond the New Sociology* (London, and New York: Routledge & Kegan Paul).

————. (1988). Symbolic economy of identity and denial of labor: Studies in high school #1, in Lois Weis (ed.), *Class, Race, and Gender in American Schools* (Albany: State University of New York Press), 302-315.

————. (1990a). Citizenship in the semiotic society, in Bryan S. Turner (ed.), *Theories of Modernity and Postmodernity* (London: Sage), 164-175.

————. (1990b). School is society, public lecture, University of Rochester, Rochester, NY.

————. (1991). Afterword. Collective/self/collective: A short chapter in the professional middle class story, in Wexler (ed.), *Critical Theory Now* (London: Falmer), 242-250.

————. (1992). *Becoming Somebody: Toward a Social Psychology of School* (London and Washington, D.C.: Falmer).

Wexler, Philip, Martusewicz, Rebecca, and Kern, June (1987). Popular educational politics, in David W. Livingstone (ed.), *Critical Pedagogy and Critical Power* (South Hadley, Mass.: Bergin & Garvey), 227-243.

Wexler, Philip, Whitson, T., and Moskowitz, E. (1981). Deschooling by default: The changing social functions of public schooling, *Interchange*, 12 (2-3), 133-150.

Wheelis, Allen (1949). Flight from insight, *American Journal of Psychiatry*, 7, 915-919.

————. (1950). The place of action in personality change, *Psychiatry*, 13 (2), 135-148.

————. (1956). Will and psychoanalysis, *Journal of the American Psychoanalytic Association*, 4 (2), 285-303.

————. (1973). *How People Change* (New York: Harper Colophon).

————. (1980). *The Scheme of Things* (New York and London: Harcourt Brace Jovanovich).

Whitehead, Barbara Dafoe (1994). The failure of sex education, *Atlantic Monthly*, October, 55-94.

Whitty, Geoff, and Young, Michael F.D. (eds.), (1977). *Society, State and Schooling: Readings on the Possibilities for Radical Education* (Sussex, UK: Falmer).

Widener, Alice (ed.) (1979). *Gustave Le Bon: The Man and His Works* (Indianapolis, Ind.: Liberty Press).

Widlocher, Daniel (1985). The wish for identification and structural effects in the work of Freud, *International Journal of Psycho-Analysis*, 66, 31-46.

Williams, Raymond (1968). The idea of a common culture, in *Resources of Hope: Culture, Democracy, Socialism* (New York and London: Verso, 1989), 32-38.

————. (1976). *Keywords: A Vocabulary of Culture and Society* (New York: Oxford University Press).

————. (1980). Base and superstructure in Marxist cultural theory, in Williams, *Problems in Materialism and Culture: Selected Essays* (London: Verso), 31-49.

Williamson, Bill (1981). Contradictions of control: Elementary education in a mining district, 1870-1900, in Len Barton and Stephen Walker (eds.), *Schools, Teachers & Teaching* (London: Croom Helm), 77-95.

Willis, Paul (1977). *Learning to Labour: How Working-Class Kids Get Working-Class Jobs* (Westmead, UK: Saxon House).

Willis, Paul, and Corrigan, Philip (1983). Orders of experience: The differences of working class cultural forms, *Social Text*, 8, 85-103.

Wilson, John (1986). Power, paranoia, and education, *Oxford Review of Education*, 12, 3-15.

Winnicott, D.W. (1951). Transitional objects and transitional phenomena, in Winnicott, *Playing and Reality* (Harmondsworth: Penguin, 1980), 1-25.

————. (1956). Primary maternal preoccupation, in Winnicott, *Through Pediatrics to Psychoanalysis* (New York: Basic Books), 300-305.

Worsham, L. (1992/1993). Emotion and pedagogic violence, *Discourse*, 15, 119-148.

Wortis, Joseph (1954). *Fragments of an Analysis with Freud* (New York: McGraw-Hill).

Wright, Elizabeth (1984) *Psychoanalytic Criticism: Theory in Practice* (London and New York: Methuen).

Wrong, Dennis (1961). The oversocialized conception of man in modern sociology, *American Sociological Review*, 26, 183-193.

Yates, Lynn (1992). Postmodernism, feminism and cultural politics: Or, if master narratives have been discredited, what does Giroux think he is doing? *Discourse*, 13 (1), 124-133.

Young, Michael F.D. (ed.), (1971). *Knowledge and Control: New Directions for the Sociology of Education* (London: Collier-Macmillan).

Young, Robert (1990). *A Critical Theory of Education: Habermas and Our Children's Future* (New York and London: Teachers College Press).

————. (1992). Postmodern politics of education, *Discourse*, 13 (1), 133-141.

Zinner, John and Shapiro, Roger (1972). Projective identification as a mode of perception and behavior in families of adolescents, *International Journal of Psycho-Analysis*, 53, 523-530.

Žižek, Slavoj (1989). *The Sublime Object of Ideology* (London, and New York: Verso).

————. (1990a). Beyond discourse analysis, in Laclau, *New Reflections on the Revolution of our Time*, 249-260.

————. (1990b). Eastern Europe's republics of Gilead, *New Left Review*, 183, 50-62.

————. (1991a). Why should a dialectician learn to count to four?, *Radical Philosophy*, 58, 3-9.

————. (1991b). *Looking Awry: An Introduction to Jacques Lacan through Popular Culture* (Cambridge, Mass., and London: MIT Press).

INDEX

LIBRARY
OF
MOUNT ST. MARY'S
COLLEGE
EMMITSBURG, MARYLAND

About the Author

STEPHEN APPEL is a lecturer in the Department of Education at the University of Auckland.

ISBN 0-89789-442-1

HARDCOVER BAR CODE

NOV 07 1997